THE
POWER OF
TRANSFORMATION

How to Find Physical, Spiritual and Emotional Wellness
And Live Life to Its Fullest

Pauline E. Lewinson

iUniverse, Inc.
Bloomington

The Power of Transformation
How to Find Physical, Spiritual and Emotional Wellness And Live Life to Its Fullest

iUniverse books may be ordered through booksellers or by contacting:

iUniverse
1663 Liberty Drive
Bloomington, IN 47403
www.iuniverse.com
1-800-Authors (1-800-288-4677)

ISBN: 978-1-4502-8003-7 (pbk)
ISBN: 978-1-4620-0046-3 (cloth)
ISBN: 978-1-4502-8004-4 (ebk)

Printed in the United States of America

iUniverse rev. date: 2/18/2011

*A just weight and balance are the Lord's: all
the weights of the bag are his work*
Proverbs 16:11.

DEDICATION

I am indebted to all the men and women God placed in my path to influence my spiritual growth and my personal and professional development.

To my uncles, the late Daniel Brown and Fredrick Sutherland, who filled in the gap for my father, I will never forget the role you played in my life.

To my grandmother, the late Regina Sutherland, who believed in me and raised me to be who I am today; thank you for your love, care and humility.

To my elementary school principal, the late Hulda Sawyers who coached and mentored me in the absence of my parents; you were an excellent role model who taught me how to persevere and have strong self-esteem, combined with integrity.

To the late Deszreen Lewinson, you were the best mother-in-law ever.

I hope to see all of you in eternity.

To the saved and un-saved people in this world, young and old-may *The Power of Transformation* provides enlightenment, be a blessing and helps you to find answers to questions you seek. I ask you to put God first in your lives so that you can experience His gift of salvation which offers, His righteousness, freedom, deliverance, transformation and eternal life.

In everything give thanks: for this is the will of
God in Christ Jesus concerning you
1 Thessalonians 5:18.

CONTENTS

PREFACE
GOD IS SOVEREIGN

Wherefore I also, after I heard of your faith in the Lord Jesus, and love unto all the saints, Cease not to give thanks for you, making mention of you in my prayers; That the God of our Lord Jesus Christ, the Father of glory, may give unto you the spirit of wisdom and revelation in the knowledge of him: The eyes of your understanding being enlightened; that ye may know what is the hope of his calling, and what the riches of the glory of his inheritance in the saints, And what is the exceeding greatness of his power to us-ward who believe, according to the working of his mighty power, which he wrought in Christ, when he raised him from the dead, and set him at his own right hand in the heavenly places, Far above all principality, and power, and might, and dominion, and every name that is named, not only in this world, but also in that which is to come: And hath put all things under his feet, and gave him to be the head over all things to the church, Which is his body, the fullness of him that filleth all in all
Ephesians 1:15-23.

The apostle Paul wrote this spiritual prayer of wisdom to the people at the church in Ephesus. I believe that when you read this prayer, you will be guided to receive the wisdom in this book that is applicable to your particular situation.

ACKNOWLEDGEMENTS

O give thanks unto the LORD; for he is good;
for his mercy endureth for ever
1 Chronicles 16:34.

I have been writing this book since December of 2004 and many times, I felt like giving up. I thank God for the times when the Holy Spirit would not let me rest until I wrote. The preparation and completion of this book were made possible through the thoughts, ideas and the help of countless individuals. I give thanks to God, my Lord and Savior Jesus Christ, for giving me life and for inspiring me to write for His purpose. I thank my Mother, Dorenda Walker and my father, Clifford Walker (deceased in 2008), for bringing me into this world and for their prayers. Thanks to Aunt Sissy, who always labored in the kitchen to prepare the meals for the family.

To my husband, Royston, who never gave up on me, has always encouraged me to reach for the stars, tells me that I can do all things through Christ Who gives me strength, and that the Lord who began a good work in me will see it to completion, I thank you.

Thanks to my daughters, Shauna and Regina, and my son, Dior, for loving the Lord, for being excellent children, for their unconditional love and support, and for being so understanding while I took time away from our family time to write. I thank my son-in-law, Therren, for demonstrating what true strength is, in the way he served his country, held on to his faith, and persevered through the difficult times that he experienced.

Dior, thank you for encouraging me to write and for giving me suggestions on the length and pages of this book, for bringing me a drink at times while I was writing, and for reminding me that my eyes needed a break from the computer.

Please know that my accomplishment is yours as well.

To all my friends who have given my family and me their love and support through the years; especially, Arlene and Paul Mattis, Bevon Blake, Caye VanWagenen, Eric and Claire Fraser Faith Thomas-Dixon, Hayacinth Forbes, Hope White, Jennifer Cunningham, Joyce and Raymond Jarrett, Julette Matcham, Dr. Marilyn Broadus-Gay (my prayer partner), Marisa Espinoza, Melbertine Reid, Rose Rutland, Ruby and Roy Stewart, Vena and Todd McDonald, and the Young's family-thank you for your continued prayers and encouragement. Marie Lorminey, my mentee and my nephew, Tyshawn Walker-thank you for loving God with all your hearts, and for showing me how to take love to another level. To my niece, Marva, thank you for always checking up on me to make sure I am doing alright...just to name a few.

Thanks to all my siblings who contributed to my life in one way or another, especially my sisters, Grace and Zelin, who loved and nurtured me after my parents migrated to Great Britain when I was only three years old.

Thanks to Ms. Smith, my English professor at the University of Connecticut, who advised me to keep writing.

Thanks to all the pastors of my earlier years, and to the more recent ones: Reverend, Robert Martin, Pastors, Kim Brown, Ben Barfield, Ralph Orduno and Demetrius Miles, for the deposits you have made to enhance my spiritual growth.

Last, but not least, I wish to thank all the people who have contributed to the editing of this book. Sandy Sprague I cannot thank you enough for the final editing.

I will be forever grateful to all of you.

INTRODUCTION

*God created man in his own image, in the image of God
created he him; male and female created he them*
Genesis 1:27.

*And be not conformed to this world: but be ye transformed
by the renewing of your mind, that ye may prove what is
that good, and acceptable, and perfect, will of God*
Romans 12:2.
*Take notice! I tell you a mystery (a secret truth, an event decree
by the hidden purpose or counsel of God). We shall not all fall
asleep [in death], but we shall all be changed (transformed)*
1 Corinthians 15:51 (AMP).

*Come to Me, all you who labor and are heavy laden, and I will give you rest.
Take My yoke upon you and learn from Me, for I am gentle and lowly in heart,
and you will find rest for your souls. For My yoke is easy and My burden is light*
Matthew 11: 28-30 (NKJV).

The Power of Transformation, is filled with life-altering ideas that are based on biblical truths. I will share with you biblical principles that I have applied to my life and actions that I have taken to transform my life. I decided to write this book for four reasons:
(1) I have been a believer all my life and recently, I have been experiencing a life transformation through in-depth reading, studying and application of God's Word. I am lead by the Holy Spirit and compelled to share with you: God wants you to change your way of thinking and heart so He can transform your life;
(2) I have been given the script by the Holy Spirit line by line and precept by precept. I have always had a desire to write a book and attempted to do so many times, but just could not bring it all together before now. I believe that nothing happens until the right time, as determined by God. There is a message of truth in this book for you;
(3) I seek to answer questions that people have asked me over the years such as: How do you find that inner peace that I see in you? How have you stayed married for such a long time? How do you raise girls? Are

you still saved after all these years? What is your secret for looking so happy and young?

(4) I have spent hundreds of hours seeking God's direction in the writing of this book and I believe that people's lives will be positively impacted after reading it. The main purpose of this book is to win the un-saved people of this world and to help believers mature, transform their ways of thinking and become stronger in their faith and walk. If I can do it, so can you. The questions I have listed above, are questions that every believer who applies biblical principles and are serious about their walk with God, should be able to answer without hesitation. I had been saved for many years, but I was not fully surrendered to Christ. Since I confessed all my sinful mistakes and made the decision to live a surrendered and sanctified life in Jesus Christ, God has been literally taking me through a daily process of transformation. It is not easy, as He shaves at my flesh, prunes me like a tree and peals me like a banana. I am at peace with Him doing these things because I know He is doing them for my good. He is grooming me to meet the Bridegroom.

All my life I have had a burning desire to live a life that pleases God and to see others do the same. Due to circumstances, I have failed many times in my attempts to live such a life. I also desire to live above mediocre standards and create an abundant and fulfilling life in all areas, according to the promises of God. I have made up my mind that I will not settle for anything less than the person I was created to be and I will do nothing less than I was created to do. I will use the righteousness that God has given me through His son Jesus Christ to glorify Him and live life to its fullest.

In transitioning from one career to another and making some changes in my life, I asked many people (friends and family), to fill out a questionnaire that a mentor had given to me. This is a questionnaire that she had used when she was making a life transition. I decided to use this tool as she recommended. The purpose of the questionnaire was to see whether or not the respondents' impressions of me would match what I felt were my current life's assignments-writing, life transformation coaching and inspirational speaking.

This was an eye-opening exercise. It was very interesting how different people's perceptions of me were. One friend, in particular, who is a few years older than I am and who was one of my role models when I was growing up responded to two questions as follows:

Q: What are two things you wish I would change about myself? (Be honest!)

A. "The air of sophistication which tends to let others feel that you present a picture of being above them. You present the image that you would tend to look down on other people who do not measure up to your standards. In other words, you would appear to be more in the Elite group, rather than be with the "Roots." Whatever that meant to her, I am not sure.

Q: What do you see as my driving force? In other words, what do you think makes me tick?

A: "Being among aristocrats. Surprise, I don't think you are! I think this is a really good exercise. because I know you, these are attributes that are unique to you; I do not find them as a problem. However, other people, who do not understand this, might have a problem with it." Well, that would be their problem.

From this I learned a few things: Ask for what you want, and you will receive something, even if what you get is far different from what you expected. Do not take anyone, or anything personally, or for granted, and always, always be sure you know who you are, so you do not have to accept who another person tells you, you are. People may perceive you differently from the way you perceive yourself, or from the way that you are inwardly, but it does not matter. There is no perfect person. God is the only One Who is perfect, Who truly knows a person's heart and does not judge you. Always remember that God created you in His likeness and image, so it is okay to BE you.

What is of utmost importance, is having good intentions, a good heart and love for everyone, no matter what. Look for the lesson in every circumstance. First have a good and personal relationship with God, as this *will* make the difference. I was somewhat astonished by my friend's answers, but after giving some thoughts to them, I respected her candidness and accepted them as her perception of me. After all, she has a right to her opinion. I realized there was a lesson in it for me. The lesson was that I must be consciously aware of the message I send.

My purpose is to influence, and impact lives positively, not only through my words, but most importantly, through my actions. The last thing I want is for my message to be misconstrued. My intention is never to debase or offend anyone. I am an encourager and I always want the best for everyone. Sadly, what I have realized is that not all people want the best for themselves or for others. Unfortunately, a person's boldness, honesty and ability to speak truth will always be misunderstood by some.

Coming from a place of empowerment, and inner strength allows me to accept constructive criticism, and to use negative ones to my advantage. I refuse to let what people say, or do have a negative effect on me. Of course, there was a time when the negative things that people said or did, indeed mattered. I have however taken a different stance-I have chosen to dispel any unfavorable comments, and actions that are made toward me. You can choose to do the same. The choices we make now, will help to shape our future.

Chose today not to be embarrassed by anything that happened in your past. Focus on how to be your authentic self. This might mean that you will stop worrying about pleasing everybody, and seek to please God, instead. In order for transformation to take place in our lives, we must please God. Pleasing God will strengthen your faith. The Bible says: *without faith, it is impossible to please God*. Even with extraordinary faith, love, peace and all the other good natured things, it is impossible to please everyone. So why be concerned about pleasing others? It is much more beneficial, and easier to please God.

If you are not functioning out of your authentic self, and you are playing the role of someone else because you are concerned about what others say or think of you, your life will be miserable. We can be inspired through the grace and mercy of God to turn things around in our lives and start living life to its fullest. In turning over the pages in my life, I learned that I am not a victim of past circumstances. I only accept and agree with things that inspire or uplift me. I believe people should keep improving and progressing, and as they do, they should help others who are willing to do the same.

While others may see "an air of sophistication," I see desire, determination, persistence and confidence. When I think of the price that Jesus paid at Calvary to set me free, and His promise in John 10:10, I repudiate any actions of judgment from anyone.

I share the information regarding the questionnaire with you, because I know that many people are stuck in a place of uncertainty, physical and emotional paralysis and mediocrity as a result of the words that others have spoken to them. Also because of misconceptions, and unnecessary burdens that they have carried from their past. Scripture warns that life and death are in the power of the tongue. When you understand this principle, you will not accept everything that people tell you, or you will not allow anyone to speak words of death to you, or act towards you in ways that are contrary to who you are in Christ. It is very important to protect your self-esteem, self-image, dreams, life and destiny.

We all have unique qualities by nature of design. Own your personal and unique qualities that you have received through God's grace. While our uniqueness may be bothersome to others, it is our responsibility to embrace it, and not seek to be like anyone else. It is okay to be the defective bean in the pod or the yellow flower in the garden of red daffodils. I accept myself just the way God has made me, and you should too. When you accept yourself as you are, then you will be able to accept others as they are, live in God's will and access the promised abundant and blessed life.

As a numinous believer, I pray on a continuous basis, confessing my sins, and asking the Lord to crucify my flesh, and remove anything in me that displeases Him. I also ask Him to use me for His divine purpose for my life daily. I believe that as I allow Him to do His will in my life, He eliminates the things that He does not want in me. God said: *As many as I love, I rebuke and chasten: be zealous therefore, and repent* (Revelation 3:19). For that, I am truly grateful and blessed.

I put a lot of energy into being productive, making continuous progress, and helping others to improve their lives as well. That is my purpose. I influence the lives of others at the deepest possible level, and as much as they would allow me to. I am passionate about it, and I am determined to continue doing this, for the sake of obeying God's call on my life. As a believer in the power of God, it is my duty to fully embrace His Word as they have been declared in scripture. For example 1 Peter 2:9 asserts: *But ye are a chosen generation, a **royal priesthood**, an holy nation, a peculiar people; that ye should shew forth the praises of him who hath called you out of darkness into his marvellous light.*

When you are called into this light, you simply do not allow others to dim it, much less to put it out. I also identify with people like Louisa May Alcott who said: "You are an extraordinary woman, how can you expect to live an ordinary life?" Every believer should desire to touch people's lives in the most meaningful ways as some of the most remarkable people whom I have met, read about, or seen in movies have done, as God gave them the authority to do.

I admire people such as Mother Teresa because she had an undying love for the broken hearted, and for those who were suffering, Nelson Mandela for his intellect and strength; Martin Luther King for his prophetic gifting and his great work in uniting people; Mike Murdock for the way he uses biblical wisdom to help people transform their lives; Myles Munroe for his intelligence and inspiring intellectual gift in helping people to understand the nature and character of Kingdom God, and last but not least my husband, Royston Lewinson, for his love, faith, dedication, and consistent determined approach to serving others. In addition to many Bible scholars, these are some of the countless modern-day people who have inspired me, and influenced the lives of thousands of other people.

I have often imagined how wonderful this world would be if the unsaved people would become saved. and the saved would all live in spirit and in truth, by studying and applying the Word of God. All people should set goals to grow and mature in all areas of their lives, seek the unlimited possibilities and be in agreement with the divine will of their Creator. However, more and more I have witnessed that this is not the reality for many. Too often I see people denying the existence of their Creator, and some Christians settling for lesser, rather than greatest, curses rather than blessings and death instead of life.

Without a shadow of doubt, I am accomplishing my assignment by being a teacher, counselor, wife, mother, relative, friend an edifier/ encourager, exhorter, evangelist and enthusiast. I got sucked into trying to do good, not realizing that I could not do any good on my own accord. I failed God terribly at times, by not trusting Him deeply, but He has never failed me. There have been times when slipped from the will of God, and I prayed for God to forgive me; yet I would not forgive myself. I would always go back to thinking about those times when I did something wrong and my conscience was stirred immensely. I would go back to God and ask Him to forgive me, over and over and again for the same old sin, but one day the Holy Spirit set me straight, buy letting me know that it was time to stop being a pathetic Christian.

The Holy Spirit said, "The Lord has already forgiven you and you must accept His forgiveness and move on. Why do you keep remembering the sins that Christ has already forgiven, wiped out and forgotten?" Tears filled my eyes because of the ignorance I allowed to rule my emotions. I was soon comforted, however, by the fact that one of the Holy Spirit's jobs, is to teach me. This lesson changed my way of thinking. I said, "Thank you precious Holy Spirit."

With this new insight, I stopped torturing myself with the mistakes of my past. Now I live my life embracing radical transformation daily. I understand that sin is inevitable, because of our fallen nature as a result of Adam's sin. The truth is, Christ died, I am forgiven of not only of one, but of all my sins. Due to this deliverance, I have the freedom to choose each day not to sin, but rather to live in the divine will of God. I am very excited about having a choice; it keeps me motivated, exhilarated, and wanting to be more like Jesus. When I realized that I needed to do something about my relationship with the Lord in order to become more like Him, I did. That is the best decision I ever made after the decision to believe in Jesus Christ, accept Him as the Lord my life, and to live for Him. Will you do that too?

I do believe if I had had a spiritual mentor, or a spiritual coach along my journey I would not have made some of the mistakes I made, and I might have done some things differently. For this reason I have chosen to give my service in the area of Life Transforming Coaching. My goal is to assist others in organizing their values as children of the King and as citizens of heaven.

My question to myself was, "How do I get closer to Jesus, and keep this desire that I have to please Him for the rest of my life?" The answer was revealed to me through the Holy Spirit: I should search the Scriptures, ask for revelation and meditate, and the Lord would show me how. I began a journey of in-depth Bible reading, meditating on the Word, fasting and praying and asking the Lord for revelation, and divine direction. It is amazing to me that I found so many truths in the Word, truths that I had never heard or read before I started to spend more quality time reading the "Good News". In addition to the truths

I found in God's Word, I enjoy personally hearing Him as I navigate my way through the Scriptures and through life.

Each day as I read the scriptures with the help of the Holy Spirit, it became clearer, and clearer to me that I could not continue to straddle the spiritual fence. I mean that I could not continue to say, "yes" to both the old man, *sin,* and to the New Man, *God,* at the same time. I did that for a while, but it was certainly not to my advantage. I made the decision to give up double-mindedness, and to begin to put more focus on obeying the Scripture: *choose you this day whom ye will serve* (Joshua 24:15). Since I decided to live only on God's Truth–the Word, I can feel, and see that the burden of my sinful nature is decreasing. I have a burning desire to renounce satan's tactics, repent, and please God.

Matthew 11:28-39, is the catalyst for what I am about to say here. Jesus said that I could come to Him if I felt overwhelmed, and He would give me rest, and that I should take His yoke, because His yoke is easy, and His burden is light. I needed to find an easier way, so I decided to leave the things of the world that had prevented me from being the best that I could be for Christ's sake. In return of me giving my burdens to Him, He gives me His increased anointing to experience His greatness.

As I began to get deeper into seeking God's divine plan for my life, I learned so much more than I did in the many years of living the "religious type" Christian life… skimming the surface of the Bible, only when it was convenient for me, instead of setting aside quality time to read, study, meditate, and apply the Word every day. I was doing things that pleased my flesh. I tried to take control of everything, without seeking the guidance of the Holy Spirit. I was doing things this way not because I wanted to, but because all the years that I had been going to church, I had not been taught how truly important it was to fully surrender to the ways of the Lord. I was not aware of the extraordinary value of the Bible, and the benefits of studying and applying its principles. I believe the church should really place more emphasis on the study of God's Word.

I have learned more about the nature of God in the last ten years of my life than I learned in the first forty-three. I even left the church that I was attending, after establishing these new standards by which I am committed to living. Previously, I felt that my spirit was dying, and I needed more spiritual sustenance than I was getting at the church I was attending at the time. When I left, my spiritual growth was enhanced, and my life began to change in many ways. Please do not misunderstand me; I am not saying that the church was responsible for my relationship with Christ, because it was not. For me, that particular church did not nurture me with the Word in a way that helped me to grow spiritually. I knew that I needed to have a personal relationship with God in order to have spiritual growth, and enjoy the freedom that salvation offers, and this church did not help me achieve this goal.

I believe it is the will of God that we share with, teach and counsel one another as it is written His Word: *Let the words of Christ in all their richness, live in your hearts and make you wise. Use His words to teach and counsel each other. Sing psalms and hymns and spiritual songs to God with thankful hearts* (Colossians 3:16).

My prayer is that this book will find its way into the hands of people who are ready to be transformed, both the believers of God's Word, and unbelievers alike. Paul said in Philippians 4, that he had not reached perfection, but kept working toward that day when he would finally be all that Christ Jesus saved him for, and wanted him to be. This scripture caught my attention many years ago, it is my inspiration and I have come to know many people who are working toward this end, and what a joy this is!

On the other hand, I still see many of my Christian brothers and sisters who are doing the exact opposite of what Paul wrote about in this passage; some of the very same things that I used to do before I made the conscious decision, through the grace of God, to live a transformed life, physically, spiritually, emotionally, and financially. I am compelled to play a significant role in assisting others in understanding what it means to be created in the image and likeness of God, to see the image and likeness of the Creator within themselves, to exercise His righteousness, become spiritually awakened and alive, delivered, set free, surrendered to God's will, and to His process for their lives.

If you are a believer who is unsure of who you really are in Christ, and you are still vacillating, or if you are an unbeliever who has doubts about your spirituality, you will find information in this book that will help to free you from the strongholds of your mind and your flesh; information that will transform your way of thinking and doing. You will allow the Holy Spirit to consume your soul and teach you how you can apply biblical principles, develop a personal relationship with God through His Son, Jesus Christ, let your light shine and live life to its fullest.

The Holy Spirit has impressed upon me to share this information with you, and I believe it is my duty to obey. My prayer is that you receive the contents of this book with an open heart and mind, so that you may find the best way sooner, rather than later. I am committed to this assignment to teach and coach, and I have a plan to carry it through to the fullest extent. I know that the lessons I am learning on my spiritual journey, some of which I have shared throughout the pages of this book will help you and me, as we continue our process of transformation. Let us live lives of holiness and sanctification. I am grateful to God for allowing me to write this book for such a time as this. *Now this I do for the gospel's sake, that I may be partaker of it with you* (1 Corinthians 9:23).

PART I

THE GIFT OF ENCOURAGEMENT

CHAPTER 1
THE STRUGGLING BELIEVER

*I beseech you therefore, brethren, by the mercies of God, that ye present
your bodies a living sacrifice, holy, acceptable unto God, which is
your reasonable service. And be not conformed to this world: but
be ye transformed by the renewing of your mind, that ye may prove
what is that good, and acceptable, and perfect, will of God*
Romans 12:1-2

*Therefore if any man be in Christ, he is a new creature: old
things are passed away; behold, all things are become new*
2 Corinthians 5:17.

*You are the light of the world. A city on a hill cannot be hidden. Neither do
people light a lamp and put it under a bowl. Instead they put it on its stand,
and it gives light to everyone in the house. In the same way, let your light shine
before men, that they may see your good deeds and praise your Father in heaven*
Matthew 5:14-16

*Verily, verily, I say unto you, He that believeth on me, the
works that I do shall he do also; and greater works
than these shall he do; because I go unto my father*
John 14:12.

*Ye have not chosen me, but I have chosen you, and ordained you, that ye
should go and bring forth fruit, and that your fruit should remain: that
whatsoever ye shall ask of the Father in my name, he may give it you*
John 15:14.

Wherefore comfort yourselves together, and edify one another, even as also ye do
1 Thessalonians 5:11.

But ye are a chosen generation, a royal priesthood, an holy nation,
a peculiar people; that ye should shew forth the praises of him who
hath called you out of darkness into his marvelous light
1 Peter 2:9.

If you love me obey my commandments
John 16:15.

So let us stop going over the basics of Christianity again and
again. Let us go instead and become mature in our understanding.
Surely we don't need to start all over again with the importance of
turning away from evil deeds and placing our faith in God
Hebrews 6:1 (NLT).

Many believers struggle in their walk with Christ because they have not fully realized who they truly are in Him. They have not renewed their minds, taken on the new creature status or committed to living by the standards set forth in the Holy Bible. They have not maximized, applied their faith or grasped the meanings of the powerful Word. I am speaking of people who believe in the Holy Trinity, where there is one God, with three personalities; namely God the Father, God the Son, and God the Holy Spirit. God the Father, El Shaddai- the Almighty and all sufficient God, Who is the Maker or Creator of all human beings and things. He loves us so much that He sent His only Son to die for our sins. His Son, Jesus, Who is the second person of the Trinity, willingly obeyed the Father and died on the cross at Calvary. Jesus paid the ultimate price on the cross for our sins. He is our Savior, and because of this, we are indebted to Him (to obey and surrender our all to Him). Therefore we should love, believe, grow, mature and live for Him. In other words, we should have a personal relationship with Him and stay away from sin. We, should not just say we believe and not live according to His principles.

Jesus came to earth and lived among men; so He knows what it is like to be both God and man (God incarnate). He set a standard by which we (believers and His followers) are to live. He went back to heaven to be with His Father. It is recorded in the Bible that He stays by the right hand of His Father, interceding on our behalf. Before Jesus left the earth, He promised to send the Holy Spirit to live in, guide, teach, and counsel us. The Holy Spirit is the third person of the Trinity, and has a most significant presence in the believer's life. I know all this already, so why are you telling me? Because as simple as it sounds, there are those who do not get it. We need the Holy Spirit to help us as we perform the work we have been assigned to do until Christ returns. The Word declares: *But the Comforter, which is the Holy Ghost, whom the Father will send in my name, he shall teach you all things, and bring all things to your remembrance, whatsoever I have said unto you* (John14:26) *But you have received the Holy Spirit, and he lives within you, so you don't need anyone to teach you what is true. For the Spirit teaches you everything you need to know, and what he teaches is true—it is not a lie. So just as he has taught you, remain in fellowship with Christ* (1 John 2:27) NLT.

Believers are called to abide in Jesus, which mean to become His bosom friend by accepting His unconditional love, obeying His Word and having a relationship with Him. It is making the decision to live a sanctified and holy life, even though it requires a great deal of commitment. Jehovah-M'Kaddesh, who helps us with sanctification, is always ready to sanctify and help us to live holy whenever we are ready. We have been given this command: *Love the LORD **your** God, and to serve him with **all your heart** and with **all your** soul* (Deuteronomy 11:13). Therefore we are to remain in a sanctified and supernatural relationship with Jesus, bearing and sharing in His suffering until He comes, not only when it is convenient for us, but consistently. The reason we must make the decision to live holy is so: *That the righteousness of the law might be fulfilled in us, who walk not after the flesh, but after the Spirit* (Romans 8:4). Believers should have no fear or worry about how to live right. God already assured us that He is our righteousness. He demonstrated this in John 3:16 and in our daily experiences with Him. However, we cannot claim His finished work and not live by His Word.

Sometimes believers get confused—they believe that because Jesus died for our sins, we can live any kind of life we feel like living, without taking responsibility for our actions. Paul said "No"(Romans 6:15). *What **shall** we say then? **Shall** we **continue** in **sin**, that grace may abound?* (Romans 6:1). Christ finished work alone should be sufficient for us to obey and live by God's Word. We cannot sit or live a sinful life thinking that we have nothing to do because Jesus did it all. We still have to do our part until Jesus returns to take us with Him. So do not miss the point and get too comfortable, thinking that because Jesus finished His work, yours is also finished. You have to surrender to Christ, love everyone, forgive, stop yielding to sin/satan/flesh and follow the mandates of the scripture. Yes, we live by faith, but *faith without works is dead* (James 2:20*)*.

When my son was four years old, he asked me, "Mom, why did God send His Son, Jesus to die? Why didn't He come and die Himself?" At the time he asked me the question, I had no idea how to answer him. I told Him that because God is the Father He knows what is best and He always does the right thing. Later I learned in a Bible class that Jesus came because God is a Spirit and He needed to send a body with which mankind could identify.

When I found this out I attempted to explain it to my son and he said, "I still don't get it." I told him not to be too concerned about it, because he will understand it one day. In the mind of a four year old, a father should be protecting his child, not giving him up to death. I was telling him the story of the Crucifixion when he posed the question. Needless to say, I was stunned. I thought to myself, "I had never even conceived such a question and here he is at such a young age, asking this of me."

If a child can be this eager to learn more about the character of God, why should believers not be? From the experiences of Jesus' life leading to His crucifixion, resurrection and ascension we learned that Jesus lived a sinless life, doing everything that God His Father asked Him to do. He said He did nothing unless His Father asked Him to. This is the example for us believers to follow in order to become holy. If anyone tells you it is effortless because Jesus already did the work, do not believe them. You have work to do and it is important for you to understand that and to find out what your specific assignment is.

Jesus knew that by ourselves we would not be able to follow in His footsteps, so He left with us the Holy Spirit, Who is with us constantly, teaching, counseling and guiding us. I often ask myself, why do I have to have fleshly desires to do things that make me feel good, but are not necessarily in line with the kind of character I want to build as a child of the living God? The answer to this question is that, although I have the privileges of a believer, I am still subject to sin, because of the fall of my ancestors, Adam and Eve. Paul elucidates this for us in Romans 3:23: *For all have sinned, and come short of the glory of God.*

What an assurance we have in knowing that we sin, but God justifies us! Justification applies to every believer. It helps us believers to understand that we are justified only by faith in Christ Jesus and not by our works. It is not by the work we do that God gives us justification, but through our faith in Him. Nevertheless, we must not neglect the work. It is impossible to receive justification by ourselves, or from any other source, except from God. The Scripture declares: *No one is righteous-not even one* (Romans 3:10). Justification, according to The Strong's Exhaustive Concordance of the Bible, is: the act of divine grace which restores the sinner to the relationship with God that he would have had if he had not sinned: pardon of sin. The word is used also to denote the state of the sinner after he is restored to divine favor. It is from the Hebrew word *guel*, which means "splendor of God." This sounds like something every believer should desire to have. Do you want to have the splendor of God and to live a serene life?

Believers must be prepared at all times. One question I often ponder is this: If the rapture was to take place right now, would I be caught up to be with Jesus? If you ask yourself this question and you are unsure of the answer, it is a good time to re-examine the foundation of your life, your character and your spiritual status. Ask God to remove and cast from you those things that are in violation of your relationship with Him. God can use us to do the things He has prepared for us to do, only when we release those things that have spiritually flawed our characters. Believers are chosen and are called to love, obedience, gentleness, justice, mercy, persecution, favor, sanctification, purification, holiness, forgiveness, blessings, promises and as peace-makers. Sin is not an option for us, even though it is inevitable in our human flesh. When I look back at my life, and look at the 10 Commandments, it seems as though I have committed all the sins there are to commit, but I also read in the Word that there is no sin I could ever commit that God would not forgive, except if I blaspheme the Holy Spirit (Matthew 12:31-32). There must come a time in every believer's life that he/she must to study the character of Christ in order to avoid sin and be like Jesus. This is the transformation I am alluding to. As believers in Jesus Christ we ought to encourage and build up one another. According to principles, every believer should be an encourager and a brother's keeper.

On the contrary, we pull down or tear one another apart. That is what we have been conditioned to do. Believers should be exhorting rather than fighting against other believers, evangelizing rather than pretending, interceding rather than gossiping, pulling down or tearing apart, being accountable and seeking confidants in this department rather than being wishy-washy and just sliding by, having gratitude and appreciation rather than complaining, being confident rather than timid and indecisive, taking action rather than procrastinating, living in abundance rather than in poverty, being consistent in our walk rather than being inconsistent, building characters rather than destroying them, being an enthusiast for the Word of God rather than being matter-of-fact about it, acknowledging rather than criticizing, empowering rather than belittling and living in the spirit rather than yielding to the flesh.

Believers must deepen their relationships with the Lord by being honest first to themselves and then with Him. We should make concerted efforts each day not to sin against Him, by: *Casting down imaginations, and every high thing that exalteth itself against the knowledge of God, and bringing into captivity every thought to the obedience of Christ* (2 Corinthians 10:5). God loves us more than any human being can. We need to be confident in the unconditional love Jesus has for us. We do not need to haphazardly seek love, but rather be satisfied in knowing that no other love can compare to the love of God for His children. The most important thing for the believer is to have a consistent personal relationship with God, through the application of biblical principles in daily living.

Have you ever been in church and felt as though the pastor was preaching directly to you when he preaches on topics that addressed issues of which you knew you were guilty? I have been there, but these days I do not feel guilty when a pastor preaches about what I call a "hot spot" (something that convicts me). Instead, I am rather thankful for the messages that help me to make changes in my life and enable me to grow and get closer to God in many ways. The word declares in Hebrews 3:13: *But encourage one another daily, as long as it is called Today, so that none of you may be hardened by sin's deceitfulness* (NIV).

My prayer is that God will put someone who needs to hear about Him in my way every day.

The apostle Paul said: *So let us stop going over the basics of Christianity again and again. Let us go on instead and become mature in our understanding. Surely we don't need to start all over again with the importance of turning from evil deeds and placing our faith in God* (Hebrews 6:1) NLT. In other words, let us have some growth, some maturity in our spiritual lives, improve on what we already know, strive for excellence and work toward perfection. Although we will never be perfect in this life, I believe it is worth working toward it.

Sometimes we allow circumstances to prevent us from being all that we are capable of being. This is one of our greatest handicaps in the body of Christ. If you have overcome some major issues in your life, use those experiences to help protect others from falling victims to the same situations. Sometimes I say to myself, if I had only known what I know now, I would never have done what I did then, but what I have learned is that God allowed me to go through those experiences for His purpose, not mine and so that I might use them to bring Him glory. This verse is my assurance: *And we know that all things work together for good to them that love God, to them who are the called according to his purpose* (Romans 8:28).

It should not be our concern as to whether or not people listen to us. The believer's responsibility is to tell his or her testimony, for Christ's sake. Yes, people will judge you, but you have to get to that point where you do not let fear of what people may say or do impede you from doing what you need to do. For example, the apostle Peter said that if you were called to be a speaker, you should speak as though God Himself was speaking through you, speaking boldly and proclaiming the Gospel knowing that God will not judge you, even though you deserve His judgment: *If any man speak, let him speak as the oracles of God; if any man minister, let him do it as of the ability which God giveth: that God in all things may be glorified through Jesus Christ, to whom be praise and dominion forever and ever Amen* (1 Peter 4:11).

When I speak of the believers, I am addressing the people who have believed in Jesus, accepted Him as their Savior, confessed their sins and have become *new*. They were baptized as an outward indication to the world that they are now saved and have a personal relationship with the

Messiah through faith, trust, love and obedience. True believers engage in other practices, such as reading and applying the Word of God in daily living, taking the Holy Communion, worshipping in everything, sharing fellowship with the saints and experiencing the blessings of the Lord. The dictionary describes a true believer as a person who professes absolute belief in something; a zealous supporter of a particular cause. What cause are you zealous about?

God did not save us only, for our own comfort and ease. He expects us to have spiritual growth, become kingdom builders and live life to the fullest. Jesus said: *I am come that they might have **life** and that they might have it **more abundantly*** (John 10:10). Unfortunately some of us live questionable lives every day, causing people to pull further away from God instead of getting closer to Him. We never get to that turning point, which I call transformation.

There was a time in my life when I did not understand the deeper things of God, even though I was saved. I was ignorant to a whole lot of the truths that I should have known as a Christian. For instance, I used to supervise a young lady who I will call "Linda." Linda took her Bible to work every day, and she religiously read it at every break she had. Other staff members complained to me about it, because the young lady would also read her Bible during naptime while the toddlers were resting on their cots.

I knew it was a good thing to read the Bible, so I did not address the complaint, since the children were not being neglected; but I was thinking that she definitely had an obsession with the Bible. What I did not realize was that this woman had something that we did not have. She had an unfathomable love for God and that made her stay in His Word. I am grateful that today, I can say I have found this trait in myself. I am obsessed with reading and hearing the Word at every chance I get. This is indeed my greatest pleasure joy.

Now I understand what the voracious Bible reader was experiencing. I am at that very place in my life, right now, where I have an insatiable appetite for reading the Bible. Saturating myself with the Word is like an addiction. I can hardly put the Bible down. I am absolutely in love with the Word of God. This is truly a good place to be, and I invite you to join me here. As a result of this obedience, God has revealed things to me that I never in my wildest dream imagined were in this great book.

I can tell you one amazing thing I have learned from it is this: *The thing that hath been, it is that which shall be; and that which is done is that which shall be done: and there is no new thing under the sun.* (Ecclesiastes 1:9). I no longer search for answers outside the Bible, because all the answers to our questions are in there.

I actually completed a detailed study of Genesis when I first started writing this book. I found that the contents of the book of Genesis are so everlastingly rich that I think everyone owes it to himself/herself and deserves to get a detailed study of this foundational book. Genesis sets the precedence for all of the other books that follow. I see the intricacies of God's magnificent design and creation. I am amazed at how God weaved mankind into this glorious masterpiece called the World. I know that my life will never be the same again. I see the beauty of God's grand creation in a much different, brighter, richer light than I ever have. I can now appreciate the creeping, crawling creatures that I once detested. With a new concept and understanding of the Holy Spirit, I find it much easier to exist in and appreciate nature, though I had to have my husband kill the rattle snake that showed up in our yard.

The Apostle Paul's passion for a spirit-filled life ignited my spirit when I read what he wrote in Galatians 5:16-24: *This I say then, Walk in the Spirit, and ye shall not fulfill the lust of the flesh. For the flesh lusteth against the Spirit, and the Spirit against the flesh: and these are contrary the one to the other: so that ye cannot do the things that ye would. But if ye be led of the Spirit, ye are not under the law. Now the works of the flesh are manifest, which are these; Adultery, fornication, uncleanness, lasciviousness, Idolatry, witchcraft, hatred, variance, emulations, wrath, strife, seditions, heresies, envyings, murders, drunkenness, revellings, and such like: of the which I tell you before, as I have also told you in time past, that they which do such things shall not inherit the kingdom of God. But the fruit of the Spirit is love, joy, peace, longsuffering, gentleness, goodness, faith, meekness, temperance: against such there is no law. And they that are Christ's have crucified the flesh with the affections and lusts.*

Every believer should enjoy the Spirit filled life, because according to John 3 we are born of the water and the Spirit, and Romans 8:11 says: *But if the Spirit of him that raised up Jesus from the dead dwell in you, he that raised up Christ from the dead shall also quicken your mortal bodies by his Spirit that dwelleth in you,* and finally, 1 John 2:20 says: *But ye have an unction from the Holy One, and ye know all things.*

John went on to give further explanation that Jesus came to baptize the believer with the Holy Spirit. He said: *And I knew him not: but he that sent me to baptize with water, the same said unto me, Upon whom thou shalt see the Spirit descending, and remaining on him, the same is he which baptizeth with the Holy Ghost* (John 1:33). The same spirit that raised Jesus from the dead is the spirit that we as believers have today. This fact will never change because:

Jesus Christ the same yesterday, and today, and forever (Hebrews 13:8). The Holy Spirit is powerful and awesome. Although every believer has this Spirit, not all believers allow the Holy Spirit to have free reign in their lives. Paul wrote these words for a reason: *Quench not the Spirit* (1 Thessalonians 5:19), and Matthew in quoting John the Baptist said: *indeed baptize you with water unto repentance, but he that cometh after me is mightier than I, whose shoes I am not worthy to bear: he shall baptize you with the Holy Ghost, and with fire* (Matthew 3:11). If we should not quench the spirit and if Jesus baptized us with fire when He gave us the spirit, why then are we so cold and quiet about the Holy Spirit? Who can sit still in fire? One example of how a person does not give the Spirit full reign over his life is seen in pastors who do not live what they preach. They live double standard lives and in reality are dishonoring God and doing an injustice to the people they lead. In fact, there are warnings against pastors who disobey, scatter and destroy God's sheep: *Woe, be unto the pastors that destroy and scatter the sheep of my pasture! saith the LORD* (Jeremiah 23:1). I pray for any pastor who would fill people with unbelief and ignore or encourage immorality, because he would be guilty of corrupting the world.

When a pastor destroys God's vineyard by compromising or condoning with church members who live in sin, such as adultery, fornication, homosexuality and other forms of obvious sinful acts, God holds him responsible, because when He chooses a person to lead His flock, he expects integrity and good character. He gives wisdom and expertise to impart undiluted wisdom, knowledge and understanding as it is written in the Holy Word.

He expects a pastor to sow good seeds that will build a strong foundation for a lifetime of commitment to His Kingdom. People are required to live a life of good conduct and reverence in the church. The spiritual foundation of the church should be strong. Paul wrote: *Don't team up with those who are unbelievers. How can goodness be a partner with wickedness? How can light live with darkness? What harmony can there be between Christ and the devil? How can a believer partner with an unbeliever?* (2 Corinthians 1:14-16 and 17a) *Therefore, come out from them and separate yourselves from them, says the Lord.* The Bible warns that Christians have to cleanse themselves from the things that can defile their bodies and their spirits. God requires much from whom He has given much:

For unto whomsoever much is given, of him shall be much required (Luke 12:48).

Those who are chosen for such an important role as pastor, should not continue to support or be silent about moral issues. Silence does not allow progress and upward movement. The main purpose of the church or the body of Christ is to set good biblical standards and help the rest of the world to come to Christ. Another thing that concerns me about the church is the failure of pastors to recognize and use the gifts that people bring to the church. Some pastors are too afraid to delegate work to their member, because they seem to think they can do everything on their own or that they think that relinquishing some of the duties is going to reduce their self-acclaimed power. They either are ignorantly overlooking the essence of the body of Christ which is to employ all the gifts to build up the Kingdom or they are simply selfish. They expect their members to support them, placing all kinds of demands on them, wanting them to support their visions, yet ignoring that the members have personal visions, as they do. Pastors study and seek wisdom on these issue by applying Philippians, Corinthians and other scriptures as necessary. I once heard Zig Ziglar, my favorite inspirational/motivational speaker, say: "The main thing is to make the main thing, the main thing." That is just another way of saying, stick to the original plan and do not become distracted by other things around you. The original plan of the believer is obedience to God's Word. Stay focused!

How can we do this in a world that is filled with distractions? My guess is that if we listen to the Holy Spirit, know our purpose and remain determined and focused, we can accomplish our spiritual goals. Isaiah said it best when he announced: *Because the Sovereign Lord helps me I will not be dismayed. Therefore, I have set my face like a stone, determined to do his will. And I know that I will triumph* (Isaiah 50:7). As David did, we too can *encourage ourselves in the Lord, our God* (1 Samuel 30:6).

If you are in a church where the pastor avoids preaching the Word as it is written in the Holy Bible, does not challenge you to grow spiritually, physically, emotionally, financially and compromises with sin, that is an indication that you need to find another place to worship. Look for a church where the unadulterated truth is being taught, where there are outreach ministries, where you will be challenged to grow spiritually, where you can worship and glorify God freely without any inhibition. When looking for a church, here are a few things to look for; are the members allowed to use their spiritual gifts for God's glory? Are there visible signs of the workings of the fruits of the spirit: love, joy, peace, patience, kindness, goodness, faithfulness, gentleness and self control, being practiced in the church, as it is written in Galatians 5:22-23. Are the Commandments being followed, the Beatitudes and the entire teachings of the Bible being embraced and showing clear signs of manifestation?

Disciples should set an example for others to follow Christ and be conductors with renewed minds that seek after the things of God, while bringing everything else under subjection. In an effort to bond with Jesus, they should have an extension of the Holy Communion. Some churches serve it once per month, but you can have communion at your home with your family or by yourself, as you are led. God's Word declares: *For as often as ye eat this bread, and drink this cup, ye do show the Lord's death till He comes* (1 Corinthians 11:26).

The church is supposed to be the example for the world and if the people of the world do not see the people in the church living according to the fruits of the spirit, this could hinder them from coming to the church to receive Christ. We must take a stand for the uncompromising truths of the gospel and against the behaviors of the world that have infiltrated the church. If the church does not speak out against the evils in society, who can and who will?

Christians, let us work together and make every effort to live a life with the hope of moving into the perfection that Paul talks about. We know that God has already cleansed us from our sins, once and for all, therefore sanctification and holiness are what we need to ensure, possess and maintain. It is written in 1 John 5:18:*We know that whosoever is born of God sinneth not; but he that is begotten of God keepeth himself, and that wicked one toucheth him not.* Read 1Thessalonians 4:1-12, also.

We must set our affection on the things of God. With God's help we must examine our hearts and see if there are any wicked ways in us. We must identify that one thing or those many things that is/are preventing us from living a holy life that is *acceptable* to God. Time is of the essence, and we must decide if we are going to go "all in," as my former Pastor, Ben Barfield encourages his congregation to do. The Word declares: *know ye that the kingdom of God is nigh at hand.* (Luke 21:31). Since no one knows exactly when the return of Jesus will be, it makes sense to be prepared at all times. To be prepared at all times means to consciously live a holy and sanctified life through the application of biblical principles and in preparation for the second return of Jesus Christ. Identify the conditions to which you need to pay attention to and do what it takes to make this happen.

Once you have identified what the issues are, immediately address them by asking: What do I need to do about these issues? "Nothing happens until change happens." First you can begin by admitting to yourself that you have these challenges, confess them to the Lord and then ask Him to help you deal with them, after you have given Him thanks for forgiving you. Make the decision to refrain from sinning over and over again. If we are not careful, our end could be as described in this verse: *But many Israelites—those for whom the Kingdom was prepared—will be thrown into outer darkness, where there will be weeping and gnashing of teeth* (Matthew 8:12). This will happen to believers who settle mediocrity and for straddling the fence, or living on the edge, instead of fully committing to Christ. Scriptures warn that we should be fully clothed, we should be prepared and ready, that if Christ comes suddenly He will find us, not living in sin, but fully ready to go with Him. What are you doing to ensure this? Are you one of those Christians sitting on the fence living a happy go lucky, nonchalant kind of life?

We need to deliver to the world using the power of the Word we have been given by *El Shaddai* (the almighty and all sufficient God). In order for us to do this work we must do a character check often, asking ourselves pointed questions, such as; Am I seeking God's guidance in my decision making processes? Do I put God first in everything I do? This scripture gives direction and clarity in this area: *But **seek** ye **first** the kingdom of God, and his righteousness; and all these things shall be added unto you* (Matthew 6:33). Can you imagine what would happen to believers if we really put God first?

Another area in which we might fall short is in knowing our purpose in the church. Here again, it would help if we ask these questions of ourselves. Do I understand the vision of the church? Am I loyal to the work of the Lord, and how committed am I to the church in helping it to accomplish its vision? Am I fighting with my brothers and sisters? Am I lying, grudging, stealing, cheating, being unforgiving, harboring bitterness and un-forgiveness, being hypocritical, double-minded or rebelling against the Holy Spirit? These character traits do not image God's character. Our character should be impeccable, exuding righteousness with integrity and confidence. As Believers we have a great deal of work to accomplish. The word declares: *Blessed are the pure in heart: for they shall see God* (Matthew 5:8). The journey of a believer is a struggle, but the good thing is that God never leaves us nor forsakes a believer. Even when we shove Him to the side, he is always there to see us through our difficult times, just as he did for Peter. As a young believer, I learned this gem somewhere along the way and for some reason, it has stuck with me. It goes like this: "Some people go to church to laugh and talk, some to gain a lover, some their faults to cover, but few go there to worship God." I thought-how true and how sad!

I know we could think of many other interesting reasons why people go to church; unfortunately, many of the reasons are contrary to God's intention for the church. The bottom-line is that it is not about those people; it is about you and God. A person who finds a true and personal relationship with God does not let what people say or do become a hindrance to their serving God. To serve God, obey His commands and stay in His will are personal choices. There is a saying that goes, "If you do good, people talk, if you do bad they also talk, so all you have to do is to serve God and give them more to talk." We have to be true to ourselves and to God: *For God is a Spirit, so those who worship Him must worship in Spirit and in truth* (John 4:28).

Too many people blame others as a means of taking the easy way out. How long will you point the fingers at others? Until we begin to examine our own lives, be honest with ourselves, and make the decision to fully obey and trust God, we will always point our fingers at and blame others. If we continue to do this we cannot have the peace and joy that we need to enter that place in paradise. My grandmother used to say, "Big finga neva sey, look yah, it always sey, look deh." Translated from the Jamaican dialect, it means, we blame or throw darts at everyone except at ourselves, or that we always see others' faults, but never our own. Even though our big finger is closest to us, we point it outwards to blame others because we refuse to see our own faults, the *specks in our own eyes,* as the Bible puts it.

The Word of God promises us joy and peace. If we seek God's Guidance He will give it to us and He will deliver us, set us free and protect us from satan's traps. John 8:36 declares: *If the Son therefore shall make you free, ye shall be free indeed.* In this freedom there is a renewing of the mind that will allow you to let your light shine and live life to its fullest.

PRINCIPLES FOR DAILY APPLICATION

(1) Begin by renewing your mind/thought life. Stop believing the lies you hear playing in your head. Be sure to read and meditate on God's Word daily, this will help you to filter out the rubbish and get a good understanding of what the Word is saying to you. According to scriptures, the Word is God inspired and God breathed. Therefore, do not reject any part of it or allow the enemy to snatch it from your heart? Do not harden you heart; receive the message with joy, be excited about It, and allow it to sink deeply into your heart. When you have the Word implanted in you and situations, such as persecution, trials and other problems arise, you can stand firm because you know what you know. Do not allow the cares of life or attraction of wealth to distract you.

Stay focused and ask the Lord to forgive and *transform* you into the person He created you to be. Do a daily *integrity* check to make sure your *character* lines up with your Father's. God's Word says: *Ye are the light of the world* (Matthew 5:14) *Therefore, Let your light so shine before men, that they may see your good works and (be led) to glorify your father who is in Heaven* (Matthew 5:16). Are we really doing this as believers?

We are also told that we are the salt of the earth: *Ye are the salt of the earth: but if the salt has lost his savour, wherewith shall it be salted? It is thenceforth good for nothing, but to be cast out, and to be trodden under foot of men.* (Matthew 5:13). We all know that food without flavor is tasteless, so is the life of the believer who does not reflect the image of God. Write these scriptures in your heart.

(2) Live the *truths* of the Bible. It will please God and show in your life when you apply the Word. Believe the promises in the Word and claim the Blessings of Deuteronomy 28. Do not be a counterfeit Christian. In the book of Mark we are told: *Salt is good: but if the salt has lost his saltness, wherewith will ye season it? Have salt in yourselves, and have peace one with another* (Mark 9:50). We need to be well equipped in order to help the people who are still seeking to find the truth in this troubled world. I have heard many people (unsaved) say that they are trying to find the Truth or that they are seekers of It. What are they seeking for? The Bible clearly states: *seek God*. The reason they cannot find what they are looking for is because they are looking in the wrong places and at the wrong things. I often share some of my testimonies about why I believe in Jesus and how I know the Truth. I also advise them to take the time to look within themselves and in the Bible in order to find all that they seek. Unfortunately, if they do not look in the Bible, they will be forever *seeking.*

(3) Forgive yourself and forgive others then *expect* the *unexpected.* Be willing to change with the times, get rid of the old mind-set, of the traditional strongholds, intellectual and celebrity spirits, un-forgiveness and all generational curses. Accept God's forgiveness of all sins in order to be confident and celebrate the new you in Christ. We are reminded by Paul:

Therefore if any man be in Christ, he is a new creature: old things are passed away; behold, all things are become new (2 Corinthians 5:17).

Acts 13:38-40 tells the importance of forgiveness for those who desire to go to heaven. Un-forgiveness is one of the biggest problems we face as human beings. It causes anger and hatred and it is makes us sick. This can be difficult for many, because we are sometimes too hard on ourselves, but we must practice forgiveness, if we want to inherit God's Kingdom.

(4) Surrender to your purpose (the will of God) and do not rebel. As this popular quote from God's Word goes, "to whom much is given much is required." This is suggestive of the high expectation God has for the believers. Rebellion has to become a thing of the past for us, because we now know God and understand that if we do not obey His Word, He'll bring His wrath upon us. Romans 1:32 declares: *Although they know God's righteous decree that those who do such things deserve death, they not only continue to do these very things but also approve of those who practice them* (NIV).

(5) Do not gossip. Gossip is a common thing among people, not only in the work place, but in the church as well as in other places. It is the act of discussing people's private matters with others and spreading rumors. It is ugly and dirty, stay away from it. I like to pick on the church, because we should know better. Let us say, for example, a sister or a brother in the church, at home or at work comes up to you and starts to talk about another person; if you choose to engage in the conversation, that is called gossiping. If you chose to listen, even if you do not partake in the conversation, you are a recipient of that gossiper's sin, and it becomes your sin too.

The right way to handle such a situation, then, would be to dismiss the conversation by informing the gossiper that you are not interested, or simply excuse yourself and walk away. You have the right to walk away from anything that is offensive to you, or is against the will of your Father. It is written in Ephesians that we are to keep the unity of the spirit in the bond of peace: *Endeavoring to keep the unity of the Spirit in the bond of peace.*(Ephesians 4:3). Hypocritical behaviors cause strife, not peace. If you feel that you have been offended by someone, address the person directly. You may be considered, abrasive, blunt or insensitive. Do not let that prevent you from doing the right thing, as long as your motive is love and genuine concern for the welfare of the individual.

(6) Jesus promised: *And I will give unto thee the **keys** of the **kingdom** of heaven: and whatsoever thou shalt bind on earth shall be bound in heaven: and whatsoever thou shalt loose on earth shall be loosed in heaven* (Matthew 16:19). Believers must take these keys and run with them in order to win the race that is set before us. Work continuously on your image to become more like Jesus in, attitude, patience, perception, behavior, belief system, love yourself, God and others, apply the fruits of the spirit, the commandments, study the beatitudes, worship God in the beauty of holiness and advance the Kingdom in every way possible.

Learn to use the authority God gave you to have confidence in yourself and to have dominion over all things. There are no limits for the believer, except the ones we place on ourselves. The truth is we are unstoppable. Remember: *the kingdom of God is within you* (Luke 17:21). Matthew reminds us: *Be ye therefore perfect, even as your Father which is in heaven is perfect.* (Matthew 5:48). Read Romans Chapter 12. I have found it to be a great source of encouragement about being a living sacrifice for the sake of Christ. Always remember; life's troubles and struggles are preparing you for your destiny.

(7) Pray, pray, pray always and again, I emphasize; study the Bible and meditate on the Word. You can write scripture verses on 3x5 or smaller cards, and memorize them daily. It is imperative that you use the Bible as the tool that directs your life. Read it regularly and confess you sins daily. Joshua had remarkable wisdom about the Word; here is what he advise: *This book of the law shall not depart out of thy mouth; but thou shalt meditate therein day and night, that thou mayest observe to do according to all that is written therein: for then thou shalt make thy way prosperous, and then thou shalt have good success* (Joshua1:8).

Be sure to read the book of Genesis in its entirety for yourself. Study the Ten Commandments in Exodus 20. Read Ephesians 4. Open your Bibles often and ask God to direct your reading. You can enhance your biblical knowledge and spiritual life by finding a group such as Bible Study Fellowship (BSF) to learn more about this great Word. BSF is free.

Oh, taste and see that the Lord is good: Blessed is the man who trusteth in Him!(Psalm 34:8).

As the songwriter wrote, "I feel like a fire is shut up within my bones." I can say that I feel the joy of the Lord within me. It gives me strength and I cannot contain this joy; I must share it with you as I am compelled to do. I hope you too are inspired to share the Good News. Sharing the Gospel is my passion. In order to share your passion or the Gospel, you have to study: *Study to shew thyself approved unto God, a workman that needeth not to be ashamed, rightly dividing the word of truth* (2 Timothy 2:15).

Get familiar with passages such as Galatians 6:8, Hebrew 12:1

(The Fruits of the spirit), John 15:5, Ezekiel 18:30-31 (the Holy Spirit) Matthew 1:18-20, James 5:11, 2 Timothy 2:3 (Patience and endurance). Please get deeper into the Word... read the entire Bible.

Study the Desiderata.
I learned the Desiderata when I was a child, and these words have resonated in my spirit ever since. They have actually become a part of how I think, say, do things and live my life. This is an encouraging, character building poem. May God bless you, my sisters and brothers!

THE DESIDERATA

Go placidly amid the noise and haste and remember what peace there may be in silence. As far as possible, without surrender be on good terms with all persons. Speak your truth quietly and clearly; and listen to others; even the dull and ignorant; they too have their story. Avoid loud and aggressive persons; they are vexatious to the spirit. If you compare yourself with others, you may become vain and bitter; for always there will be greater and lesser persons than yourself. Enjoy your achievements as well as your plans. Keep interested in your own career however humble; it is a real possession in the changing fortunes of time. Exercise caution in your business affairs; for the world is full of trickery. But let this not blind you to what virtue there is; many persons strive for high ideals; and everywhere life is full of heroism Be yourself. Especially, do not feign affection. Neither be cynical about love; for in the face of all aridity and disenchantment it is perennial as the grass. Take kindly the counsel of the years, gracefully surrendering the things of youth. Nurture strength of spirit to shield you in sudden misfortune. But do not distress yourself with imaginings. Many fears are born of fatigue and loneliness. Beyond a wholesome discipline, be gentle with yourself. You are a child of the universe, no less than the trees and the stars; you have a right to be here. And whether or not it is clear to you, no doubt the universe is unfolding as it should. Therefore be at peace with God, whatever you conceive Him to be, and whatever your labors and aspirations, in the noisy confusion of life keep peace with your soul With all its sham, drudgery and broken dreams, it is still a beautiful world. Be cheerful. Strive to be happy.

Max Ehrmann 1927

PRAYER:

Dear heavenly Father, I thank You that You are Jehovah-M'Kaddesh, Who sanctifies us. I Thank You for interceding for my brothers and sisters in Christ. I pray oh Lord that we will no longer settle for a mediocre life, but a holy life that is acceptable to You. Thank You that we are the head and not the tail, the first and not the last, at the top, and not at the bottom. We let our light shine in your Shekinah. As Paul said, we know *that we follow after, if that I may apprehend that for which also I am apprehended of Christ Jesus I count not myself to have apprehended: but this one thing I do, forgetting those things which are behind, and reaching forth unto those things which are before I press toward the mark for the prize of the high calling of God in Christ Jesus Let us therefore, as many as be perfect, be thus minded: and if in anything ye be otherwise minded, God shall reveal even this unto You* (Philippians 3:12-15).

Oh Lord, although sometimes we feel like Elijah felt-all alone, we have the assurance of Your Word, that You will never leave us nor forsake us. Thank You, God for rescuing us from the pitfalls of the enemy and making us more than conquerors. I pray as Jeremiah prayed: *thou hast made the heaven and the earth by thy great power and stretched out arm, and there is nothing too hard for thee* (Jeremiah 32:17). Thank You, for You are the great and powerful God, the Lord Almighty. You have all wisdom and do great and mighty miracles. We know that You are aware of the conduct of all Your people, and You reward us according to our deeds. I thank You Lord that we do not want for anything, because You are Jehovah Jireh and You provide everything that we need. Lord, in faith I surrender to You this very moment.

Remove anything in me that is not of You and replace it with all of You. Lord, I thank You that we are strong through Your mighty power, we have Your full armor of protection and we are standing firm ready to fight the warfare of the enemy, regardless of all his tricks and tactics that he will try to use against us.

Father God, I thank You that Your Word teaches us that we are not fighting against our brothers and sisters, but against the wicked spirits, powers of darkness and evil rulers and authorities that live in the world we cannot see with our naked eyes. Thank You for equipping us with the shield of faith and opening our spiritual eyes to see the unseen and for helping us to put on the Helmet of Salvation, the breastplate of righteousness, the sturdy belt of truth and the shoes of peace. We decree and declare that the fiery darts of the enemy has been stopped, as Ephesians 6 informs us.

Most of all, God, I thank You for the sword of the spirit, which is Your Word. Thank You for loosening my feet and setting me free, so that I can run and tell others the Good News! Thank You Lord that I pray in the Holy Spirit, I am sanctified through the blood of Your son Jesus, and I am watchful and alert. I will pray without ceasing, in Jesus' name, Amen.

CHAPTER 2
THE UNBELIEVER

For God so loved the world, that he gave his only begotten Son, that
whosoever believeth in him should not perish, but have everlasting life
John 3:16.

Come now, and let us reason together, saith the LORD:
though your sins are as scarlet, they shall be as white as snow;
though they are red like crimson, they shall be as wool
Isaiah 1:28.

But seek *ye first the **kingdom** of God, and his righteousness;*
and all these things shall be added unto you
Matthew 6:33.

And they will go away into eternal punishment,
but the righteous will go into eternal life
Matthew 25:46.

*Come unto me, all ye that labour and are **heavy laden**, and I will give you rest*
Matthew 11:28.

For the wages of sin is death; but the gift of God is
eternal life through Jesus Christ our Lord
Romans 6:23.

Are you saying that you are not worthy? God is saying I need you, you are mine, and I love you more than you would ever know. There is nothing that you have ever done or could ever do that would cause God not to receive you if you want Him in your life. You belong to Him, but He has given you free will to choose. There are only two choices, God or satan. The one you choose will determine if your destiny will be good or bad. Do you know Jesus? If not, you must read the Holy Bible in order to get to know Him for yourself. I can share my experiences with you, but there is nothing to compare with knowing Christ for yourself. Jesus is your wonderful Savior. I have heard some people say they have read the Word, and they know God, but they do not believe in Jesus. My advice to anyone who is in this predicament is that you pray hard and ask God to help you to understand His Word. Jesus said: *I and my Father are one* (John 10:30). He also said: *I am the way, the truth, and the life: no man cometh unto the Father, but by me* (John 14:6).

Read the entire Bible, and by this I mean both the Old and the New Testaments, because the Bible says that you cannot know the Father and not know the Son. The lesson of His salvation is found in the Old Testament. The Old Testament points to Jesus' coming, gives character witnesses, wisdom and much more... To know the Son you must read the New Testament, because that is where you will find the testimonies, miracles and all about the life of Jesus Christ, the only begotten Son of God and the One whose life we are called to emulate. Would you not want to get to know the Man whose Father created you and the One who died for your sins? Memorize John 3:16: *For God so loved the world, that he gave his only begotten Son, that whosoever believeth in him should not perish, but have everlasting life.* Take a look at Isaiah 1:28, God says, COME NOW. Will you answer His call today?

I know that some of you reading this book have already heard God's message and have not believed it and some have not yet heard God's Word. For those who have not, please understand that I have studied God's Word in the Bible and He reveals Himself to me through them. That is what qualifies me to give you this message. Why does He reveal His secrets to me? Because I believe in Him, I study, meditate on, and apply His Word daily. I have known Him since I was a young child and what I have found is that He has never left me since. John, the one who came to prepare the way for Jesus, wrote: *This was to fulfill the word of Isaiah the prophet: Lord, who has believed our message and to whom has the arm of the Lord been revealed* John 12:38 (NIV). There are those who have heard God's Word and have refused it; therefore they cannot understand why others can write with confidence about the benefits of having faith in Christ Jesus. When you accept and are living for Christ, you will have the same privileges.

There are some people who believe the Messiah has not yet come and while they are waiting for His first arrival, others are waiting for the second coming of Jesus. If you happen to be one of those (still waiting for the first), please do not be mistaken-Jesus has already come and will be returning for His second coming. Read Romans Chapter 10, if you are one of those persons who believe that Jesus is still hanging on the cross, or that He has not yet come to earth. *The Lord is risen* indeed (Luke 24:34). This is too good to be kept a secret. The Bible says that everyone should taste for him or herself and see that the Lord is good.

You may have every material thing you desire and are experiencing a joyful life, but if you do not know Christ, that is just a temporary feeling, and when it leaves you, there will be a feeling of emptiness and void. This joy that I am talking about is the one the Bible tells about. It is a joy that will last forever. It is living water and when you drink of it you will thirst no more living

Do not miss God. How much more does God have to do to prove His existence and mighty power? Have you already forgotten the natural disasters of 2005 and former years, and the recent earthquake in Haiti, that affected an estimated three million people, the unprecedented hurricanes, such as Katrina and Rita; the terrifying tornados, tsunamis, earthquakes, floods and uncontrollable fires? In the daily news we hear of devastating things happening worldwide, not to mention the wars and rumors of wars that are constantly echoed in the media. Did you ever think a black man would become President of the United States of America (USA)? I did not! Barack Obama is black and he is the President of the USA. Considering all circumstances, this is one of the greatest miracles of our time. Have you not seen how violent man has become? How much longer do you think God is going to allow these evil things to happen? Do you remember the Flood in the days of Noah, the incident with the Tower of Babel, or the destruction of Sodom and

Gomorrah? Do you think these are all myths? These things happened in the beginning of time, and according to the Bible, "as it was in the beginning, so shall it be in the end." Luke 21:28 tells us, *So when these things begin to happen, stand straight and look up for your salvation is near!* (NLT). Are these things of no significance to you?

Our God is such a patient God; He often waits and waits and waits, in order to give the people more than enough time to turn from their wicked ways. Paul in Romans 2:4-7 pleads: *Don't you realize how kind, tolerant, and patient God is with you? Or don't you care? Can't you see how kind He has been in giving you time to turn from your sin?" But no, you don't listen. So you are storing up terrible punishment for yourself because of your stubbornness in refusing to turn from your sin. For there is going to come a day of judgment when God, the just judge of all the world, will judge all people according to what they have done* (NLT). He will give eternal life to those who persist in trusting and obeying Him, those who seek the glory and honor and immortality that only God offers. Pay attention to these verses: 2 Peter 3:9 informs: *The Lord is not slack concerning his promise, as some men count slackness; but is longsuffering to us-ward, not willing that any should perish, but that all should come to repentance.* What do the people do instead?

Jeremiah 19:15 answers: *they stubbornly refuse to listen* (NLT). The result is: Judgment and destruction. Proverb 8:35-36 explains this further: *For whoso findeth me findeth life, and shall obtain favour of the LORD. But he that sinneth against me wrongeth his own soul: all they that hate me love death.* I also came across the following verses and when I read it I asked myself, why would anyone want to experience such agony? *There will be weeping and gnashing of teeth, for you will see Abraham, Isaac, Jacob, and all the prophets in the Kingdom of God, but you will be thrown out* (Luke 13:28) (NLT). *And in hell he lift up his eyes, being in torments, and seeth Abraham afar off, and Lazarus in his bosom. And he cried and said, Father Abraham, have mercy on me, and send Lazarus, that he may dip the tip of his finger in water, and cool my tongue; for I am tormented in this flame* (Luke 16:23-24). *Then the rich man said, 'Please, Father Abraham, at least send him to my father's home. For I have five brothers, and I want him to warn them so they don't end up in this place of torment* (Luke 16:27-28) (NLT).

God has promised that He will save us from many disasters if we turn from our evil ways. The Lord told Jeremiah to warn the people of Judah and Jerusalem, say to them: *This is what the Lord says: I am planning disaster against you instead of good. So turn from your evil ways, each of you, and do what is right (Jeremiah 18:11)* (NLT). Read the books of Isaiah, Joel, Zephaniah and Zechariah and John. If you have decided that you do not want to continue in your unbelief or rebellion against Jesus; if you do not want to follow satan and perish, or if you want to give your life to Jesus who already gave His life for you, all you need to do is to take these simple steps which I have outlined for you.

First, you must **admit or confess to Jesus** that you are a sinner. This simply means to tell the Lord that you recognize you are a sinner. How do you know that you are a sinner? It is written in the Bible that we are all born in sin: *Behold, I was shapen in iniquity; and in sin did my mother conceive me* (Psalm 51:5). Therefore, we must be born again if we want to enter the Kingdom of God: *Ye must be born again* (John 3:7). We must confess our sins. It is written in 1 John 1:9: *If we confess our sins; He is faithful and just to forgive us our sins and to cleanse us from all unrighteousness.* If we were not sinners there would be no need for confession. It is also written in (Romans 3:23), *For all have sinned and have come short of the glory of God* and in (1 John 1:8) it says that, *If we say we have no sin, we deceive ourselves, and the truth is not in us.*

It is also important to understand that you cannot get rid of your sin on your own, but by faith in God and by His grace, love and mercy. This is evidenced in Titus 3:5 where it is asserted that, *He (God) saved us, not because of the good things we did, but because of His mercy. He washed away our sins and gave us a new life through the Holy Spirit.* John 3:16 sums it all up: *For God so loved the world, that he gave his only begotten Son, that whosoever believeth in him should not perish, but have everlasting life.*

If you refuse to rid yourself of sin and continue living in it, then the price you will pay is death as it is written in Romans 6:23: *For the wages of sin is death, but the free gift of God is eternal life through Christ Jesus our Lord.*

You must **believe** that Jesus Christ is the only one who can save you from your sins and that God gave His only Son, Jesus Christ, to die on the cross at Calvary for you. You may be asking: How can I believe in Jesus when I have not seen Him with my physical eyes? Let me ask you this: Can you see your mind? Do you believe you have a mind? If you believe you have a mind, which you cannot see, you can believe in Jesus although you have not seen Him. The beauty and splendor are in the life He lived, the work He performed, His death and resurrection and in the fact that He is by God's right side, always interceding for us.

Believing in Jesus is using the measure of faith that God has given to every single person. What is faith? Hebrew 11:1 explains: *Now faith is the substance of things hoped for, the evidence of things not seen.* It is also written in the Word: *Neither is there salvation in any other: for there is none other name under heaven given among men whereby we must be saved* (Acts 4:12). Jesus died and was buried. God raised Him after three days, to prove that death was defeated. Although Jesus lived a sinless life, He chose to be punished in our place, so that our sins may be forgiven. This is evident in the scripture that says: *For Christ also hath once suffered for our sins, the just for the unjust, that He might bring us to God, being put to death in the flesh, but quickened in the Spirit* (1 Peter 3:18).

Once you have a talk with Jesus and let Jesus know that you believe in Him and that you accept Him into your life, He will forgive you of all your sins and will invite you to spend eternity with Him. *He is the one that all the prophets testified about that everyone who believes in Him will have their sins forgiven through His name* (Acts 10:43) also, Jesus said, *I assure you, those who listen to my message and believe in God who sent me have eternal life. They will never be condemned for their sins, but they have already passed from death into life* (John 5:24).

You must **repent** of all your sins. God's Word says: *Repent ye therefore, and be converted, that your sins may be blotted out, when the times of refreshing shall come from the presence of the Lord* (Acts 3:19). *If we confess our sins, He is faithful and just to forgive our sins, and to cleanse us from all unrighteousness* (1 John 1:9). In addition: *If you confess with your mouth that Jesus is Lord and believe in your heart that God raised Him from the dead, you will be saved you.* (Romans 10:9).

Welcome to the family of Christ. Know that you are not on this new journey by yourself. Many other believers are praying for you and want to assist you in any way they can. Do not hesitate to ask any questions you may have.

If you have still not accepted Christ after reading the preceding paragraphs, please think about these thoughts that follow. Do not be like Pharaoh, who at the repeated request of the Lord, stubbornly refused to let the people of Israel go. He listened to and watched the magicians who were able to do some of the same things that God had done to show His power and might. Please do not be fooled by these things, because it was through God's permissive will that these magicians were able to do the things that they did with their secret arts. Today we see that God has given man (saved or unsaved) the ability to do many great things. Some people abuse this freedom and do all sorts of abominable things, such as seeking; fortune telling, physic readings, astrology, palm readings and the likes to find out things about themselves, instead of looking to God, and reading His Word to find the answers that he has so carefully established for us. God is the only One Who has the true and everlasting answers to everybody's questions. In the time of Pharaoh the magicians were successful in getting people to believe in them, and the same things happen in our day. God gives people a certain amount of power to do whatever they chose to do, but He also takes that power whenever He wants.

There was a time when the magicians failed, because God was not about to have them, nor the people around them, continue to believe that the power was their own. God took that power away and they were unable to continue performing their acts. The wicked Pharaoh hardened His heart even more against God. He was not fazed by all the plagues that God had sent upon them. Pharaoh did not heed any of God's commands until God ordered all the firstborn sons and animals to be killed. Pharaoh woke up during the night and realized that there was a death in every single household in Egypt, including his own; then he decided to obey God and let the people go. Can you think of anyone in our society today who reminds you of the Pharaoh? This brings to mind another man in the Bible-Jonah. He was a prophet of God, but one day God gave Jonah an assignment that he did not want to carry out. Jonah did not realize, as many of us today, that he could not run away from his destiny.

God called Jonah to go and preach the Word to the people who did not know God and Jonah refused to go. He did not care if that particular group of people were saved, so instead of listening to God and going five hundred miles east to Nineveh, he decided to go two thousand miles west to Tarshish. Does this resonate with you? Do you see how that man was clearly running away from God and from His assignment? Are people running away from God and their purposes in our day? It was beyond Jonah's comprehension that God would want to save a group of people who were so wicked and had no time for him (God). He-like many of us today, did not understand God's mercy and grace. That is why it is written in the Bible that our thoughts are not like God's and neither are our ways like His. God did not allow Jonah to get away with his disobedience. He sent a powerful storm to rock the boat on which Jonah was trying to escape. This illustration is ironic, because it appeared that Jonah was the only one on the boat who knew the true God, and the other occupants were praying to their gods, but those gods, of course, could not save them, so they cried out to Jonah's God, and He saved them.

If you are still having doubts or questions about whether or not you should accept the Lord Jesus Christ as your Savior, I would like to recommend that you get the movie, *The Passion of Christ* and watch it, if you have not already seen this movie. Also read Matthew Chapter 24. I copied Matthew Chapter 24 from the King James Version of the Holy Bible and placed it in this book, just in case you do not have access to a Bible. You will find it in Chapter 25. It is evident in the Word that when people repeatedly turn their backs on God, He brings His wrath upon them; but when they turn from their disobedience, He embraces and blesses them.

Some people may feel that they have not accepted Christ; they have everything they want and live any kind of way, yet nothing bad has happened to them. What they have not realized is that God gives people time to turn from their iniquities to Him. He is a just God and the Bible says; He reigns on the just as well as on the unjust. He also waits for full manifestation of evil, before he brings His destruction upon them. So the reality is; they are not getting away with it; it is only a matter of time. For insight on this, read Isaiah 63:1-6.

Many people have excuses for not serving God. I have heard people say, "I don't go to church, because church people are hypocrites, liars, and so forth." I know that some people have been hurt by church folks, but I believe for people to say that they do not go to church because of other people's behaviors, that is a "cop-out." Unfortunately, that is the choice many people make, so that they can continue to live in sin. One of the purposes of the messages given in church is to convict you and help you live right.

For example, if you are an abuser of substances and the sermon for the day is about substance abuse, the message may convict you and cause you to give up that bad habit because of your new awareness that your body is God's temple and you should keep it pure. You will have many questions when you decide to live for Christ, and you will find some people along the way who will be able to answer some of your questions. You will discover some of the answers for yourself as you read God's Word, but you will also find that you will not get the answers to every question you have. Do not get discouraged or start to think that something is wrong with you or the pastors or teachers who do not have all the answers to your questions. Some things are not meant for us to know just yet, perhaps later and perhaps never. Some things are tests to challenge our faith, so we must apply faith in certain instances.

We have to believe in things we cannot see. Remember what Hebrews 11:1 says? *Now faith is the substance of things hoped for, the evidence of things not seen.* I have heard people ask many questions which indicate their doubts about the existence of God and His Son. I believe that their issues are due to lack of faith and refusal to accept God's creation as it is. All they have to do is stop, look around them, take a deep breath and see and embrace God's magnificent creation. Based on the following scriptures, some things were not meant for us to know. It is written: *There are secret things that belong to the Lord our God, but the revealed things belong to us and our descendants forever, so that we may obey these words of the law* (Deuteronomy 29:29). John the apostle wrote in the concluding verses of John 21:24-25: *This is the disciple which testifieth of these things, and wrote these things: and we know that his testimony is true. And there are also many other things which Jesus did, the which, if they should be written everyone, I suppose that even the world itself could not contain the books that should be written. Amen.*

This might well be one of the reasons why eighteen years of Jesus' life are unaccounted for in the Bible. I believe that Jesus was such a hard worker that everything could not have possibly been recorded about Him. However, everything that we need to know in our lifetime has been carefully laid out for us in the Holy Bible. We do not need to analyze, intellectualize, contradict, criticize or continue with endless scientific studies, attempting to discover things of which we were never meant to have knowledge.

I guarantee that when people find the truth, the only truth and "nothing but the truth;" they will also find security, peace, freedom, purpose and fulfillment. If people do not know the truth, they will continue to have a craving and desire for it. They will have a huge "hunger and thirst" after it, because they were created to be like Jesus and they cannot truly know Him until they accept Him for who He is. The truth is to know Jesus and accept Him as the One and only Lord of your life. *And ye* **shall** *know the* **truth***, and the* **truth shall make** *you* **free** (John 8:32).

PRINCIPLES FOR DAILY APPLICATION

(1) The first thing you need to do is to believe in Jesus. **Believe** in God, the Father, Jesus the Son and the Holy Spirit. Together, They are called the Holy Trinity. When you believe in Them you will start to think differently and see things in a different way. Light will come into your dark world. *Therefore if any man be in Christ, he is a new creature: old things are passed away; behold, all things are become new* (2 Corinthians 5:17). *Abraham believed and the Lord counted him righteous* (Genesis 15:6). **Believe** *on the* **Lord Jesus Christ***, and* **thou shalt** *be* **saved***, and thy house* (Acts 16:31).

(2) Accept Jesus into your life and let Him guide your path. If you allow Him to, He will show you the way. ***But seek*** *ye first the* **kingdom** *of God, and his righteousness; and all these things shall be added unto you* (Matthew 6:33). Help others to know that they too can accept Jesus in their lives. Share your testimonies with others.

(3) Confess your sins by simply telling Jesus you are sorry for your sins that you may have knowingly or unknowingly committed. The devil will work hard for you to commit sins, but you have to make a conscious effort not to yield to his temptations. Jesus was aware of satan's temptations and He did not let satan's tactics hinder Him from doing God's will. When you do sin, you must confess them to God, accept His forgiveness and move on. The reasons for confessions are found in the following scriptures. *For all have sinned, and come short of the glory of God* (Romans 3:23) *That if thou shalt confess with thy mouth* the Lord Jesus, and shalt believe in thine heart that God hath raised him *from the dead, thou shalt be saved. For with the heart man believeth unto righteousness; and with the mouth confession is made unto salvation.* (Romans 10:9-10).

(4) Stay away from the dark things of this world (sin) because God is light and there is no darkness in Him at all. Live for God by applying His Word to your life. Find a church that teaches from the Holy Bible and attend it often. Get to know God and people who share the same faith at a deeper level. By worshipping together with them that will help you help to learn how you can advance the Kingdom of God. *But if we walk in the light, as he is in the light, we have fellowship one with another, and the blood of Jesus Christhis Son cleanseth us from all sin.* (1 John 1:7). *Not forsaking the* **assembling** *of ourselves together, as the manner of some is; but exhorting one another: and so much the more, as ye see the day approaching* (Hebrews 10:25).

(5) Get a Bible if you do not already have one and begin to read it daily. It will give you guidance on how to live your life for Christ. If you cannot afford to buy a Bible, walk in to any church and let the pastor or someone know that you would like a Bible. They will give you a free one or tell you how to get one. When you have the Bible, do not set it down to collect dust. Read it every day and you will get to know Jesus better. He will open up to you through His Word and you will discover His divine plan for your life. *Thy word is a* **lamp** *unto my* **feet***, and a light unto my path* (Psalm 119:105). *This book of the law shall not depart out of thy mouth; but thou shalt* **meditate** *therein day and night, that thou mayest observe to do according to all that is written therein: for then thou shalt make thy way prosperous, and then thou shalt have good success* (Joshua 1:8).

(6) Share your faith, deliverance story, new found joy, hope and your gift of eternal life. Sharing the Word of God is a commandment that Jesus left for his disciples when He departed from the earth and ascended to sit at the right hand of God, the Father in heaven. He informed the disciples that God gave Him all power in heaven and on the earth. Jesus commanded them: *Go ye therefore, and teach all nations, baptizing them in the name of the Father, and of the son, and of the Holy Ghost: Teaching them to observe all things, whatsoever I have commanded you: and, lo, I am with you always even unto the end of the world. Amen*

(Matt.28:19-20). *Jesus forgave one woman's sin and warned her: Go, now and sin no more"* (John 8:11) *For if we **sin** willfully after that we have received the knowledge of the truth, there remaineth **no more** sacrifice for **sin**s* (Hebrews 10:26).

(7) Pray, pray, pray as often as you can and make sure you pray at least twice per day; when you first wake up in the morning, and before you go to sleep at night. Ask God to show you the plan He has for you each day and give Him thanks before going to bed, no matter what kind of day you had, good or bad; give Him thanks. *Pray without ceasing* (1 Thessalonians. 5:17). Tell God about everything: your joys, sorrows and pain.

PRAYER:

Say this Prayer if you are ready to accept Christ as your Lord and Savior.

Dear Heavenly Father, I believe that You are the Christ, the only begotten Son of God, and I accept You as my Lord and my Savior. I am sorry for all my sins and I give them all to You this very moment. I renounce my past life with satan and I surrender to Your will. Thank You, for releasing me from all of my sins. Thank You for dying on the cross for my sins. I am grateful to You for Your grace and mercy toward me. You said that You are the One Who blots out my transgressions, for Your own sake, and remembers my **sins no more.** I am glad that Your Word is sufficient for me and Your foundation is solid, sure and true. Thank You, for my new life and new beginning that separates me from iniquity and brings me closer to You. Please help me to use my faith as the instrument that will keep me grounded in my relationship with You and help me to feed on Your Word so that I will learn how to trust, obey and live for You for the rest of my life-Amen.

PART II

EFFECTS OF TRANSFORMATION

CHAPTER 3
DIVINE DESTINY

For I know the thoughts that I think toward you, saith the LORD,
thoughts of peace, and not of evil, to give you an expected end
Jeremiah 29:11.

The steps of the Godly are directed by the Lord. He
delights in every detail of their lives.
Psalm 37:23.

And this is His plan: at the right time He will bring everything together
under the authority of Christ-everything in heaven and earth
Ephesians 1:10.

Seek His will in all you do and, he will direct your path
Proverb 3:6 (NLT).

*There **is** a way which seemeth right unto a man, but*
*the **end thereof** is the ways of **death**.*
Proverbs 14:12

Do you know who you are, where you came from, why you are here, what you are here to do and where you are going when you leave here? Every individual should be able to answer these questions with a certain degree of certainty. One day I decided to examine my life and to make sure I could answer these questions. Once I realized what my true purpose in life was, I was compelled to get rid of, and change some things that I once thought were important. I became excited about my purpose and passion, and embraced the fact that I am not a spiritual

39

or religious fanatic, as some may say. I am an individual with a divine assignment and a passion for Christ. I do believe it is important that we ask ourselves questions as a form of self-evaluation.

Have you ever given serious thoughts to the reason you are here? Or have you ever asked yourself, where am I going when I leave this earth? and what will it take me to get there? The day I asked these questions of myself, I knew I had to encourage my clients to ask themselves these same questions. I ask these questions often because I want to be sure I am taking the right actions, staying focused and travelling on the path to my divine destiny. I also want to continue helping others make sure they are doing what God has placed them here to do. Sometimes we have to abandon some of the things that we are currently doing, because we did not get the authority from God to do them. The things we attempt to do that are not ordained by God for us, will lead to failure.

I began to seek the Lord for clarity of purpose by praying this simple prayer daily: "Lord, I do not have clarity about everything that I need to do today, but I am making a commitment to do the things that I can. Please do not allow me to do anything that is not a part of your plan for my life. I come as an empty vessel before you. Use me as you will-Amen." This prayer gives me peace to know that I am depending on God, and not just doing things on my own. I believe this is good practice as Jesus never did anything without the Father's direction.

As I began to rely on, and hear more clearly from the Lord, my purpose became clearer to me. My desire is to accomplish my purpose here on earth just as Jesus and His disciples accomplished theirs. I believe that Jesus has set the standard; the blueprint has been written and I am determined to follow it. I want to be able to say to Him what he said to His Father (God). Jesus said: *I have glorified thee on the earth: I have finished the work which thou gavest me to do* (John17:4). Jesus was so sure His work was done that He even proclaimed it right before He died. His unforgettable words were: **It is finished** (John 19:30). Likewise, our work will not be finished until we die or until Jesus returns. Would you like to be able to say this with surety at the end of your earthly journey?

If your answer is *yes*, Romans 12 is a necessary application for you. Verses one and two declare: *I beseech you therefore, brethren, by the mercies of God, that ye present your bodies a living sacrifice, holy, acceptable unto*

God, which is your reasonable service. And be not conformed to this world: but be ye transformed by the renewing of your mind, that ye may prove what is that good, and acceptable, and perfect, will of God (Romans 12:1-2). Our reasonable service is to submit to the will of God. In order for us to do that we must change the way we think, separate from worldly pleasures, and saturate ourselves in the treasures of the Kingdom.

In order for us to bring glory to our heavenly Father, we have to believe that God's purpose is best, and we must accomplish those things He has assigned us to do. Statistics have shown that more than eighty-five percent of people are not fulfilled in their work. This is incredible, and something is definitely wrong with this picture. Many people today seem to be going about aimlessly. They have no direction, and they do not know their purpose in life. My grandmother used to say, "God has a plan for every man." It is essential to discover what "your" purpose is and execute the plan.

He does have a plan that is unique to each individual, but too often we have allowed our circumstances to interfere with God's plans. Sometimes we are so desperate to be like another person that we miss out on what is right for us. God has always had great plans for us. This declaration from God by the prophet Jeremiah gives insight into the plan God has for us. He declared: *"For I know the thoughts that I think toward you, saith the LORD, thoughts of peace, and not of evil, to give you an expected end."* (Jeremiah 29:11). What a great promise this is! We can rest in this assurance, knowing that we are promised the best life, full of abundance, success, prosperity and health. Further insight into this great plan can be found in many parts of the Bible, such as in Deuteronomy 28, Psalm 139 and 3 John 1:2.

If you understand that God has a plan for your life, you will not allow the conditions of your life, past or present to prevent you from reaching your divine destiny. When you know "God's" purpose, you will know "your" purpose and you will stay within the boundaries of God's plan for your life. This will bring peace and joy. You will know when and how to tap into His unlimited resources, using the power, authority and wisdom He has given you. God designed it and you chose how you will maximize it. I agree with this statement by Mike Murdock

"Choice is the divine paint brush God gives every man to design his own world." How will you choose to use your paintbrush to design your world?

The paths to our destinies do not have to be difficult, but they will be, if we make the wrong choices. It is a sad thing to think that there are many people who have prepared themselves for life, but they are unemployed, unengaged in their life's work or hate their jobs. If you do not know what your purpose is, pray for divine revelation and clarification. Praying for clarity of purpose will enable you to become more aware and focused. You will be better able to handle the distractions, lies and schemes of the enemy, whose job is to keep us from achieving our destinies. The enemy's job is to make you do the opposite of what God has planned for you to do.

Distraction is one of the tools the devil uses to prevent people from engaging in the wonderful plan that God has for them. Satan, the thief, nefarious deceiver and chief destroyer wants to take away everything that God has deposited in His people. John alerts us: *The thief cometh not, but for to steal, and to kill, and to destroy: I am come that they might have life, and that they might have it more abundantly* (John 10:10). The thief is the devil.

Do not reject God's plan; it is only through His plans that you will get to that place of self-actualization, enlightenment or more accurately stated - the place in your life where you have finally realized God's purpose for you, you have surrendered and are actually living for Christ daily, through the direction of the Holy Spirit. This is what we must all strive for. If we do not pay close attention to God's instructions, the prince of the air will distract us into following his lies, and before we know it our dreams will be dead and will and have disappeared into thin air.

Many people have wasted time creating their own plans, and therefore, never fulfill God's plan. As a Life Coach, I understand what Dr. Myles Munroe, an excellent speaker and best- selling author, meant when he said; "The greatest tragedy in life is not death, but rather it is going through life not knowing your purpose."

Are you living life purposefully? We are promised an abundant and blessed life if we live life with purpose. What is the quality of your life like? God desires excellence in the lives of the believers, because He is a God of excellent standards. The Bible says, *But covet earnestly the best gifts: and yet shew I unto you a more excellent way* (1 Corinth. 12:31) Our goals should then be to achieve excellence always. How do we do that? Put God first in everything that we do and love Him and love everyone. Then He will show us how.

I believe that the most significant reason for experiencing lack of clarity in knowing our purpose is because we have not allowed the Holy Spirit to teach, lead or guide us. We often find it difficult to make decisions about choices, because we are making decisions independent of the Holy Spirit. When faced with a situation it always helps to pray about it and seek the Holy Spirit's Guidance. This will help in making a realistic choice, based on the benefit to be derived from that decision; the one that would bring glory to God.

When we do not maximize our God-given potentials, we end up in a vicious cycle of confusion and frustration. We want to be like this person or that person and what we end up doing is ignoring our own gifts and talents. What benefit is there in aspiring to be like someone else, instead of embracing the person God created you to be? It is okay to admire other people, but it is not okay to desire so much to be like them that you lose track of your purpose or lose your identity. It is better to strive to be like Jesus; in so doing, you can never go wrong. Always remember; you are uniquely designed for a specific purpose. Find out what your purpose is and stick with it, regardless of what doubts or discouragement comes.

If you are feeling intimidated about what God has told you, that is normal. You have to figure out a way to get over the intimidation so you can run with the vision, because according to Habakkuk, the vision is only for a time. *For the **vision** is yet for an appointed time, but at the end it shall speak, and not lie: though it tarries, wait for it; because it will surely come, it will not tarry* (Habakkuk 2:3). Try not to miss it. Instead of dodging and finding excuses as to why you cannot carry out your assignment, it is better to trust and obey God and keep asking Him until you have the answers you seek. Taking the escape route did not work for Jonah and I doubt it will work for any of us. The kind of relationship we have with God does affect our destinies. God is patient with us. He gives us many chances and the freedom to make choices, but it is up to us to act upon them wisely. God wants us to follow His plan and instructions as we accomplish our daily tasks. Isaiah warns:

It will all happen as I have planned. It will come about according to my purposes (Isaiah 14:24*)*. In the end, it will come about according to *His* purpose, not *my* purpose or *your* purpose. Psalm 33:11 says: *The counsel of the LORD standeth for ever, the thoughts of his heart to all generations.* Jesus said: *I must work the works of Him that sent me, while it is day: the night cometh, when no man can work.* (John 9:4).

Although God has the master plan, we must also have a plan to carry out God's plan in the earthly realm. The important thing to realize is that our plans are secondary to His. He reminds: *My son, let them not depart from your eyes. Keep sound wisdom and discretion. So they will be life to your soul. And grace to your neck. Then you will walk safely in your way, and your foot will not stumble* (Proverbs 3:21-23). The word says to plan and when you execute those plans, fulfillment will come. If you have a thought, write it down, because it is not a plan until it is tangible. A thought can easily slip away and might never come back to you. If you write down your goals and put it on a shelf or in a drawer somewhere, nothing will happen. You must act on it to see manifestation. Keep it in your purse, wallet, palm pilot or on your desk where it is easily visible.

Fear dominates our lives, when we allow the divisor of all evil to control us with his lies. This is a big mistake on our part. We should refuse to settle for the plans that satan devises. We must fight for our destinies. A gentle reminder for us is this: *There are many devices in a man's heart; nevertheless the counsel of the LORD, that shall stand* (Proverbs 19:21). Paul said God created us for His Pleasure: *Having predestinated us unto the adoption of children by Jesus Christ to himself, according to the good pleasure of his will* (Ephesians 1:5). God is so faithful to us that we should not give satan a chance.

An example of how faithful God is and how amazing and perfect His plans are for can be seen in the life of Abraham. Abraham was determined to accomplish God's plan, even though it took a long time to be realized. He waited on God, obeyed trusted and walked in His purpose. As a result, to this day, his descendants live an abundant and blessed life. This is the life promised to all believers, who applies the faith principle, embrace the Holy Spirit's guidance and live the spirit filled life. The following truths about the Holy Spirit as John recorded are helpful to us in understanding the purpose of the Holy Spirit: *But* the **Comforter**, *which is the Holy Ghost, whom the Father will send in my name, he shall teach you all things, and bring all things to your remembrance, whatsoever I have said unto you* (John 14:26). *But when the Comforter is come, whom I will send unto you from the Father, even the Spirit of truth, which proceedeth from the Father, he shall testify of me* (John 15:26).

This is a good place to interject an important aspect of purpose. Do you have a vision, a mission statement and a plan for execution? Habakkuk said to write the vision and make it plain: *And the LORD answered me, and said, Write the vision, and make it plain upon tables, that he may run that readeth it* (Habakkuk 2:2). Every individual should have a vision and a mission. Your vision is a mental picture of what you want to accomplish and your mission is your plan to accomplish it. You may create your vision statement from the desires of your heart. Think about the things you value and really want to do. What are those unaccomplished things that keep tugging at you? What are the things you think about when you should be sleeping at night? What is keeping you from being fully satisfied and having complete peace? Those are the things you should take to heart, begin to work on them and do not stop until you have your desired results. In the end we should be able to proclaim as Paul did: *I have fought the good fight, I have finished my course, I have kept the faith.* Paul was able to make that announcement, because he accomplished his assignment, just as Jesus did His. We can do as Jesus and Paul did, having the tolerance and asking God for the capacity to function in the will of God, regardless of adversity.

People who are engaged in their calling do not have to stay up at nights thinking or grow weary in well doing, because they enjoy what they do and they know they will reap if they faint not. When you are at this place in your journey with a purpose, you may sometimes like the Giving Tree, where you do and do, give and give and you get nothing back from the human being to whom you are giving your service. Do not let that discourage you, because God will reward you and He has promised you great things if you do not give up. God will never fail you. He says when He begins a good work in you He will see it to completion: *Being confident of this very thing, that he which hath begun a good work in you will perform it until the day of Jesus Christ* (Philippians 1:6). Timothy also informed: *If a man therefore purges himself from these, he shall be a vessel unto honor, sanctified, and meet for the master's use, and prepared unto every good work* (2 Timothy2:21).

I took a few psychology classes in undergraduate school. From one particular class, I learned something that has stuck with me until this day. It made a lot of sense to me. Abraham H. Maslow had a theory which suggests human beings are motivated by unsatisfied needs and that lower order needs must be met or satisfied before one is motivated to progress higher up the needs pyramid to become what one is capable of becoming. For some reason this resonated with me, and I believe if a young person thinks in these terms, he or she will have something to work toward. This would help in understanding that everything in life is a step by step process which when followed accordingly will result in success. Maslow put these ideas on a pyramid or a triangle, with the base of the triangle representing the lower level needs and the top of the triangle representing the higher level needs which is the need for self actualization. He named the hierarchy of needs on the triangle as follows:

The first level, he named physiological needs. The second is the need for safety and security. The third is the need for love and belonging. The fourth level is self–esteem, where he noted that there are two versions of self-esteem need- a lower and a higher one. He proposed that if significant problems arise during any of these phases of development and some of these needs are not met, a person may become fixated and remain in that stage for the rest of his or her life.

Finally, Maslow talked about the need for self–actualization, which cannot be met until all the lower needs have been satisfied. To be self-actualized is to know your purpose and be engaged in it. It is the realization of yourself and who you really are. It is discovery and acceptance of where you are from, what you are here to do. It is taking inspired action to do your life work, disallowing the past to interfere with your present or future. Most importantly, you are no longer guided by the world systems, but by the system of God's kingdom. Your have faith and trust in His system and hope in where you are going. I believe the key to self-actualization is surrendering to one's purpose and applying Matthew 6:33: *But seek first his kingdom and his righteousness, and all these things will be given to you.*

Let us take another look at Abraham and Sarah for a moment. They are early examples of how God's extraordinary plan and process work in people's lives. God promised to give Abraham and Sarah a son. They waited for a long time and still had not received their promised son. They were well up in age, and perhaps thought Sarah was too old to bear a child, so they decided to help God by using their maid, Hagar, to produce the son that God had promised them.

They trusted God with all their hearts, but because they were human beings, they allowed themselves to be tricked by the desires of their flesh. They lied and separated from God during that waiting period. If only they had sought God's guidance; they would not have made the mistakes they made.

When I look back at my own life I see many times when I separated from God and did things outside of His will. Just as God kept His promises to Abraham and Sarah, even though they did things against the will of God, He keeps His promises to us also when we too fall from grace. If we want to please God, we must understand that God has made everything, including us for His own purposes, according to Proverb 16:4: *The LORD hath made all things for himself: yea, even the wicked for the day of evil.* Jesus assures: *The thief cometh not, but for to steal, and to kill, and to destroy: I am come that they might have life, and that they might have it more abundantly* (John 10:10). If we are not operating in God's will we are operating in the will of satan. We are warned in 1 Peter 5:8: *Be sober, be vigilant; because your adversary the devil, as a roaring lion, walketh about, seeking whom he may devour.* If we leave ourselves open to satan's scheme he will destroy us as he did Job and many others. Imagine this little conversation between Jesus and satan:

Something happened in the life of Job: *And the LORD said unto Satan, Whence comest thou? Then Satan answered the LORD, and said, From going to and fro in the earth, and from walking up and down in it.* (Job 1:7). This is serious business, as satan still has that same position today. He still sees everything that we do and he wants to snatch every good thing from us and keep us confused about our destinies. Nevertheless, he is powerless and defeated. We can use the power and authority that God has given us to combat every trick of the enemy. The omnipotent God took the adversary's power away and made him a coward. Unless you give him power to deceive you and control your life, he is absolutely unable to have any control over you. You may read the proof of satan's demotion by God in Isaiah 14:12-15, Ezekiel 28:12-18 and in Revelations 12:7-8. God has all the power. He casted satan, the *father of all lies* out of heaven. *Not by might, nor by power, but by my spirit, saith the LORD of hosts* (Zechariah 4:6).

Commit always to your purpose, take inspired actions and be obedient in whatever your current engagement is and seek God's direction. Coupled with consistent prayer you will eventually become clearer and clearer of what your life's purpose is. You will have confidence, be unshakable and unstoppable in your natural strength, and you will be empowered by supernatural inspiration.

An email pal sent me this message at a time when I was seeking more depth into my purpose. The words in the email helped me to stretch my imagination and I would like to share it with you:."In everything you do, have a purpose. Make sure the quality of your intent is one of truth, honor and love. Prepare to pursue your purpose with prayer. Ask for guidance, protection and direction. Ask that closed doors be opened and the purpose of those that remain closed be revealed. Give thanks for your answered prayers by proceeding without any doubt. Keep your purpose in mind, trust the guidance you receive, have faith in your ability to succeed and accept all that comes your way. If your purpose is clear, your prayers are backed by faith, your outlook sure and positive, never, ever look back. You may meet bumps and turns in the road, but your obstacles shall all be removed." The email concluded with this African American folklore:

"Plan purposefully, prepare prayerfully, proceed positively and pursue persistently."

PRINCIPLES FOR DAILY APPLICATION

(1) If you have any doubt at all about who you are, why you are here and where you are going; do yourself a favor and find a coach or a mentor to help you figure these things out. When you have figured them out and begin to work toward that end, always consulting Jehovah-Shammah-the God Who is always there to assist you, you will live your life in peace and harmony. When you are living purposefully, God will show you the most excellent way. Everything will become clearer. Paul tells us in Romans 8:9: *But you are not controlled by your sinful nature. You are controlled by the*

Spirit if you have the Spirit of God living in you. (And remember that those who do not have the Spirit of Christ living in them do not belong to him at all.) (NLT). The point is, you must embrace the Holy Spirit, move out of darkness and into the lighted path of your destiny.

(2) Write down your vision and mission statements. Establish a plan of action with measurable and achievable goals. Look at them daily and take actions accordingly. Your plan should line up with God's plan because if it does not, there will be chaos. Your plan should have a beginning and an end in mind. If you do not know where you are going, you will end up nowhere. Let Jehovah-Rohi, the Lord your shepherd guide you. If you know God's purpose for your life you will have a better understanding of your purpose.

(3) Seek God's guidance and approval in everything you do. If you try to do things without God's approval, you will experience burn–out, stress, accomplish little and do mediocre work. Letting God in is the key to understanding and accomplishing your divine purpose. It makes a lot of sense to take some time to think about your life and change directions if needs be, zero in and focus.

(4) Take responsibility and accountability for all your action**s**. Take control of the situations in your life, listen to the Omniscient God. He knows everything, so you can never go wrong with listening to Him. Let the Holy Spirit guide you and you will see that there are no boundaries or limits around you. You will be unstoppable. We do not always have the full picture of when, how and why to make the next move, but it is always smart to begin. When you begin, revelation will follow. There is no need to be of concern, because we are under the leadership of an all-knowing God and the Holy Spirit who, as we allow them, assume the responsibility for making our loads lighter. I have heard it said: "When you don't know where you are going, you often end up where you don't want to be."

(5) Make self examination a habit. Examine yourself and the conditions of your life as you move forward on your journey to fulfillment. The result of self examination is the ability to function where you are, with what you have, as well as an awareness of the areas in which you need to develop and grow. Many people are stuck in one of the lower stages that Maslow wrote about. They are not proactive enough to take the necessary steps to move to the next stage. Some people are unaware that they are stuck and need to get help. God accomplishes His purposes regardless of how frail we may be, how little faith we have or how much we think we know and can do without first consulting Him. The bottom line is, if we can deny ourselves, take up the cross of Christ and follow God's plan, we will find true fulfillment.

(6) Admit your weaknesses, be honest about the things you need to address, do not be too proud or shy to ask for help, do not procrastinate; act swiftly to make changes.

(7) Pray, Pray, Pray and ask God to direct your path daily. Let Him know you come as a willing vessel, ready to fill up with whatever He has for you to do. Give Him thanks.

PRAYER:

Dear heavenly Father, I thank You for creating me with a divine purpose and for all of the answers I need to my questions about how to connect with You and fulfill my destiny that is written in the Bible. Thank You for Romans 11 verse 36 which tells us, everything comes from You, exists by Your power and is intended for Your glory. Please give me deeper insight, revelation and clarity as I read Your Word and seek to fulfill your plan for my life. I pray, oh Lord, that You will give me deeper and complete understanding of Your will for my life, so that I may not waste time trying to find out on my own. Thank You for giving me spiritual wisdom, so that I can learn how to trust in You and lean not on my own understanding.

Help me to understand the importance of finding and sticking with Your plan, because Your plan is far greater than mine, and it is the ultimate and perfect plan for me. No matter how wise or well advised my earthly plan may be, it can not measure up to Your divine plan for me. Please let me not go to my grave without accomplishing Your plan for my life here on earth. Oh Lord, we have many plans but Proverbs 19:21 reminds us: *Many are the plans of a man's heart, but it is the Lord's purpose that prevails.* Forgive us Lord for our rebellious and disobedient actions toward Your plans. Please help us to listen to the Holy Spirit and allow Him to guide, counsel and teach us through the processes of our lives journey. All honor, glory, dominion and power to You, in the name of Jesus, Amen.

CHAPTER 4
A NEW MIND AND SPIRIT

Finally, brethren, whatsoever things are true, whatsoever things are honest, whatsoever things are just, whatsoever things are pure, whatsoever things are lovely, whatsoever things are of good report; if there be any virtue, and if there be any praise, think on these things
Philippians 4:8.

If your sinful nature controls your mind, there is death. But if the Holy Spirit controls your mind, there is life and peace
Romans 8:6

For who hath known the mind of the Lord, that he may instruct him? but we have the mind of Christ.
1 Corinthians 2:15-16.

*For as he **thinketh** in his heart, so is he...*
Proverbs 23:7.

And be not conformed to this world: but be ye transformed by the renewing of your mind, that ye may prove what isthat good, and acceptable, and perfect, will of God
Romans 12:2.

And be renewed in the spirit of your mind
Ephesians 4:23.

I believe transformation is a complete lifestyle change and making a decision to maintain purity and self-control. With this as my focal point of interest; the first thing I did to align with my process of transformation was a mind check and then some alterations. I knew I had to make some significant changes in the way I think, as true transformation would be dependent upon me restructuring my mind. The way I used to think was too narrow, I needed to broaden my mind, so that I could be more productive and successful in every area of my life. I needed to release myself from worry, fear and self-limiting beliefs. I had to affirm myself with who God said I am and stop believing the lies of the enemy.

I see the mind as being the most powerful tool that anyone possesses and it can make or break an individual. I wanted to make sure that this dangerous weapon would not get in my way as I work at revolutionizing my life. I wanted to make sure it was being used for the purpose of which the Creator created it. A pistol can destroy anyone who is caught in its line of fire, yet it is used as an instrument to keep peace and order in the law-enforcement arena; in a similar way, our minds can cause us to do evil or good, beyond our wildest imaginations. Our minds, wills, emotions and physical bodies are in constant conflict, and if we are unaware of this truth, we are in serious trouble.

When we battle with our minds, we create all kinds of vain imaginations. A few verses in Paul's writing in Romans have helped me to understand the battles that I sometimes find going on in my mind: Paul said: *Now then it is no more I that do it, but sin that dwelleth in me. For I know that in me (that is, in my flesh,) dwelleth no good thing: for to will is present with me; but how to perform that which is good I find not. For the good that I would I do not: but the evil which I would not, that I do* (Romans 7:17-19).

How confused Paul seems to be! This is indeed a true picture of how we human beings suffer in the flesh. Paul, the transformed apostle is experiencing battles of the flesh and spirit. He does not understand why this is happening because he is now a saved man. He does not want to have the experiences of his sinful nature anymore, but it is inevitable because he is a human being. These are the same kinds of battles that believers experience on a daily basis in today's world and the way to deal with them is to be conscious of this truth. Like Paul, I have found myself many times in circumstances where I may judge a situation, feel rejected or worried, and I ask myself why I am doing this if I am a "transformed" person. This has helped me to understand that even though I chose to consciously live in a transformed state of being, my human nature gets in the way at times. I am not perfect, and will not be until Christ comes, and I will continue to encounter disappointments as I journey through this life.

Have you ever found yourself in similar situations? It is essential that we evaluate our thoughts if we are struggling and having mind battles as the one described above. Are your thoughts from your Creator or are they from the enemy? Are they fearful, scary, wrong, condemning, judging, deceitful, insecure, frustrating, anger provoking, or are they good thoughts? Consider your mind a jump drive, wipe it clean of all the old stuff and fill the space with new thoughts and information. Allow yourself to be renewed in the spirit of your mind. I heard the story of a woman who had amnesia after an accident. When she began her new life it was far better than the one she had before. There was no memory of her past to hold back anymore.

Someone once said that our thoughts and our actions determine who we are and who we become. In the recording of the *Strangest Secret* by Earl Nightingale, he states: "You become what you think about all day long." What are you thinking about today? Are those thoughts inspiring, healing, or blessing your mind? How are they affecting your attitude? Are you satisfied with where you are in mind, body and spirit? How are the people in your life influencing you? There is an old adage: "Show me your friends, and I will tell you who you are." Who are your friends? Friends and family members can influence your thinking and unfortunately, in a negative way, to say the least. What kinds of influence do they have on you? Are they encouraging or being supportive of you? What is the atmosphere like when you are spending time with them? Do you choose a satisfactory environment that is conducive to love, peace, joy and harmony?

Have you thought about writing a journal; recording the good and bad things that you experience on a daily basis? I have found that going back and reading my journals helps me to relax, smile, cry, and even to reminisce in awe. I often do other things such as praying frequently, reading books on personal development, visiting a sick person to pray and read with them, or even pick up the phone or sit and email the person who has been on my mind. These are just a few things we can do to redirect and refocus the thoughts of our minds. When you recognize that destructive thoughts are occupying your mind, speak to them and tell them that you reject them in the name of Jesus. Unimportant thoughts can keep us captive for a long time if we do not deal with them. Many of these thoughts are the prisons and shackles of our past that may have caused us to behave in a manner that is unacceptable to our Creator, ourselves and to others. These thoughts need to be freely let go, so we can attract and settle only for good thoughts and emotions. When undesirable thoughts try to take residence in my mind, I remind myself that the devil has no place in my head, because he is my stomping ground and under my feet is where he belongs. Approaching the battles of mind in this way has made a significant difference in my life. It could make a difference in your life too.

"You are what you think," is another popular phrase. Recently someone in my Toastmasters' group shared this tale that a man told to his grandson: She stated that one Evening, an old Cherokee told his grandson about a battle that goes on inside people. He said, "My son, the battle is between two wolves inside us all. One is Evil. It is anger, envy, jealousy, sorrow, regret, greed, arrogance, self-pity, guilt, resentment, inferiority, lies, false pride, superiority, and ego. The other is Good. It is joy, peace, love, hope, serenity, humility, kindness, benevolence, empathy, generosity, truth, compassion and faith." The grandson thought about it for a minute and then asked his grandfather, "Which wolf wins?" The old Cherokee simply replied, "The one you feed." This question is a great one for each of us to ask: Which wolf am I feeding?

In order for us to serve the good wolf, our will should be submitted to God's, because the Bible says in 1 John 4:4: *Ye are of God, little children, and have overcome them: because **greater is** he that **is** in you, **than** he that **is** in the **world**.* Our minds are of utmost importance to us and should be treated as such. The Apostle Paul warns in Romans 12:1-2, that we should offer our bodies as living sacrifices, holy and pleasing to God. He said that we should not be conformed to the things of this world, but we should be transformed by the renewing of our minds. We have to use our minds to relate to Christ. As I mentioned before,

Paul himself had great struggles, in his mind and from his experience and teachings, we can learn how to deal with the mind battles with which we struggle. Peter is another example of a Bible character who had battles of the mind. He was a disciple of Jesus, but he denied Jesus and cried when he realized what he had done. Can you identify with Peter? It seems as though Peter was pretty much as we are today in our humanness. If we are to please God and live in righteousness, we must take control of our thoughts.

There is a story in the Bible about a man who had two sons. The younger son, known as the Prodigal son, got it in his mind that he was grown and no longer wanted to live at home with his family, so he asked his father for his portion of the inheritance. His father gave it to him, and the son took the money and left home. He squandered all the money, got involved with swines, and lived and ate with them in their pen. After living in this condition for awhile, repentant thoughts started going through his mind. One of his thoughts must have been; "My father is rich. What am I doing living among swines and eating with them?" This man realized that God had a better plan for his life, so he gave up his horrible lifestyle and decided to go back to his father's home. He refused to let the enemy continue to mess with his mind. The enemy will put it in our minds that we are unworthy or worthless when we make mistakes, because he wants us to stay in the pits and in shackles. We can chose whatever life we want, but there are consequences.

Cultivate strong minds by thinking about how God gave His only Son as a sacrifice so that you can have love instead of hatred, hope, instead of hopelessness, abundance instead of lack and joy instead of sadness. God is our source and He is our strong tower. A transformation of the mind and a new focus will make it easier to recognize and to minimize selfish, ignorant or destructive thoughts by which we are often plagued. You have seen what it is like when gutters get blocked by debris, and the water is not able to flow through its right course. The same concept applies to what happens to our minds when we do not clear out the old ways of thinking. When our minds get blocked, we are unable to take in the new and insightful thoughts that can make a difference in our lives.

Have you ever felt something in your spirit or witnessed something that you know is of God, and then you felt these little doubts creeping in? Those other thoughts are from the enemy, and sometimes they seem very real, making it difficult to decipher which voice is real. It is at that moment you need to tell the enemy to take his ideas and go back to hell. Take immediate control and do not allow them to manifest. Remember, according to John 10:10, satan comes to kill, steal and destroy. He is constantly trying to take out the good things that God has placed in our spirit.

Do you remember in Job 1:7 when God asked satan *"From where do you come?" So Satan answered the LORD and said, "From going to and fro on the earth, and from walking back and forth on it."* (NKJV). This is the reason we have been advised to*: Be sober, be vigilant; because your adversary the devil, as a roaring lion, walketh about, seeking whom he may devour* (1 Peter 5:8). We have weapons to combat satan. Read Ephesians 6:12-19 and John 10:10.

When we allow the enemy in our lives he brings diseases, destroys relationships, marriages, churches, dreams and purpose. He keeps us imprisoned in the shackles of our past and paralyzes us with fear. It is quite common that when people are faced with adversity, they have confusion in their minds and begin to ask questions such as, why does God allow this to happen? If this question ever crosses your mind, read the book of Job and your answer will be crystal clear. There are reasons we go through trials and tribulations. For example:

(1) If you are not saved, it is possible that God might be trying to get your attention to remind you that His purpose for your life is that you would serve Him.

(2) If you are saved and not living right, it is likely that God might be calling your attention to the fact that you need to get right with Him.

(3) If you are living righteousness of God, that would mean that you are applying your faith and are pleasing God. You are doing His will according to what His Word teaches us to do, such as; obeying, loving everyone, forgiving, living holy, abiding by the spirit and following through with what God has commissioned us to do according to Matthew 28:18-20, Mark 16:15 and Luke 24:47. It is possible that He is testing you to see if you are ready of if He can trust you to do greater

things in your walk with Him. Trust God and be patient. He always knows what He is doing. Disciples follow; read Matthew Chapter 10. Just as Jesus sent out His disciples to be witnesses for Him long ago, He sends us to be witnesses for Him today. Disciples also understand the meaning of Romans 8:28.

Fear can stop us from fulfilling our assignments, but the scripture says that in Him there is no fear. Jesus told His disciples in Matthew 10:28: *Don't be afraid of those who want to kill you. They can only kill your body; they cannot touch your soul. Fear only God, who can destroy both soul and body in hell* (NLT). There are several scriptures addressing the issues of fear, such as 2 Timothy 1:7 and 1 John 4:18, but I use this verse because one of mankind's greatest fears is the fear of death. But here we see clearly that even if someone kills our bodies while we are doing God's work, our souls belong to God. What greater hope or promise can we have? It is important to study and keep the words from the Holy Bible in our hearts.

If we live our lives with our mind's eye open, readiness to slay the giants and willingness to die for the sake of Christ, then we will have nothing to worry about and we can enjoy the freedom that life offers. Be willing to keep your mind focused on Christ and live each day as if it were your last. We know that we have a blessed assurance, a great promise, and hope of one day inheriting the Kingdom of God. Jesus assures us: *In my Father's house are many mansions: if it were not so, I would have told you. I go to prepare a place for you. And if I go and prepare a place for you, I will come again, and receive you unto myself; that where I am, there ye may be also* (John 14:2).

PRINCIPLES FOR DAILY APPLICATION

(1) Recognize the chatter that goes on in your mind. The sub-conscious mind is very powerful. It does most of the thinking. Engage it with thoughts that allow you to set your heart on God, and listen to His Word through the Holy Spirit. Do not worry about what man says. It is not about looking good in public. It is about abiding by the will and Word of God. God looks at our hearts and honors what we do from our hearts. Starting today, decide how you will use your mind for the rest of your life. Read 1 Samuel 16:7.

(2) Examine your heart daily and search for things that might be holding you back from being all that you can be in Christ. Look for those beliefs that you have held that have caused damaged to your progress in relationships, life, health and well being or in your professional and personal growth. Matthew 7:1-5 and 2 Corinthians 10:5, help us to bring things into perspective and take destructive thoughts and imaginations into captivity. Allow the Holy Spirit to lead you in your thought processes.

(3) How will you decide to use your mind today and for the rest of your life? Your decision will determine your direction and your future. Be the captain of your mind and anchor your thoughts in goodness and Godliness. Use your super conscious mind, because it receives direct inspiration from God. This mind illuminates you, helps you to know the truth, things as they really are and not as they falsely appear to the senses. When you know the truth it sets you free. Read about this in John Chapter 8.

(4) Let your mind focus on God, think of divine wisdom and allow your wisdom to guide you. Do not doubt that you possess this wisdom and inspiration. To quote Les Brown: "Feed your mind and allow your doubts to starve to death."

(5) Keep your mind's eyes on Jesus, not on the devil. We have a choice to listen to the Holy Spirit or to the devil. We have been given only two choices; the flesh that has a sinful/bad nature and the Holy Spirit which is from God and it is good. Lay down your flesh and allow the Holy Spirit to take control. Keep your mind sharp and ready to combat satan's attacks which are certain to come. When he comes to you with lies, such as, "you are unworthy, you are sick"or any other kinds of negative thoughts, your response should be a suitable scripture such as, "Jesus carried my sickness and diseases, by His stripes I am healed "or", it is God's will that I should prosper and be in good health." When Jesus was fasting in the wilderness and satan tempted Him with food, Jesus responded to satan by telling him: *Man shall not live by bread alone, but* *by every word that proceedeth out of the mouth of God* (Matthew 4:4), *and Thou shalt not **tempt** the **Lord** thy God* (Matthew 4:7).

(6) Believe that you are a conqueror. I believe that if David could conquer a lion, a bear and then slay Goliath, I can keep my mind clear of garbage and I can conquer all the evil things that satan throws in my path. The devil works constantly for us to have strife with one another. Instead of criticizing people or scheming against them, pray for and bless them. Take the responsibility to guard your heart and your thoughts. Napoleon Hill said, "You are searching for the magic key that will unlock the door to the source of power; and yet you have the key in your own hands, and you may use it the moment you learn to control your thoughts." Better yet Jesus said: *And I will give unto thee the **keys** of the **kingdom** of heaven: and whatsoever thou shalt bind on earth shall be bound in heaven: and whatsoever thou shalt loose on earth shall be loosed in heaven* (Matthew 16:19).

(7) Pray, pray, pray. Seek God's directions for your quiet times, personal development, work, fellowship and leisure. God is a God of order and He will order you steps, if you allow Him to. When he orders our steps, we bypass confusion and have a sound mind. Know that God does not show favoritism and what He did for David; He will do for you, for me and for every believer who lives a holy life and seeks after His glory, anointing and righteousness. God is very kind, tolerant and patient with us, but we are often stubborn, seeking our own desires, impatient, and disobedient to Him. Bear in mind that God will judge us according to the things that we have done. Be sensitive to the workings of the Holy Spirit in your life. Sin messes up our minds, and the Bible warns: *Now turn from your sins and turn to God, so you can be cleansed of your sins. Then wonderful times of refreshment will come from the presence of the Lord, and He will send Jesus your Messiah to you again* (Acts 3:19-20).

PRAYER:

Dear heavenly Father, I thank You for Your Word that warns us in Romans 12:2 that we should not be **conformed** to this world, but that we should be transformed by the renewing of our minds, so that we may prove what is that good acceptable, and perfect will of God. Father, I confess to You that I have had thoughts about things that are not acceptable, perfect or in Your will. Lord I am sorry, so very sorry, and I promise to guard my thoughts, do the right things and please You. I will use my mind each day to glorify You. Lord, I promise to think on things that are true, honest, just, pure, lovely, and are of good report as Paul listed in Philippians 4:8. Thank You Lord for helping us to become aware that we should challenge the conversations that go on in our heads and the conflicts that they have caused within our hearts and bodies. Thank You for the comfort we find in Your Word, as we submerge our souls in them, and use them to re-program our lives. Most of all, thank You for transforming my mind and for creating in me a clean heart and giving me a whole new life, Amen.

CHAPTER 5
AN UNDYING LOVE

*For God so loved the world, that he gave his only begotten Son, that
whosoever believeth in him should not perish, but have everlasting life*
John 3:16.

*But I say unto you, Love your enemies, bless them that
curse you, do good to them that hate you, and pray for
them which despitefully use you, and persecute you*
Matthew 5:44.

This is my commandment, That ye love one another, as I have loved you
John 15:12.

*And above all things have fervent love for one another,
for "love will cover a multitude of sins*
1 Peter 4:8 (NKJV).

*My little children, let us not love in word, neither
in tongue; but in deed and in truth*
(1 John 3:18).

*Beloved, let us love one another: for love is of God; and every
one that loveth is born of God, and knoweth God*
1 John 4:7.

As I struggle on my journey to sanctification, I am realizing that
God is dealing with everything in me that is not of Him. Day
by day, He crucifies my flesh and shows me things about myself that I
need to work on in order to live a sanctified life. When he spoke to me

about *love*, I asked, "Lord, how can I possibly love everyone, especially the people who have caused me pain and anguish?" I pleaded, "Lord, I simply cannot do it. It is hard to love everyone. Surely, you understand I already love the people I need to love." But no, He was not about to let me off this easily.

After this internal conversation, the Holy Spirit took me to scriptures in the Bible that did not only show me that God loved me first, but that He commands me to love even my enemies and that He would help me to do this, because He knows that I could not do it on my own. The process is very simple. The first step is to love God unconditionally and ask Him to help you love yourself and others unconditionally. This has to be practiced daily. Think carefully about how you can demonstrate love in your daily living and look for opportunities to show love to others consistently. By this I do not mean to let people walk all over you, use or abuse you, because some will, if you let them. They will take your love for weakness or for granted. I did not grow up hearing the words, *I love you,* and I sure did not get many hugs either, as that was taboo in the culture in which I grew up. God has changed that in my present life as I put forth the effort to hug my husband and my children as often as possible. We also exchange the three words; *I love you,* every day. We have also extended these habits to friends, relatives and even to strangers.

The Bible has been a very helpful resource to me, because when I read it, it makes me want to love more. 1 Corinthians, Chapter 13 has become one of my favorite passages. It teaches about love. I looked up LOVE in the dictionary and found several definitions, but for the purpose of this book, love will be discussed according to these meanings that relate to God and humankind:

(1) Love is a strong affection for or an attachment to another person based on regard or experiences or interest;

(2) God's benevolence and mercy toward man;

(3) Man's devotion to or adoration of God and the feeling of benevolence, kindness or brotherhood toward others. These three meanings cover a multitude of things about love.

When we understand the meaning of love and what Peter said about it in 1 Peter 4:8, we have to make love a priority. When we love, we will not hate or be envious of others. I am addressing hate because it is the opposite of love, and when we do not love we hate. We can dispel hate by embracing love. Hate is not always a negative thing; it is okay for us to hate the things that God also hates. The Bible does say that God hates certain things. To find out the things that God hates, read Amos 5:21, Malachi 2:16, Proverbs 6:16-19 and Isaiah 1:13-15. When you read these verses, you will notice that God does not hate people, He hates some things. Whenever you are tempted to envy or hate people, you can ask God to pour out His anointing upon you, so you can love them instead; even if you must hate their actions that are evil.

Hate, envy and jealousy are dangerous. They always get in our way of love. Since we are commanded to love others; we should rid ourselves of hate, envy and jealousy. They should not exist in the life of the believer. I read in Proverbs 14:30 that: *A sound heart is the life of the flesh: but envy the rottenness of the bones.* Envy and jealousy go hand in hand. They create havoc in people's lives, cause illnesses in the mind and body, and anger to rise up in people. Anger interrupts love. The Bible warns against anger in Psalms. It says: *Stop being angry! Turn from your rage! Do not lose your temper—it only leads to harm Psalm 37:8* (NTL). You may say, "but Jesus displayed anger." He did, but He never sinned and we have been warned: *Be ye angry, and sin not* (Ephesians 4:26). Paying close attention to, and living by what the Scriptures say, can truly move people to live a life of joy, as Proverb 17: 22 declares: *A merry heart doeth good like a medicine: but a broken spirit drieth the bones.*

We can avoid these devastating situations by putting into practice the teachings of the Bible and by simply practicing love daily, as it is demonstrated in 1 Corinthians 13:

Though I speak with the tongues of men and of angels, but have not love, I have become sounding brass or a clanging cymbal. And though I have the gift of prophecy, and understand all mysteries and all knowledge, and though I have all faith, so that I could remove mountains, but have not love, I am nothing. And though I bestow all my goods to feed the poor, and though I give my body to be burned, but have not love, it profits me nothing. Love suffers long and is kind; love does not envy; love does not parade itself, is not puffed up; does not behave rudely, does not seek its own, is not provoked, thinks no evil; does not rejoice in iniquity, but rejoices in the truth; bears all things, believes all things, hopes all things, endures all things. Love never fails. But whether there are prophecies, they will fail; whether there are tongues, they will cease; whether there is knowledge, it will vanish away. For we know in part and we prophesy in part. But when that which is perfect has come, then that which is in part will be done away. When I was a child, I spoke as a child, I understood as a child, I thought as a child; but when I became a man, I put away childish things. For now we see in a mirror, dimly, but then face to face. Now I know in part, but then I shall know just as I also am known. And now abide faith, hope, love, these three; but the greatest of these is love. (NKJV).

Loving others will make us see their needs and force us to pay attention and help them. As God helps us to love those who we are tempted to have envy and hatred for, we will discover that love will make us do to, and for others the same things that we would do, or want for ourselves, which is always the very best. Love will make us rejoice and celebrate in the victories of others. Love is taking Matthew 25:45 into account. It reads: *Then shall he answer them, saying, Verily I say unto you, Inasmuch as ye did it not to one of the least of these, ye did it not to me.*

In referencing the Greek meanings of different types of love, I found some explanations in Wikipedia that solidify the meanings of four types of love:

Agape love, as I understand it, is the spiritual love that Christians have for one another. According to C.S. Lewis, "this kind of love is like the relationship between Jesus and His beloved disciples. It is a rational love that is not based on total self-interest; a Christian is supposed to love someone who is not necessarily lovely or loveable." It is the love depicted in John 3:16 and Matthew 5:44. I believe that this love sticks closer than a brother. It is the kind of love Abraham had for God, the Prodigal son's father had for him, Ruth and Naomi had for each other and Boaz had for Ruth. It is the kind of love that Mordecai had for Esther and Dorcas had for people in need. This love is secured, it links people together. It is holy and pure like the love of God. This is sincere love and the type of love that we must strive to have for one another. This love can never fail.

Eros is passionate love, with sensual desire and longing. Although Eros is initially felt for a person, with contemplation it becomes an appreciation of the beauty within that person, or even becomes an appreciation of beauty itself. It is the love a husband has for his wife. Plato, the philosopher, said that Eros helps the soul recall knowledge of beauty and contributes to an understanding of spiritual truth. Lovers and philosophers are all inspired to seek truth by Eros.

Philia means friendship in Modern Greek, a dispassionate virtuous love. It includes loyalty to friends, family and community. It requires virtue, equality and familiarity. In ancient texts, *philia* denoted a general type of love, used for love between family, between friends, a desire or enjoyment of an activity, as well as between lovers.

Storge means affection in Modern Greek; it is natural affection, like that felt by parents for off spring. It is rarely used in ancient works and then almost exclusively as a descriptor of relationships within the family. This is the type of affection that family members share with each other.

The Greek philosophers described love in these ways long ago. Their work may be ancient, but concepts and principles such as these that relate to God's Word never changes. Love is something that we give and receive. The greatest of the commandments should not be ignored or taken for granted. According to scriptures, as we seek first the kingdom of God, everything else is added. Likewise, if we love first, everything else will become easier to do.

Five reasons we should practice and make love a priority are: (1) To accept people the way they are, as God accepts us just as we are; (2) To learn to forgive ourselves and others, as the Lord has forgiven us; (3) To celebrate others' successes with them as we like celebrating our own and having others celebrate with us; (4) To learn to give and take and to treat others as we would like to be treated (The golden rule); and (5) To practice giving freely and often without looking for any reward.

Believers of the Word and the laws of God should be obedient to God's greatest command to love one another, as well as to obey all of the other commandments. We are reminded by John that we should not pretend to love others, but we should love authentically: *My little children, let us not love in word, neither in tongue; but in deed and in truth* (1 John 3:18). In reading John 3:16, we experience, first-hand, the revelation and the evidence that God's love for us is matchless: It reads: *For God so loved the world, that he gave his only begotten Son, that whosoever believeth in him should not perish, but have everlasting life.* This sacrificial death of the son of God on the cross at Calvary is the highest and most significant demonstration of love that there has ever been.

We are further enlightened on the topic of love through this scripture in John 21:15-20, where Peter and Jesus had a dialog about love. The importance of love is strongly felt in verses 15 and 17, when Jesus asked Peter, not once, but three times, "Do you love me?" Jesus commanded Peter to Feed His lamb, since he said he loved Jesus. Just as Peter kept His commandments, so should we. In 1 John 4: 7-10, the apostle writes: *Beloved, let us love one another: for love is of God; and every one that loveth is born of God, and knoweth God. He that loveth not knoweth not God; for God is love. In this was manifested the love of God toward us, because that God sent his only begotten Son into the world, that we might live through him. Herein is love, not that we loved God, but that he loved us, and sent his Son to be the propitiation for our sins.*

Love is an unconditional commandment from God, and like any other commandment, you can chose to love or hate. When we make the choice to obey God's commandments, we must make the commitment to truly obey. We must act upon this commandment and each individual has his/her part to play. 1 John 5:3 states: *This is love for God: to obey his commands. And his commands are not burdensome* (NIV) Loving God means keeping His commandments and his commandments and not seeing them as burdensome. God does not want us to love only the people who love us, but He wants us to love the ones who we consider to be our enemies as well. I know that this is difficult to do, but it is what the Word of God declares. Therefore, there is no room for compromise or to question whether or not we should love others.

The Gospel of (Matthew 5:43-46), declares: *You have heard that it was said, 'You shall love your neighbor and hate your enemy.' But I say to you, love your enemies, bless those who curse you, do good to those who hate you, and pray for those who spitefully use you and persecute you that you may be sons of your Father in heaven; for He makes His sun rise on the evil and on the good, and sends rain on the just and on the unjust. For if you love those who love you, what reward have you? Do not even the tax collectors do the same?* If we truly love others, we would correct them, and if they truly understand the meaning of love, they would not get offended, and vice versa.

We sometimes allow fear to prevent us from correcting or pointing out to others their faults. When that kind of fear comes upon us we should dispel it by remembering 1 John 4: 18-19: *There is no fear in love; but perfect love casteth out fear: because fear hath torment. He that feareth is not made perfect in love. We love him, because he first loved us. If a man says, I love God, and hateth his brother, he is a liar: for he that loveth not his brother whom he hath seen, how can he love God whom he hath not seen?*

Proverbs 27:5-6 also help us with this matter by assuring: *Open rebuke is better than secret love Faithful are the wounds of a friend; but the kisses of an enemy are deceitful.*

In essence, sin is lack of love. Love will protect us from sin. Job said, *You gave me life and showed me your unfailing love. My life was preserved by your care* (Job 10:12). When we obey God's commandments and follow His principles, his favor will be upon us. Remember that the greatest of His commandments is **LOVE**. When we love our brothers and sisters as God commanded, we have joy and peace. Paul said in (Ephesians 4:2-7) *With all lowliness and meekness, with longsuffering, forbearing one another in love; Endeavoring to keep the unity of the Spirit in the bond of peace. There is one body, and one Spirit, even as ye are called in one hope of your calling; One Lord, one faith, one baptism, One God and Father of all, who is above all, and through all, and in you all. But unto every one of us is given grace according to the measure of the gift of Christ.*

Love will humble us to the point of respecting our brothers and sisters, while revealing the truth that we are all created in the image and likeness of God and should therefore be able to get along with one another, and live in unity. Living in unity does not mean that we will not have differences, but we will conquer and overcome them. With love, we have the power to reconcile when disappointment comes. Be aware that disappointment is not always a bad thing. There is an old adage: "Every disappointment is for good." One songwriter conveys comfort through his Song when he wrote: "You don't have to worry and don't you be afraid. Joy comes in the morning, troubles, they don't last always." and Romans 8:28, says: *And we know that all things work together for good to them that love God, to them who are called according to his purpose.*

Be at peace with yourself and know that you are a child of the King. Forgive, be forgiven and allow love to flow naturally as a stream of living water. Holding on to past grudges and hurts, can cloud your ability to show love to others and even to love yourself. Do not think and dwell on the negative things in your past, because that is what the enemy wants. He tries to constantly remind us of our ugly past. When we leave a crack through which he can stick his nose, he has a party, and while he is having a grand time we are having a pity parties. Say goodbye to the past hurts and pity parties, or continue to hold on to them and miss out on enjoying the greatest thing we can ever have-God's love.

Love will direct us to give God praise. The Psalmist said, *From the rising of the sun unto the going down of the same the LORD's name is to be praised* (Psalm 113:3). God loves us so much, we should praise Him at every chance we get. He covers our deepest secrets, no matter what they are; whether drug addictions, abortions, fornications, adultery, lies, stealing and all other sins. It does not matter what the sin is, when you turn your life over to Christ, and live for Him, He covers them. One of the benefits of the believer is that the believer does not have to worry about their sins anymore. He did this to take the burdens from us, so that we may lighten up and do the work that he left us here to do. He wants us to stop operating in darkness and ignorance. All human beings and some animals want to be loved, and it is very important to remember that true love comes from God and that before we can love anyone, we must first love ourselves.

Love always wants the very best for others and does no injustice. It rejoices in the victories of others. The scriptures say: *But there will be glory and honor and peace from God for all who do good – for the Jew first and also for the Gentile. For God does not show favoritism* (Romans 2:10-11). I like how Paul explains it in verse 11: *For there is no respect of persons with God.*

God sees us all in the same way-sinners saved by grace and anticipating a future with Him or sinners going to hell to have a future with the devil. He knows all about us. He knows every single hair on our heads. He knows when we are hating, and when we are loving, when we are sinning and when we are living right. He knows our beginning and our end. God wants us to love, have faith, trust and live in obedience to His Word. He has promised to reward us according to the ways in which we live our lives. Paul wrote:

For all who are led by the spirit of God are children of God. (Romans 8:14). God blesses the people who patiently endure testing. Afterward they will receive the crown of life that God has promised those who love Him. (James 1:12).

PRINCIPLES FOR DAILY APPLICATION

(1) Love God, love yourself and love others. In order to do these three things you must first accept and feel God's love for you. Practice, practice. Every day, tell your loved ones that you love them. Love will teach you how to accept people just the way they are, like God accepts us just as we are. It is patient and kind. Read 1 Corinthians 13:4; 1 John 4:8.

(2) Start with forgiveness. Is there anyone you need to forgive? Do yourself a favor and take care of that. Learn to forgive. Love will teach you to forgive yourself and others as the Lord has forgiven you. See Matthew 18:22.

(3) Love will teach you to celebrate other people's successes with them as you like celebrating your own. Love does, and wants the very best for everyone, regardless. Matthew 5:44; John 13:34-35.

(4) Love will instruct you to give and take, and to treat others, as you would like to be treated. Love is "the golden rule" Matthew 7:12; 22:37-40,

(5) Love will train you to give freely and often without looking for a reward. Love is the only debt that we owe to each other according to Romans 12:10;
13:8.

(6) Chose love and it will take away your fear according to John 4:18, Deut.30:20.

(7) Love will help you to obey God's Word, have faith, trust, hope and will make you want to wait for eternity according to Deuteronomy 11:13.

PRAYER:

Dear heavenly Father, please forgive me of all my sins and help me to become more like You. You sent your Son, a sinless Man to earth in the flesh, just for my sake. You loved me so much that You allowed Your Son to die so that I might live. I thank you for loving me. You are the epitome of true love. Please help me to love like You, unconditionally. Thank You for showing me every example that I need to exercise unconditional love. You taught Your disciples about true love and I thank you that I can learn from Your teaching. In my weakness, I sometimes find it difficult to love others who do not show respect for You, and those who have caused me pain, but I know that Your Words compel me to love even my enemies. I ask You to bless those who make it difficult for me to love them. I thank You that You loved me first and You even love me in spite of all of my faults. Please help me to live by Your example and practice Your way of love daily, so that I may love others regardless of their faults. Thank You, that when I am incapable of loving others by myself, I can love them through You. I love You Lord, and I give You honor, glory and praise, forever, Amen.

CHAPTER 6
CHANGE IS INEVITABLE

*Then Jacob said unto his household, and to all that were with him, Put away
the strange gods that are among you, and be clean, and change your garments*
Genesis 35:2.

*If a man dies, shall he live again? All the days of my
appointed time will I wait, till my change come*
Job 14:14.

*And he answered and spake unto those that stood before him, saying, Take away
the filthy garments from him. And unto him he said, Behold, I have caused
thine iniquity to pass from thee, and I will clothe thee with change of raiment*
Zechariah 3:4.

*Therefore if any man be in Christ, he is a new creature: old
things are passed away; behold, all things are become new*
2 Corinthians 5:17.

Why do people resist change when change is inevitable? In order for
transformation to take place in our lives, we must be willing to
change some things. Change sometimes calls for a new way of thinking.
It is a shift in your paradigm. It is becoming aware of the things that
are negatively affecting your life and taking the necessary actions to
correct them. When people say that they do not have the strength, the
determination, the discipline, or the will to change, they are discounting
or underestimating the power of almighty God, through whom we
can do all things. Paul contends in Philippians 4:13: *I can do all things
through Christ who strengtheneth me.* You can change the undesirable

things in your life if you believe you can. Within you are all the tools you need. You have to personally make the decision to change before change can actually occur.

Adam R. Gwizdala gave a vivid expression of change in the following statement: "Everything in life changes you in some way; even the smallest things. If you do not accept these changes you do not accept yourself. For through these changes bring new and greater things to you, making you wiser, as time progresses. To avoid these changes is a loss. You only live your life once. Do not waste a minute of it avoiding things. Let them come to you, and learn from them. There is always tomorrow."

When I look back at periods in my life, I have to consider myself both a product and an agent of change, because I have had many changes in my life and each change produced results. My first big change took place when I was three years old. My parents took me from one parish (Saint Andrew) on the island of Jamaica, to another parish (Portland). They left me with my grand-mother while they migrated to Great Britain.

I would not see my mother again until I was about eleven years old, and my father when I was seventeen years old, and in college. I did, however, have regular correspondences with them in the form of letters, since I did not have the luxury of a telephone. Change came again when I left for another part of the country to attend high school. It was a boarding school, Carron Hall in Saint Mary, Jamaica. When I told my children about boarding school, they said I went there because I was bad. I told them I was not a bad child but was not as fortunate as they are and that was the opportunity that came to me. It was a part of my destiny, I suppose.

The next big change I faced was dealing with the death of my beloved grandmother in 1980. I had just finished my Teaching Internship, through Short wood Teachers' College, in Kingston, Jamaica and got hired as a first grade teacher when I got the news that my Grand-mother, Regina, had passed away. I felt as if a part of me left with her. After her death, I clung to the hope of spending the rest of my life with my lover. Our friendship got stronger and we began to spend more time together. Our union produced our first daughter, Shauna, our bundle of joy.

Change knocked at my door again when Shauna was one year old.

This time it was bittersweet. I was getting ready to leave the man I loved to join my mother, who was now living in the United States, after her divorce from my father with whom she had lived for many years in Birmingham, England. This move took Shauna and me to Connecticut. The first thing I noticed as my sister, Grace drove me home from Bradley International Airport, was the dark street. I was thinking: "Is this the America, the country to which I had been so excited about coming?" I was not expecting that the street would be dark. I thought there was light on every street in America. I also thought that I would see more mansions than dilapidated houses. My ignorance of course! After that initial shock, I sunk into reality and began to embrace my big change, enjoying the beauty and opportunities that America offers.

This was to be the first time that I lived with my mother since I was three years old. I was twenty-four years old, and my one year old daughter and I were going to be living in the same house with my mother and my two teen-aged brothers whom I had never met before, except through photographs. I was excited about a union and reunion, where the family would bond. I had hoped that it would be a fantastic experience, but as you may imagine, this arrangement did not last for too long. Our lifestyles were too different. Grace agreed that Shauna and I could move in with her and her family, and we did. Life in Connecticut was different from life in Jamaica. I will give you one example that comes to mind. While it was very relaxing and laid back in Jamaica, it was fast paced here with a lot of hustling and bustling. I arrived in Connecticut in June 1983 and spent the first three months getting acclimated to the climate, the people and my big change before going to work at the Connecticut Institute for the Blind in Hartford in September of 1983. I will never forget, one cold morning when I stepped out the door to catch the bus for work and there was this white stuff on the ground.

I had never seen snow before, except in movies and in books. I had no idea how to walk on it, so I went back inside and told my sister that it was snowing and I did not know how to walk in the snow. I was hoping that she would offer to give me a ride work. Instead, she told me told me to walk carefully, so I would not slip and fall. I was stunned; I could not believe that as confused as I looked, she did not offer to drive me to work. I rushed back outside, fixing my eyes on the fluffy white stuff.

As I frantically made my way back to the bus stop, I prayed that I would not fall. Luckily I caught the bus and made it to work on time. I did not like the idea of having to punch a clock when I got to work and before I left. I did not have to punch a clock when I was teaching in Jamaica, so I had to get adjusted to this change, as well. Worst of all, if I were seven minutes late, I was penalized. It dawned on me that life is not going to be as easy for me as it was when I was in Jamaica. It took me a while to get adjusted to the American way, such as joining a line for everything. I must admit though, that overall, many of the changes have been positive.

Two years later, I experienced progress which came as a result of change. I was able to rent an apartment and purchase a used car. This to me was exciting, because if I had still been in Jamaica at that time, I would not have been able to purchase car on the salary I was making as a teacher. Things got much better when Royston, now my husband, gave up living in Jamaica and joined Shauna and me. Life, for us, would continue to change and improve. With Shauna turning five years, we were getting ready to give birth to Regina, another bundle of joy.

Change knocked on our door again when Regina was nine and Royston was offered a job in Virginia. By then, I was comfortable with our way of life, my job and my pay as a site manager for the Hartford Head Start program. We had met some wonderful people and made great friends, especially at our church, North United Methodist in Hartford. I really did not want to leave all those behind. Although a difficult decision to make, I did not resist the change; I embraced it.

Within the span of five years I saw how God used that change to accomplish greater things in our lives. We built a new home, bought a new car and had our son Dior, our last bundle of joy. I completed my master's degree and our two daughters have graduated from high school. Shauna completed college and got married; Regina is a senior in college, and most importantly, we have tremendously grown in our spiritual lives. In all these flowery experiences, I had some challenges with my health, but God healed me, and all things have worked out for the best. I wrote about my illness in my book, Living in Clarity.

In 2006, another big change came. Ford Motor Company was getting ready to close its doors in Norfolk, Virginia, which meant that Royston's job was on the line. Again, with God being the center of our lives, He opened another door. Royston was offered a job in Tucson, Arizona. We are excited about the moves of God in our lives, and we cannot wait to see what He does next. Change can be exciting!

We have had experiences on the mountain top and in the valley, but we literally apply Romans 8:26-28. Verse twenty-eight helps us to endure our encounters in the valley. We proclaim as Paul did: *And we know that all things work together for good to them that love God, to them who are the called according to his purpose.* This has helped us to stop focusing on our Circumstances; we have learned to focus on the promises of God instead. We consider our experiences real changes and answering to the call of God for our destinies. Sometimes change cannot take place in people's lives because they repel it. For example, I know of people who are determined to remain where they were born and grew up with no desire to explore the unknown, so they ignore or refuse opportunities that would give them a chance to make some progress through change. If your assignment is to live at the same place all your life, that is fine, but you should be making progress there. If your life is stagnant and miserable, you may want to take a look at how to make change happen naturally in your life, instead of resisting it. Ghandi said it well in this statement, "We must be the change we wish to see in the world." Get rid of the fear that would prevent you from advancing. Ridding yourself of fear is possible if you do this: *Trust in the LORD with all thine heart; and lean not unto thine own understanding. In all thy ways acknowledge him, and he shall direct thy paths* (Proverb 3:5-6). It is also important to meditate on this verse: *For **God** hath **not given** us the **spirit** of **fear**; but of power, and of love, and of a sound mind* (2 Timothy 1:7).

Change cannot be pushed on anyone who does not really want to change. A person has to know why he or she wants change and believe that it is possible. There is an old adage: "You can bring a horse to the water, but you can't make it drink." Sometimes it is easier for us to point our fingers at other people, expecting them to change. Think of yourself as an ambassador for the Kingdom of God. Use this thought to begin your own process of change in the areas of your life where it would make a difference if you change something.

Change does not happen overnight; it is a gradual process that requires patience. I believe every change is a step in the direction of your destiny. It would not be too difficult to accept change if we could get out of our self-centered mind-sets and look at the big picture as Paul puts it: *forgetting those things which are behind, and reaching forth unto those things which are before, I press toward the mark for the prize of the high calling of God in Christ Jesus* (Philippians 3:13-14). You may not feel it now, but once you begin the process of change you will realize that layers will begin to peel off of you. When I decided to make some serious changes in my spiritual life and I began to embrace the changes, I could literally feel the layers peeling off and it continues to happen to me daily. Sometimes I am tempted to resist it, but the Holy Spirit reminds me of the commitment I have made to embrace change when I am faced with it.

This is a responsibility that I have to assume for myself as an individual. I seek God's guidance through the process and He gives it to me. If you cannot seem to think of what you need to change to live a better life, then it is possible that your spirit is dying and you are therefore not able to see these things within yourself. The flesh that is influenced by satan and the spirit that embodies everything that comes from the Father are in constant battle. It is important to know that the enemy uses this trick to keep us bound and resistant to change.

It is evident in both the Old and the New Testaments that the enemy is rampant and he is all over the place, trying to out-do God. What we need to do is resist the devil and make him frustrated. Let him know that he is fighting a losing battle. We must believe that he has limited power and he was defeated by Jesus. James, the brother of Jesus and author of the book of James said: *Submit yourselves therefore to God. **Resist** the **devil**, and he will flee from you* (James 4:7). As the story is told in the book of Job, God asked satan where he had been and satan told God that he was roaming all over the earth watching everything. Lucifer still has the same position today. As he does his job, he finds people who are willing to work for or with him and he uses them to create havoc in their own lives as well as in the lives of others. There is also a warning in 1 Peter 5:8 that we should be watchful of the enemy's schemes and tricks, so that he will not devour us. John 10:10 reminds us that the enemy comes to kill steal and destroy. We must be aware that satan is real, he is not a fairy tale as some people have said.

On the other hand, John 10:10 assures that our Father in heaven comes to give us the most abundant life. He has promised us a rich inheritance, but He cannot release it to us if we lack the willingness to change-if we refuse to let go of the old stuff and free ourselves from mental bondage. Until you decide to let go of self-defeating belief and habits, embrace change and maximize your God given love and potential, the idea of changing anything in or about your life will always be uncomfortable to you. In order to see possibilities, we need to take responsibility for our own thoughts and actions. Norman Vincent Peale said, "No matter how dark things may be, raise your sights and see possibilities; always see them, for they are always there."

At times when I observe people's behavior it makes me wonder: Do people really want to change for the better? If they do, why then do they point their fingers at others, blame others for their conditions and complain when prominent people make suggestions or give strategies to impact change in society? Or why do they ostracize people when they take actions to affect change? Why do people have to apologize when they make comments about the truth? If we really want change, we must first change the way we think, the way we perceive things and the way we act upon them.

There are stories in the Bible that show the power of change. Starting in Genesis and ending in the New Testament, we see that change brings great results. It was necessary for God to change Abram's name in order for him to walk into his destiny. God changed Abram's name to Abraham and his wife's name from Sarai to Sarah, and great things happened for them as a result of the changes. One of the most incredible events was the birth of their son, Isaac in their old age. Jacob's name was changed to Israel and Saul's name was changed to Paul. In all of these circumstances, great things happened after the changes were made.

In modern day society there are numerous stories of people who have achieved extraordinary success, because they embraced change and persevered through trials and tribulations. Some of us look at people who are successful and become jealous of them and will do anything to see them fail, but how much more productive would we be if we directed that jealous, player-hating energy toward finding out what changes we could make in our own lives to foster success and to serve humanity better? Why not be in harmony with change?

We are often indecisive and find it difficult to make decisions about making changes, simply because we do not effectively apply our faith to ask and allow the Holy Spirit to guide us through this inevitable process, nor do we possess the patience to wait for the answers. According to Ecclesiastes 11:4, *Farmers who wait for perfect weather never plant . If they watch every cloud, they never harvest.* In other words, if we wait for the perfect condition, we will never accomplish anything and for many of us change remains just a thought. Our lives will always be full of challenges, but we must not allow them to discourage or cripple us from making the changes we need to make in order to accomplish and fulfill our destinies. There must come a time in our lives when we stop sitting back and waiting for things to just happen.

It says in the Word that faith without works is dead. We must take action! We know the relevance of change, but we still do not change. If you are ready for a change, make a list of all the things in your life with which you are displeased, dissatisfied or would like to see happen differently. Think about how God may feel about those things in your life and ask Him for help as you move toward making those changes. Keep the list with you, and start working from it. As you complete an item, cross it off your list and move to the next. Do not abandon the list until you have attained your desired results.

Spend time in the Word and the Holy Spirit will direct you. Once you have begun to make changes, do not quit. No matter how difficult they may seem. Do not let the devil interrupt your process with His lies. The Bible says: *In all thy ways acknowledge Him and He shall direct thy path* (Proverbs 3:5-6). If you do this and ignore satan's lies, you will begin to see the glory of God manifesting in your life.

All things are possible and God's plan for you is different from the one He has for me. He does not and mostly likely will not remove your chain in the same way that he removes mine or another person's. We have to remember that God does not deal with everyone in the same way; however, He is a just God, Who is Omnipotent, Omnipresent and Omniscient. Do it now, make the decision to change. This might mean that you have to get away from some people and some things. As the saying goes, "Feel the fear and do it anyway." Put your hope and trust in the Father. I love this quote from the inspiring speaker, Zig Ziglar: "The foundational quality of all change is hope." If you have hope, you can expect to see changes. Chances are that you need to change something in your life if you feel that something is missing, if you feel you have no joy, if you are financially stressed, if you are in conflict with yourself, God or with others, or if you have doubts and fear.

It takes courage to change bad habits into good habits. But as Helen Keller said, "Courage cannot be developed in ease and quiet. Only through experiences of trial and suffering can the soul be strengthened, vision cleared, ambition inspired and success achieved." When we are content with our current state, regardless of what it is, we understand that God loves us, no matter what state we are in. We will live in the expectation that change is inevitable and therefore it is to our advantage when we embrace it. Paul said that a lot of things do not matter anymore: *What counts is whether we really have been changed into new and different people* (Galatians 6:15).

PRINCIPLES FOR DAILY APPLICATION

(1) If you are dissatisfied with your life the way it is now, identify and acknowledge the things that are making you dissatisfied or unhappy. Make a clear decision to fix them by accepting and embracing change. Your destiny might be wrapped up in the next change you make. If you resist change, you may stunt your growth and abort your destiny.
(2) When you know what you want to change or restructure and you know the reasons why, believe that you can change anything in your life, by putting your mind to it, taking consistent action and remaining focus. If you continue to resist change, how are you going to experience growth and advancement? Life is very short, so the time to act is now. It is important though to know where you are going, because this will make your change in direction worthwhile. If you are already in a bad situation, why would you be afraid to try something new? You might think that if you change, it could make your situation worse, but remember it could and mostly would also make it better; especially if you ask and listen to your inner guide. Think about this question: What would you do if you knew that you would succeed at everything that you do? Whatever your answer is, it is time to release all doubts and uncertainties.
(3) If you are not allowing the Holy Spirit to guide your life, start utilizing this wonderful Person of the Trinity to help, guide and teach in every situation. When you feel overwhelmed, ask for help from

people you know who are where you want to be. Have faith, pray, trust and enjoy the process. Know that you can do all things according to Philippians 4:13.

(4) Make a commitment to do a self evaluation from day to day to ensure that you are experiencing the changes you desire and move on. Let go of anything that gets in your way of progress such as the victim mentality that has held you back for so long. In letting go you will enjoy better mental, physical and spiritual health. As the Apostle Paul did, we can get rid of our chains. Do not be fooled by your chain, it is only temporary, see what you can learn from it and move forward. If you do something and fail at it, do not give up, at least, try for a few times.

(5) Accept the responsibility that comes with change and know that all things are possible, even when they are uncomfortable and seem impossible to you.   ***all things*** *are* ***possible*** *to him that believeth* (Mark 9:23).

(6) When you begin to make changes, you may be faced with new challenges, consider the challenges as part of the process and know they are there to make you grow stronger. Do not get discouraged and give up. Continue what you started because you: *Being confident of this very thing, that he which hath begun a good work in you will perform it until the day of Jesus Christ* (Philippians 1:6). Do not look for the easiest way out of a situation, the easier way is not always the best way.

(7) Pray, pray, pray. Read the Bible, let it speak to you, have gratitude, and expect the unexpected. As I close this chapter I am reminded of the Serenity Prayer:

PRAYER:

God, grant me the serenity to accept the things I cannot change,
The courage to change the things I can,
And the wisdom to know the difference. Living one day at a time,
Enjoying one moment at a time,
Accepting hardship as a pathway to peace,
Taking this sinful world as it is, Not as I would have it.
Trusting that you will make all things right
If I surrender to your will,
So that I may be reasonably happy in this life

And supremely happy with you forever in the next.
Reinhold Niebuhr

Most gracious God, I thank You for creating in me a clean heart that makes me want to change from my evil ways and to become more like You. Lord, I want to take on Your character. Please forgive me for those times when I was too rigid and dependent upon my flesh. Thank You for the Holy Spirit who teaches me and shows me the areas of my life where I need to make changes, Amen.

CHAPTER 7
THE ESSENCE OF TIME

*And in process of time it came to pass, that Cain brought of
the fruit of the ground an offering unto the LORD*
Genesis 4:3.

*And it came to pass in process of time, that the king of Egypt died:
and the children of Israel sighed by reason of the bondage, and they
cried, and their cry came up unto God by reason of the bondage*
Exodus 2:23.

To everything there is a season, and a time to every purpose under the heaven
Ecclesiastes 3:1.

So teach us to number our days, that we may apply our hearts unto wisdom.
Psalm 90:12.

*But the hour cometh, and now is, when the true worshippers shall worship
the Father in spirit and in truth: for the Father seeketh such to worship him*
John 4:23.

Knowing the importance of time and utilizing it wisely is one of the determining factors in whether or not we succeed or fail in life. Proper use of our time is critical. In the natural sense, making a plan for every day of your life will propel you into your destiny. I was convicted of being inconsistent about my daily planning. I would wake up some days without a plan as to how I would spend my day and sometimes that proved to be very chaotic. Lack of planning could cause you to lose time and to miss out on valuable things that you could have otherwise accomplished. Be aware, however, that whatever you plan for your day could be changed at anytime, based on what God has pre-planned for you. Make your plan according to the counsel you receive from God. The Bible says: *Without counsel purposes are disappointed: but in the multitude of counselors they are established* (Proverb 15:22).

Your destiny depends on your faith, surrender, dependence and trust in God. It is crucial to know when to move and when to stay put. God's timing is perfect and if your plans can synchronize with His, yours will also be perfect. Monitoring and maximizing our time will prevent us from spending a lifetime missing out on God's plans and promises. The right time for anything, for you and for me, is *now*. If we regard everyday as the best day of our lives and focus on the present, we will no doubt experience more successes in our lives. I believe that timing is everything, especially when it comes to spiritual things. We must always be prepared and in agreement with the leading of the Holy Spirit because: The Holy Spirit will lead and guide us in the best way to execute our time. It is written in the word: *Howbeit when he, the Spirit of truth, is come, he will guide you into all truth: for he shall not speak of himself; but whatsoever he shall hear, that shall he speak: and he will shew you things to come* (John 16:13).

One might ask, why plan my time when God is in control of everything and already has a plan for me? The answer is that God is a God of order and not of chaos. The truth is that God is in control is not a reason for us to "cop out" of being responsible. There are two Greek words for time, Kairos and Chronos. Kairos time is God's time which is different from our time. Chronos time is time as we know it. Just as His ways are different from our ways, His time is also perfect. There is an example in Genesis that shows how perfect God's timing is. God asked a question and answered it with a promise that happened exactly the way he said it would: *Is anything too hard for the LORD? I will return to you at the appointed time next year and Sarah will have a son.* (Genesis 18:14).

Time was very significant in this passage of scripture, because God's Word had to be fulfilled at His appointed time. Did Sarah have her child at the time that God appointed for his birth? Yes, it is revealed in Genesis, Chapter 21. Sarah had her son at the time that the Lord promised: *And the LORD visited Sarah as he had said, and the LORD did unto Sarah as he had spoken. For Sarah conceived, and bore Abraham a son in his old age, at the set time of which God had spoken to him* (Genesis 21:1-2). There is an appointed time for everything that will come to pass in our lives, but it is possible to miss out on some things if we are not careful and savvy about how we utilize our time. Time wasting is a detriment to success and destiny. Using time wisely is wisdom. On days that I make a list of things to do, I accomplish much more than when I enter the day without a plan or a list. Accomplishing more always makes me feel better. I have heard it said that, "until you value yourself, you won't value your time, and if you don't value your time, you will not value accomplishments."

Being conscientious about time is a good way to not waste it. For as long as I can remember or as far as I can look back, I have seen people wasting time. Two things are most vivid in my mind are older men spending their days in a bar and young men hanging out on the streets. I cannot think of anything that is more irresponsible and time wasting than these two things.

When I was growing up, I thought this happened only in my community where opportunities for work were few and far between. Surprisingly, I came to the United States (the land of opportunity and abundant work), and I saw the same thing happening. This truly baffled my mind. I wondered if these people ever read Ecclesiastes 3 or any of the verses in Proverbs that explain what happens to lazy people or to people who do not work. Ecclesiastes 3 is a classic description of time to help us get a grip on how we view and use our time.

For everything there is a season, a time for every activity under heaven.
A time to be born and a time to die.
A time to plant and a time to harvest.
A time to kill and a time to heal.
A time to tear down and a time to build up.
A time to cry and a time to laugh.
A time to grieve and a time to dance.
A time to scatter stones and a time to gather stones.
A time to embrace and a time to turn away.
A time to search and a time to quit searching.
A time to keep and a time to throw away.

A time to tear and a time to mend.
A time to be quiet and a time to speak.
A time to love and a time to hate.
A time for war and a time for peace
(Ecclesiastes 3:1-8).

The word of God has made it clear that there is a time for everything; therefore, it is important for us to be aware of how and what we are doing at all times. How can we make the most of our time? We can look at the stories of many of the characters in the Bible and learn about their lives in relation to how they spent their time and what happened during their times. Many of them knew the times they were living in and positioned themselves to make the most of their time.

For example, Ruth was at the right place at the right time. She chose to stay with her mother-in-law, Naomi, and as a result, she met her Boaz. Her timing could never have been better! Rebecca was at the right place at the right time and found the love of her life. Esther understood that she was chosen to accomplish a task at a particular time, and she met with a glorious destiny. Elisha served the King at the right time and was promoted. There are many other similar examples of others who God used in special ways. When it comes to how well I use my time, I meditate on Benjamin E. Hayes' poem: *I have only just a minute only sixty seconds in it.*

Now let us think in terms of time as it relates to the Kingdom of God. Are you having a difficult time in your life at this moment in time, or do you know someone who is? In 2 Timothy 3:1, Paul sent a warning to Timothy saying: *You should know this, Timothy, that in the last days there will be very difficult times.* This is the reason we must be cognizant of the times we are in and what we should be doing. We should be equipped, resilient and prepared at all times, as were the people of Issachar. The men of Issachar, all two hundred of them, were vigilant, prepared, positioned and knew exactly what to do to help David in his battle.

Our time, Chronos, will end, but Christ's time, Kairos, will not end because it is everlasting. Peter gives a good comparison of these times in this verse: *But, beloved, be not ignorant of this one thing, that one day is with the Lord as a thousand years, and a thousand years as one day* (2 Peter 3:8). A thousand years in God's time are like a day in our time. That is why we want everything now and God says, not so fast. Wait. While we are given an opportunity to live and act in our time, we need to know that we must function on God's timetable. We should effectively use the time we are allotted in preparation for the day when we too will operate in God's eternal time. With the prophecies that have been fulfilled and the different signs that are evident in our day, I believe we are living in the last days. We cannot afford to let time slip away from us any longer.

We must grasp the essence of time and decide to use wisely the time that has been allotted to us. We need to make the best use of our time in order to fulfill our destinies. I believe that the reason some of us are so far behind, stagnant or not progressing is that we have not been good stewards of our time. The Bible says in Galatians 6:7 that *whatsoever a man soweth, that shall he also reap*. If we waste time, we will not be able to maximize our calling and get all the benefits of the Kingdom. Time wasted is time lost. We cannot recoup it. The clock is not waiting for anyone. It is ticking away minute by minute. This is an indication that we should get our lives in order. Our time is short. The time to turn to Christ is now. If you are not saved, it is time to get saved. If you are saved and living a double standard life, it is time to get serious about whom you are serving and what you should be doing to please God.

I like the way one songwriter puts it, "You better get right with God, come and do it now, under the cross of Jesus I laid my burden down." Are you right with God? Have you laid your burdens under His cross? These are necessary preparation steps. When we are prepared, if the clock stops ticking or if our hearts stop beating, we will be ready to be transcended to the other side of life. This body that we are in is temporary, but eternal life is promised to those who believe and do God's will. On the other hand, if we are not prepared to enter the Kingdom of God, He will not let us in. If we allow our hearts to stop beating and our time to run out before acknowledging Him and following His commands,

He will say to us as is described in Luke: *I don't know you or where you come from. Get away from me, all you who do evil* (Luke 13:27).

Sadly, for many, it will be similar to the case of Noah in the book of Genesis. God instructed Noah to build an ark, to save the nation from an intended flood. The people ignored all the pleas and the warnings to get on board the ark. Noah and his family were the only humans willing to get on. One day, the door closed with Noah and his family inside. The flood rushed in and everyone who rebelled and ignored the warnings perished. Unfortunately, they allowed time to slip away from them. Can you imagine how scared they were, as they cried out to God in the final minutes before the destruction? They must have cried, "God, please open up the Ark and let us in!" But the flood came rushing down and swept them away. They were too late; they allowed the window of opportunity and time to collapse on themselves. They did not repent and turn from their wicked ways, before or during the building of the Ark. I do not know about you, but I am relying each day on God's grace and His mercy, so that at the end of time, I will not hear the words like the people heard in Luke 13:27: *I know you not whence ye are; depart from me, all ye workers of iniquity.*

Time became a topic of interest to me, because too often, I saw many people, including myself, wasting precious time. Time is priceless and cannot be bought, it is free, but once it is lost it can never be regained. I like this little poem about time:

Time is …
Too slow for those who wait,
Too swift for those who fear,
Too long for those who grieve,
Too short for those who rejoice,
But for those who love;
Time is eternity. Author Unknown

People are prone to procrastination and this is disadvantageous. Procrastination is one of the biggest time stealers. It is a tool that satan uses to make us rebel against God's divine plan and prevents us from fulfilling our destinies. Be aware of the times when that feeling of not wanting to do the things you need to do, creep up on you. Speak out against it; there is power in the tongue. For example, if you get an idea to write something and you begin to say, "I'll do it later   ." As soon as you catch yourself thinking that way, say out loud, "This is a fantastic idea and I am going to write this idea down right now." At the same time ask yourself, why put it off until later when I can do it now? If you postpone writing the idea with the intention of doing it later, it might not get done. If you are a chronic procrastinator, when you wake up in the morning or at anytime you feel that this behavior is controlling you, just say to yourself, "I am a good person, I do things now." This is an affirmation from Paul McManus *Seven Great Prayers, which* I said every day to help me break the bad habit of procrastination.

In Genesis 6:3, God said, *My Spirit will not put up with humans for such a long time.* This indicates to me that God wants people to be sensitive about the time He has allotted to each of us and the way in which we use it. I agree with the person who said: "Each individual has to figure out what time it is in his or her life and not rebel against the particular thing that needs to be worked on at that particular time. Don't say you don't have enough time. You have exactly the same number of hours per day that was given to Helen Keller, Pasteur, Michelangelo, Mother Teresa, Leonardo da Vinci, Thomas Jefferson and Albert Einstein."

It is unbelievable how much time people waste in general. My hope is that you will think seriously about how you are spending your time and make the changes to break habits that rob you of using your time wisely, smartly and intentionally. We all have sixty minutes in each hour, twenty four hours each day and five hundred twenty-five thousand six hundred minutes in each year. How productive were you with those thousands of minutes last year? How are you spending them this year, and how do you think you might spend them, next year and beyond? My prayer is that we will all spend our time wisely to improve the work we have already started and to expand the Kingdom of God.

PRINCIPLES FOR DAILY APPLICATION

(1) Be aware that "procrastination is the thief of time." Do not put off what you can do today for tomorrow. "Timing is everything." Understand the times and know what you ought to be doing. Read 1 Chronicles 12:32.

(2) Find ways to work smarter, with ease and less effort. Make a daily plan or a "to-do" list and use it; however, remember not to be too rigid with your plan. Always plan with the expectation that God may change

your plan at any time. "Don't count every hour in the day, make every hour in the day count." Read 2 Peter 3:8.

(3) Know when to start and when to stop. God stopped and rested on the seventh day. There are times when we do not do enough and times when we do too much. If we allow the Holy Spirit to guide us, we will have a more balanced life.

(4) Know that there is a time and a place for everything under the sun. It is in the Word: *There is a time for everything, and a season for every activity*
under heaven (Ecclesiastes 3:1). Read Ecclesiastes verses 1-8 and Psalm 31:15.

(5) Know that using time wisely could be the difference between success and failure. Keep a journal of how you spend your time each day until you nail down the problem of time wasting. Read Acts 17:26-28.

(6) Study the poems about time given in this chapter, and read 2 Timothy 2:15.

(7) Pray that you will work with God's timing for the events that will take place in your life-both the good and the bad. Read 1 Thessalonians 5:17.

PRAYER:

Dear heavenly Father, I thank You for the time that You have allotted to me in this life. I promise to use it wisely and effectively for Your divine purpose. As I walk along life's rugged pathways, I recognize the things that have held me back from being all that You created me to be, and the misuse of time is one of these things. Dear Lord, thank You for Your grace and please forgive me. In the name of Jesus Christ I renounce the things that have clouded my vision and my mind from recognizing how important it is for me to use my time wisely. I will not rebel against You and Lord, I will not idle this eternal decision any longer. I rebuke procrastination at its root and I submit to Your will. I am decisive in taking the necessary actions toward fulfilling my destiny. I operate in Your divine timetable, and I am in synchrony with Your timing. I give honor to You my dear heavenly Father, Amen.

CHAPTER 8
LIFE'S STUMBLING BLOCKS

Again, if a righteous man doth turns from his righteousness and commits iniquity, and I lay a stumbling block before him, he shall die: because thou hast not given him warning, he shall die in his sin, and his righteousness which he hath done shall not be remembered; but his blood will I require at thine hand
Ezekiel 3:20.

Let us not therefore judge one another anymore: but judge this rather, that no man put a stumbling block or an occasion to fall in his brother's way
Romans 14:13.

Trust in the LORD with all thine heart; and lean not unto thine own understanding. .In all thy ways acknowledge him, and he shall direct thy paths
Proverb 3:5-6.

Dear friends, do not be surprised at the painful trial you are suffering, as though something strange were happening to you
1 Peter 4:12.

The dictionary's meaning of *stumbling block* is an *obstacle* or *impediment*. In the Bible the term is used to describe things that people put before themselves and God or what God puts in a disobedient person's way. In the present day, stumbling blocks are still the same. They are snares, hindrances, handicaps, or anything that impedes us in any way; it is something that gets in a person's way. In Romans 9, Paul talked about Jesus being a stumbling block in the Jews' way. The humble Jesus who came was not the Jesus for whom they were looking. Until today, some of them are still stumbling over that issue.

Although stumbling blocks may deter us from doing what we want to do, that does not necessarily mean that they are bad. They are usually there for a purpose and may be God-sent to help us in some way. The story of a man called Balaam in the Bible is an example of a stumbling block that was sent by God to protect a man. As the story goes, Balaam was a prophet who wanted to please Balek, because of the material things that Balek offered him. Balek, the King of Moab, sent some of his distinguished men to get Balaam to come and curse the Israelites whom he considered to be a threat because they were so numerous.

God told Balaam not to go, but Balaam wavered in his spirit, saddled up his donkey and set out. Sound familiar? This made God furious, so God sent an angel to block the way. When the donkey saw the angel, which Balaam had not seen standing in the road, with a sword in hand, the donkey rushed off the road into the field; Balaam beat the donkey and got him back on to the road. The angel kept appearing in the way, making it impassable for the donkey.

Balaam's anger increased and he continued to beat the donkey. As he did that, something very strange happened: *And the LORD opened the mouth of the ass, and she said unto Balaam, What have I done unto thee, that thou hast smitten me these three times?* (Numbers 22:28). When the donkey spoke to Balaam and he began to argue with the donkey, God opened Balaam's eyes, causing him to see that his donkey which had been his stumbling block was actually preventing him from getting killed. It was at this point that Balaam confessed to God, and in the end God's purpose was fulfilled through Balaam's prophecies that God commanded him to deliver. This saved the nation of Israel.

In our day we sometimes find ourselves in similar situations and because we do not always see the full picture of what God is doing, we get angry at the person, object that we feel is getting in our way. Our stumbling blocks could be our, belief system, spouse, children, supervisors, cars or just about anything. God often uses the strangest or simplest things to protect us and to get his will accomplished. Say for example you have an appointment and you go to your car only to find that it has a flat tire. You get upset, because you are going to be late for the appointment. You are not thinking at that moment that could be God's way of preventing us from getting in an automobile accident. Or have you ever been late in going somewhere and you run into a car wreck and you utter a sigh of relief because you know that had you been earlier, you could have been in that accident? Many times we do not immediately understand what is going on until later on, when we look back at events.

Several workers of the World Trade Center in New York City, were either late for work or did not show up on September 11, 2008. initially may have thought that whatever prevented them from going to work were hindrances, but in the end they gave their testimonies of how grateful they were for not having been at work at the time of the horrible devastation. Sometimes stumbling blocks make us feel as though we have no sense of direction; there is no real stability, lack of control, and no authentic sense of worth. There is no satisfying accomplishment, because something has gotten in our way. One of the reasons we fail to understand or accept stumbling blocks as a necessary part of life is that we do not put complete trust in the Lord. When we do not wait on God and we go ahead and make our own plans, we stumble over our own mistakes.

As we, stumbling blocks come in many forms. In life, we find that there are many obstacles that block or prevent us from becoming our ideal selves or realizing our purpose or unique gifts and insight from God. "We're often the victim of myths," writes Cynthia Kersey, "Myths about what are possible, myths about what we can accomplish and myths about the obstacles in our path. But where some have accepted these myths as reality, others have not and have gone on to achieve great things and live great dreams." Beware of what you believe and accept. Always do your due diligence.

Other dangerous stumbling blocks are ignorance, doubt, being out of touch with reality, being un-teachable, blaming others, worry, self-pity, selfishness, excuses, giving in to others and not finding the truth for ourselves, procrastination, laziness, denial, rejection, fear and enemy influence. Recognize these things; call them as they are, let them go, denounce them, and do not worry about them anymore. Begin to dream big, anticipate much growth and expect the unexpected. You are a powerful individual; you are a conqueror, an over-comer, and you have great potential.

Sometimes we just need a little reminder of the powerful individuals we are and how sovereign our Creator is. God can remove any stumbling block, no matter how big they seemingly appear to be to us. Stumbling blocks never mean that we should give up. Shut out the voices of the enemy, knowing that the outcome is in the accomplishment of God's divine plan for your life. Invite new actions and make affirmations; elevate your mind and spirit and expand your vision. Stop making excuses.

Make affirmations daily. Find scriptures, study them and use them to affirm yourself. Do not let stumbling blocks cripple you. If you do not try to understand stumbling blocks, they can maim you. Learn to recognize adversary's strategies that can hold you back from walking in what God ordained for your life. Having an awareness of how the opponent works will make it harder to fall victim to his tactics. You will be able to make wise decisions and resolve issues that impact your life.

Seek guidance from the Holy Spirit, Who the Father has sent us for this specific purpose. We struggle unnecessarily because we are not yielding to the Holy Spirit and making Him the most significant in our lives. When we welcome Him, He stays with us and guides us through every difficult situation. John said: *When the **Spirit** of **truth comes**, he will guide you into all **truth**. He will not speak on his own but will tell you what he has heard. He will tell you about the future* (John 16:13). If you need help, find a mentor or a coach. Every successful individual has or had a coach.

A coach can help you to stay focused. Distraction is one of the biggest stumbling blocks, but if we stay on our own path, we can recognize and roll away those stumbling blocks that are impeding our progress. As I mentioned before fear is another popular stumbling block. Fear is perhaps the worst one that robs us of our destinies. Fear can place a handicap on you and make you stay in one place for the rest of your life. It is better to choose to conquer fear with faith and remove those mounting stumbling blocks.

Fight with all your might using the weapons of awareness, vigilance, persistence, determination and consistently staying focused. This will make the devil mad. He will eventually leave you alone and go to find a more willing target. He will return, so remain mindful of this and be ready to send him back to the abyss where he belongs.

I read somewhere that, "stumbling blocks are handicaps that we have placed upon ourselves, because we do not know or understand what we do know." It is up to us to use our intelligence to turn our stumbling blocks into stepping-stones. In the book of Proverbs, Solomon acknowledges: *The heart of the prudent getteth knowledge; and the ear of the wise seeketh knowledge* (Proverbs 18:15). If we earnestly study God's Word and apply the principles to our lives, we will see that stumbling blocks are there only for a while and that ultimately we benefit from them. Paul wrote this comforting verse for us: *And we know that all things work together for good to them that love God, to them who are the called according to his purpose* (Romans 8:28). Always remember that Jesus never fails. I like this line from a song we used to sing at the Church of The First Born when I was in my early teens: "Although I falter, although I stumble, He loves me still, so I will always trust Him for He never fails."

If you take a walk back through the scriptures you will discover that God removed stumbling blocks from out of His followers' way, or He removed His followers from their stumbling blocks. For example, look at the stories of Joseph and David. In order for God to remove your stumbling blocks out of your way, you must step back and allow Him to. In order for Him to remove you from your stumbling blocks; you have to be willing to move when God says move and go where He says to go.

Another instance where God removed a stumbling block is seen Abraham's triangle. When Ishmael and his mother Hagar became a stumbling block to Sarah's and Abraham's relationship, God removed them. Hager used to be their helper and when Sarah did not bear the child God had promised Abraham, they decided to let Hagar have the child, since she was young and Sarah was old. But as it turned, that child was not the son God promised and Sarah later bore the child. So, how did remove them?

One day Sarah witnessed Ishmael making fun of her son, Isaac (God's promised seed); she turned to Abraham and demanded: *Cast out this bondwoman and her son: for the son of this bondwoman shall not be heir with my son, even with Isaac* (Genesis 21:10). Although Abraham was not pleased with this request, God told Him to do what his wife Sarah asked him to do. We know that God's purpose has to be fulfilled, in spite of what we want:

*For my thoughts are **not your** thoughts, neither are **your ways** my **ways**, saith the LORD* (Isaiah 55:8).

As was with the story of Joseph, we also see how God removed Joseph from his stumbling blocks and made him ruler over Egypt at the appointed time. God removed Joseph from his brothers who work stumbling blocks. His jealous brothers to whom he had divulged his dreams saw him as a stumbling block, so they got rid of him. Be careful with whom you share your dreams; they could become stumbling blocks on your way to achievement. Moses trusted and obeyed God. When Moses held his shepherd's staff over the water to part the red sea, God allowed the Israelites to walk through unharmed by the Egyptians. All the Egyptians who tried to cross perished. God became the stumbling block in the Egyptian's path. God will either remove you from your stumbling blocks or remove your stumbling blocks from you. He will always protect His children. He will cause your enemies to become confused and He will propel you to your destiny.

PRINCIPLES FOR DAILY APPLICATION

(1) Recognize the stumbling blocks. John 10:10 gives us a warning that the enemy comes to kill, steal and destroy, but we are comforted by another portion of the verse that says, God comes to give us life and more abundantly. Satan is always a stumbling block. We also have hope in this verse in Isaiah that promises: *no weapon that is formed against thee shall be able to prosper* (Isaiah 54:17). Use the weapons in Ephesians 6 to fight stumbling blocks that are brought on by the enemy.

(2) Determine if the stumbling blocks are for good or bad. One may think that stumbling blocks are always bad, but they are not. They may seem bad in the present, but over the long haul they may turn out to be for your good. Be careful how you approach stumbling blocks. Some can be extremely difficult. Balaam did not recognize the benefits of his stumbling block until after the crazy incidents with his donkey. As a result he became remorseful and confessed: *And Balaam said unto the angel of the LORD, I have sinned; for I knew not that thou stoodest in the way against me: now therefore, if it displease thee, I will get me back again* (Numbers 22:34).

(3) Get rid of the stumbling blocks that are hindrances to your progress.

Let them go, whether they are people, attitudes, behavior, fear, doubt, unbelief, un-forgiveness, hatred, things, or habits.

(4) Memorize Romans 8:28: *And we know that all things work together for good to them that love God, to them who are the called according to his purpose.* This will help you to get a grip when you are overwhelmed and feeling as though you are at the end of your rope.

(5) Know God's way, so you may not stumble into the path of the enemy. Be on your guard. Read 1 Peter 5:8.

(6) Make a list of the things you want to eliminate from your life, cross them off as you get rid of them and start journaling about your victories.

(7) Pray, pray, pray and ask God to help you make the best decision as to how way to handle stumbling blocks.

PRAYER:

Dear heavenly Father, I thank You that You have given me wisdom to understand that stumbling blocks are not meant to harm me, even though they may be frustrating at times. Help me to recognize them and teach me how to deal with them. I thank You that Your Word said in Romans 8:28: A*ll things work together for good to those who love you and are the called according to your purpose.* Please help me to trust in You with all my heart, acknowledge You in all my ways and to lean not on my own understanding as Your Word declares in Proverbs 3:5-6. Thank You that Your Word says whatever the enemy means for bad, You mean it for good. Thank You for the words in John 10:10 that assure us that *the enemy comes to kill, steal, and destroy, but You came to give us an abundant life.* I pray that when the enemy comes, You will lift up a standard against him. Thank You for Your promise in Isaiah 54 that no weapon that is formed against me shall ever be able to prosper. Thank that according to Ephesians 6, I can put on the whole armor of God and have divine protection from the enemy. Thank You for helping me to take my eyes off my circumstances and to keep them on *You*, now and always. Lord

I love You and put all of my trust in You as I pray this prayer in Jesus' name, Amen.

CHAPTER 9
PRAYER THE FOUNDATION

*After this manner therefore pray ye: Our Father which
art in heaven, Hallowed be thy name*
Matthew 6:9.

*For it is written, As I live, saith the Lord, every knee shall
bow to me, and every tongue shall confess to God.*
Romans 14:11.

*For every one that asketh receiveth; and he that seeketh
findeth; and to him that knocketh it shall be opened*
Matthew7:7-8.

*And it came to pass, that, as he was praying in a certain
place, when he ceased, one of his disciples said unto him,
Lord, teach us to pray, as John also taught his disciples*
Luke 11:1.

*Confess your faults one to another, and pray one for another, that ye may
be healed. The effectual fervent prayer of a righteous man availeth much*
James 5:16.

Continue in prayer, and watch in the same with thanksgiving
Colossians 4:2.

*Be careful for nothing; but in everything by prayer and supplication
with thanksgiving let your requests be made known unto God*
Philippians 4:6.

*I exhort therefore, that, first of all, supplications, prayers,
intercessions, and giving of thanks, be made for all men*
1 Timothy 2:1.

Prayer is a part of my daily life as much as faith is. I use prayer as the basis for everything I do. Prayers are our conversations with Jesus. It is a dialogue; therefore we must pray and listen for God's answers. Some people say that their prayers are not being answered, or that they do not hear from God. I know that if you stop and listen as you pray or meditate, you will hear from God. I have been praying ever since I was a little girl and more and more I realize there is no greater way to access the power, peace, mercy and security of God than through prayers. He always answers my prayers. Prayer is my foundation; what is yours?

I have seen manifestations and answered prayers on a consistent basis, so I know without a doubt that prayers really do work and they really do get answered. My prayers are not always answered immediately, but sometimes they are. At other times, it may take a day, week, month, year, and in some cases many years. Whenever they get answered, I give God the glory, honor and praise; regardless of how long He takes to answer or what answer He gives me. I know He knows what is best for me.

One of my first experiences with answered prayer came in the form of a dream. I grew up attending the Anglican Church, but in my early teens I became curious about what my friends were saying about their churches, and I started visiting other churches. There was a Seventh Day Adventist Church and a Church of God that I liked. I observed that the Adventist had some rules with which I was not familiar, but I thought they were worth exploring. I remember being confused one night after leaving a service at the Adventist church. Before going to bed that night, I prayed and asked the Lord to clear up the confusion and show me what church He would have me attend.

I had a dream that very night that I was in the Church of God worshipping. After that, I never again forced the question about which day I should worship. I assumed that since, in my dream I was worshipping at the Church of God that was where I needed to worship in reality. Before I prayed that prayer and had that dream, I read about worshipping on the Seventh Day, which would be Saturday according to the calendar, so I therefore had some concerns about being brought up to attend church on Sunday. I trusted in what the Lord had shown me in that dream. It has been thirty-five years since that remarkable experience and here I am today, back to where I was thirty-five years ago, asking God to reveal His truth to me. I keep hearing these words, *"Remember the Sabbath Day, to keep it holy. Six days shalt thou labour, and do all thy work:"* (Exodus 20:8-9). This is not to persuade anyone, either way, whether to worship on Saturday or Sunday, I simply share this to demonstrate why I believe that my prayer life and my relationship with Jesus Christ are the best things I have going for me. There is more to this story, which I may have to discuss in another book later on.

Some people are petrified about praying, especially praying publicly. I get compliments quite often when I pray publicly. I tell people that it is through the grace of God and the words that He gives me as I pray, I pray often to get closer to my Creator and that they too can pray often-silently, if that is more comfortable for them, or out loud-whichever way, just pray. The Holy Spirit will teach you. If you practice praying at home and sometimes out loud and listen to people who find praying to be easy, it will become easier for you to pray. Jack Hayford explained prayer well when he said: "Prayer is not the mystical experience of a few special people, but an aggressive act; an act that may be performed by anyone who will accept the challenge to learn to pray."

I do believe that prayer should be a part of every person's life-especially those who go to church. Matthew wrote: *It is written, My* **house shall** *be called the* **house** *of* **prayer***; but ye have made it a den of thieves* (Matthew 21:13). Some people would rather spend time in church gossiping, than praying. The house cannot be called a house of prayer if people refuse to pray. Praying as a group is very effective. It is written in the Word: *Again I say unto you, That if two of you shall agree on earth as touching anything that they shall ask, it shall be done for them of my Father which is in heaven. For where two or three are gathered together in my name, there am I in the midst of them* (Matthew 18:19-20). Praying together will get God's attention to perform significant miracles, such as healing a land.

Prayer is not always about asking God for or to do something, but what do many of us like to do when we pray? We like to ask or beg God for things. I think it is better to pray asking, than not to pray at all, but before we pray to ask God for things, we should first give Him thanks for everything that He has already given, done, is doing, will do and for all the blessings you have already received. He has given us so much! Jesus said: *And I say unto you, Ask, and it shall be given you; seek, and ye shall find; knock, and it shall be opened unto you. For every one that asketh receiveth; and he that seeketh findeth; and to him that knocketh it shall be opened* (Luke 11:9-10).

God may put a desire in your heart and you may pray for something. You may not see it happen at the time when you want it to, but do not give up. Delay does not mean that He has not heard or that He has denied your prayer. It means that God has an appointed time in which He will answer and give you what you need. Whatever you do, do not waiver or doubt when you pray. Always, have faith and hope in the promises of God. There are two verses that come to mind here: (1) *I will therefore that men pray everywhere, lifting up holy hands, **without** wrath and **doubting*** (1 Timothy 2:8)**;** and (2);*Therefore I say unto you, What things so ever ye desire, when ye pray, believe that ye receive them, and ye shall have* (Mark 11:24).

If you pray for something and it is God's will for you to have it, you will get it, even when you get discouraged and are tired of waiting. He will come through for us as He came through for Hannah when she prayed about her barrenness, Peter just at the point when he was ready to give up on fishing; He came through for Elijah when he prayed earnestly that no rain would fall, and indeed none fell for three and a half years. Then God came through again when Elijah prayed for rain to fall, and showers poured down and the plants turned green again. There is hope in every situation that might seem hopeless to us.

Jesus knows exactly which prayers to answer and not answer. He is just like His Father. God did not answer Jesus when He asked Him to remove the cup (to spare His life from death on the cross). What would have happened if God had answered that prayer? We would be forever doomed-we would not know what it is to experience grace. All the nations of the earth would be lost. There would be no remission of sin or salvation.

Jesus answers prayers in different ways and at the right time. Be alert and watchful and then you will observe how your prayers are being answered-sometimes in subtle ways and not necessarily in the ways you anticipate. Prayer keeps us divinely united with God, and many verses in the Bible tell us how to make this happen. The key to prayer is praying in the spirit and doing it God's way. Prayer is one of the open doors for the believer to meet with Jesus, communicate with Him and allow Him to work on our behalf. Every believer has the authority to go to God directly for himself or herself in prayer. The moment a person believes in God, confesses his or her sin and accepts Jesus, that person should believe what God has declared:

But ye are a chosen generation, a royal priesthood, an holy nation, a peculiar people; that ye should shew forth the praises of him who hath called you out of darkness into his marvelous light (1 Peter 2:9).

It is okay to ask people to pray with or for you, but it is of utmost importance that you pray and know that God answers your prayers directly; you do not need a mediator in a human form. You know yourself better than any person who you might ask to pray for you. You can say the best prayer for yourself. There will be certain times, however, when you will need others to intercede for you or pray with you, especially when you are overwhelmed with life's circumstances. I read in 1 Timothy 2:5: *There is one God, and one mediator between God and men, the man Christ Jesus.* Therefore you can pray directly to God in the name of His Son, Jesus.

The Bible has recorded several answered prayers. These prayers were prayed directly by the individuals needing God to act on their behalf. One that comes to mind is the prayer of Jacob in Genesis 32:9-12. Jacob, the twin brother of Esau, stole the birthright of his brother, and when he feared that his brother would come after him, he prayed to God for protection. When he delivered that prayer he was very scared, because he knew that his brother was a hunter who did not have much regard for spiritual values; this is evident in the fact that Esau sold his birthright for a meal of lentil soup and in his marrying two pagan women.

During the night, as doubt raced through Jacob's mind, he had a visitation from a man with whom he fought relentlessly. The man told Jacob that it was dawn and he should give up fighting, but Jacob was so determined, he refused to stop. Instead he offered up a short prayer. He prayed: "I will not let you go until you bless me." The person Jacob was fighting with was God. That one-line prayer removed the doubts and fear that had plagued Jacob. From that point on, he depended on, and trusted God fully.

This prayer of Jacob shows that our prayers do not have to be lengthy and drawn out for them to be answered, or for results to be achieved. Regardless of how terrible a person's character may be, God will answer that person's prayers if belief, faith and trust in Christ are exercised. I believe God hears every prayer, though He might not answer them all. Jacob had the characteristics of a person with a solid will toward the things of God and that made him a winner.

God answered the prayers of Jesus, Moses, Gideon, Elijah, Elisha, Hezekiah, Anna, Hannah, David and Jabez, among others in the Old Testament. He also answered prayers in the New Testament; of the disciples in Matthew 8:25, Luke 11:1, 17:5, and even the prayer of Jesus in Luke 23:34, as well as others. Jesus was going through the most difficult period of His life and those closest to Him were turning against Him, denying, deserting, and betraying Him. Others hated Him, mocked Him, beat Him mercilessly, put a crown of thorns upon His head, and when He was too exhausted from their atrocious treatment, gave Him a heavy cross to carry on which they eventually nailed Him. Nonetheless, before he died, he prayed a very short, powerful and effective prayer. Jesus also prayed a very long prayer in John 17 for his disciples and for all who believe in Him.

Just as Jesus told His disciples to be consistent in prayers, we are to be consistent in our prayers. Paul encourages us to pray without ceasing. In applying this principle, I have two set times when I pray: when I first wake up in the morning and before I go to sleep at night, but I also pray during the course of that day as I observe people and things around me and as the Holy Spirit leads me to pray. Prayer is powerful and we cannot overdo it. Prayer will cause things to shake up in your life as we see in Acts: *And when they had prayed, the place was shaken where they were assembled together; and they were all filled with the Holy Ghost, and they spake the word of God with boldness.* (Acts 4:31).

Did you hear that? The scripture says, they ALL were filled with the Holy Spirit after they prayed. So in order to get closer to God, receive the anointing, and get your breakthrough; you have to make prayer a priority. Believers have inherited the power of prayer, and I have often heard the saying, "prayer changes things." What an awesome gift we have as believers! Matthew 6:7-13 gives us some conditions and examples for prayer. Some people are uncomfortable with praying, but if you practice praying, like with anything else, it becomes easy to do. Once you give your life to Christ, He gives you everything you need (including the ability to pray) to become a power house and to proclaim Him at all times in every area of your life.

Consider prayer as a powerful tool and one of the greatest gifts that anyone can receive. It costs us nothing to pray- it is priceless, but when we pray we receive unlimited rewards. My prayer partner and I pray for each other and for others often and we see results. We consider ourselves intercessors, praying constantly for the salvation and healing of people globally. Sometimes it is difficult, but we always do the best we can and we always take into consideration this verse:

Confess your faults one to another, and pray one for another, that ye may be healed. The effectual fervent prayer of a righteous man availeth much (James 5:16). We look for opportunities to pray, focusing on confession, petition, supplication, intercession, thanksgiving, praise, and worship.

I received an email with suggestions for a prayer that I find helpful on those days when I struggle with finding words to pray during my prayer moments. The email stated that when you pray, you should start with your thumb, praying for your husband and children, because like your thumb, they are the closest to your heart-I add all my relatives and friends here. Next, think of your pointer or index finger, and then pray for your teachers and anyone who instructs others. I add the armed forces, lawyers, doctors, civil servants, and those who provide direct or indirect services to humanity. Next, consider your middle finger or the tallest finger and pray for our leaders, our presidents, pastors, prime ministers and so forth. Next we should pray for the sick and afflicted, this is the next finger which is the weakest. Here I pray for the homeless, poor, rejected, orphans, widows, sick, the peace of Jerusalem, and for anyone else who falls in this category and comes to mind at the time of my prayer. Lastly, pray for yourself; this is the littlest or "pinky" finger. This finger represents you, so you can now pray for yourself and know that you have already been blessed by praying for all those other people first. I think this is great advice. I hope you find it helpful, as I did.

In prayer always remember to Give God thanks, no matter what you have been through, give Him thanks, because of Romans 8:28, which declares: *And we know that all things work together for good to them that love God, to them who are the called according to his purpose.* This is hard for the human mind to comprehend, but it is true. Regardless of what we have been through, or are going true God wants good for us, while lucifer wants bad. When God said all things, He meant *all* things-even the sins we consider to be despicable, such as; addiction, fornication, adultery, stealing, murdering, hating, backbiting, backsliding and any other sins that you may name. Let us think about it for a minute. If we did not go through any of these things, what testimonies would we have? Would we be able to help others who are going through similar situations? We would be clueless, and they would be lost. We do not go through these things to keep doing them or to pretend that they never happened. Instead, they are lessons to learn from and to use in teaching and helping others.

If you have un-confessed sins, pray and confess them now, believing that God has already forgiven you. Consider those past sins as blessings in disguise; let go of their painful memories and move to the next level in your spiritual journey. This next level is where you are able to recognize sin and run in the opposite direction. The Holy Spirit within you will help you to refrain from committing sin. Do as David did. Pray as David prayed. David said: *I sought the LORD, and he heard me, and delivered me from all my fears* (Psalm 34: 4).

Our Father is aware of our weaknesses, uncertainties and doubts. He wants to deliver us from these handicaps. *Pray at all times and on every occasion in the power of the Holy Spirit. Stay alert and be persistent in your prayers for all Christians everywhere* (Ephesians 6:18). Believe in your prayer. Be consistent and persistent. Paul said that we should, *Pray first that the Lord's message will spread rapidly and be honored wherever it goes and that we should also pray that we will be saved from wicked and evil people, for not everyone believes in God* (2 Thessalonians 2:1-2). In every prayer time and at every opportunity say, "Thank you" to the Lord. He appreciates gratitude, and remembers, *prayer answers all things.*

PRINCIPLES FOR DAILY APPLICATION

(1). First of all, use the model that Jesus gave for prayer in Matthew 6:9-13. Pray often. Let prayer be the first thing you do in the mornings and last thing you do at nights before going to bed. Make confessions as you begin to pray. Confess your sins and ask God for forgiveness. Forgive others and pray sincere prayers for them. James said: *The earnest* *prayer of a righteous person has great power and wonderful results* (James 5:18) NLT.

(2) Give God thanks for supplying all your needs and exercise faith when you pray. Pray specifically for what you need and expect God to answer. Be consistent in your prayer life and never give up on God. *Pray without ceasing* (1Thessalonians 5:17). Let Jesus be the center of your life and prayer the link that divinely connects you to Him. He wants us to dominate and use the authority that He has given us. This we can do through prayer. In Mark 11: 24, Jesus said to His disciples: *What things so ever ye desire, when ye pray, believe that ye receive them, and ye shall have.* The operative word here is *believe.* Jesus' promise about receiving what we pray for *is* conditional. We must believe in order to receive.

(3) Incorporate scriptures, such as the Psalms in your prayers. I often listen to the prayer Power CD by Paul McMannus. He said if you listen to and affirm the prayers for 21 consecutive days; prayer would become a life time habit. I followed his teaching and I now pray constantly. I believe I even pray when I'm sleeping, because as I am waking up in the mornings I find myself praying while moving into my conscious state. I can attest to the effectiveness of this teaching. I highly recommend this to anyone who desires to have a closer relationship with the Lord or to become confident about praying without ceasing.

(4) Never give up. Never ever quit. Keep going to God in prayer and supplication. In Luke 18:1, Jesus told a story to His disciples about their need for constant prayer and to show them that they must never give up. If for any reason you feel like giving up, remember what Jesus also said in 2 Chronicles 7:14, that if His people who are called by His name would humble themselves, pray and seek His face and turn from their wicked ways, He will hear from heaven and will forgive their sins and heal their land. Always remember, there is nothing too hard for God to do. God told the people in Jeremiah that He is the God of all the peoples of the world and then posed this question, *is anything too hard for me* (Jeremiah 32:27)? We need to pray and intercede for the nations and peoples of the world, especially in these last days.

(5) Pray in thanksgiving and give praise to God. *Continue in **prayer**, and watch in the same with **thanksgiving*** (Colossians 4:2).

(6) Be sincere in your prayers. We are God's intercessors, just as the disciples who went before us were. The disciples specifically asked Jesus to teach them how to pray; we can do the same thing. *I exhort therefore, that, first of all, supplications, prayers, intercessions, and giving of thanks, be made for all men* (1 Timothy 2:1).

(7) Pray, Pray, Pray, Pray, Pray. There are times when we are overwhelmed or excited about certain things and anxiety sets in. When that happens, remember this principle: "Be anxious for nothing;" instead of being anxious, pray earnestly. Be like Jacob and do not give up until God blesses you.

PRAYER:

Dear heavenly Father, I come to you in the name of Jesus. I come in prayer and supplication. Lord I pray for the souls of those who are lost and for those who struggle to pray. Thank You that Your Holy Spirit teaches us how to pray and intercedes for us when we struggle to find the words to say. I know how much You love us and that You died on the cross for all of us. As You did for the disciples, please teach us how to pray. Oh Lord, I pray that You will strengthen our faith and help us to pray without ceasing. Thank You for an everlasting relationship with You through Your grace and mercy, coupled with faith. Father, I thank You for removing the darkness so that I may see Your light as I render my prayers to You in sincerity. Please help me to trust You more and more each day. Fill my cup until it overflows. Help me to accomplish Your purpose for my life, regardless of the obstacles that I might face daily. Thank You Lord for everything and praise be to Your holy name, Amen.

CHAPTER 10
WAITING IS A PART OF THE PROCESS

But they that wait upon the LORD shall renew their strength;
they shall mount up with wings as eagles; they shall run, and
not be weary; and they shall walk, and not faint
Isaiah 40:31.

Thousands upon thousands are waiting in the valley of
decision. There the day of the Lord will soon arrive
Joel 3:14 (NLT).

Rest in the LORD, and wait patiently for him: fret not thyself
because of him who prospereth in his way, because
of the man who bringeth wicked devices to pass
Psalm 37:7.

By your steadfastness and patient endurance you
shall win the true life of your souls
Luke 21:19 (AMP).

Wait for the LORD; be strong and take heart and wait for the Lord
Psalm 27:14 (NIV).

*But ye, brethren, be not **weary** in well doing*
2 Thessalonians 3:13

I have found the waiting periods to be some of the most difficult times in the process of transformation, or in life in general; yet waiting is a significant part of the process. As I look around me, I see people in action and waiting seems to be a challenge for not only me, but for others, as well. In our society waiting is not a practiced habit. I used to hear people say that patience is a virtue, but when I observe the world in motion, there are visible signs of impatience, as seen in the fast food industry and mentality, road rage and "get-rich-quick" schemes. We clamor for instant gratification, but some want to put the most important *"Thing"* on hold. The most important thing in life is to accept Jesus Christ as Lord and Savior of your life. Why wait for tomorrow when tomorrow may not come or you may not live to see it? Everything else (job, money, family or people, etc.) is secondary.

In essence, waiting means to exercise patience, faith and focus on God's plans. No matter how impatient we might be, we still have to wait on the Lord in order to allow Him to order our steps. The psalmist, David, gives us an example of what our focus should on while we wait, he said: *My soul, waits thou only upon God; for my expectation is from him. He only is my rock and my salvation: he is my defense; I shall not be moved* (Psalm 62:5-6), and again he stressed: *I wait for the LORD, my soul doth wait, and in his word do I hope. My soul waiteth for the Lord more than they that watch for the morning: I say, more than they that watch for the morning* (Psalm 130:5-6).

Although we have contrived our own plans and we want things done right now, we find that God's time frame is different from our own, and we simply have to wait on Him if we want divine order and success in our lives. Waiting on Jesus is like being in the piping hot sun in Arizona in the middle of summer, wishing for the return of autumn, or waiting for the return of spring in the bone chilling winter in Connecticut. If you live in Arizona, you wish that you could speed up the time for the monsoon rains to offer refreshing relief from the heat. Conversely, if you live in Connecticut, you cannot wait to see the sprouting daffodils offering a sign that spring is on its way. I bet if we could make time go by faster, we would; but of course we cannot. Only the creator of time possesses that capability. Waiting is no fun!

When we study the lives of the patriarchs who went before us, such as Noah, Abraham, Moses, Elijah and others, we find that they had some extremely long waiting periods through which they persevered. Even though they had questions, the expected God to answer and he did. It is upon the memories of their experiences that we can draw and find encouragement and peace as we wait in expectation.

We can rest assured that this is a time when we are in the arms of the Lord and we must trust Him completely. It is the time for us to stop doubting, so we can trust God fully and allow Him full reign over our lives. His promise to us as we wait is this: *For the vision is yet for an appointed time, but at the end it shall speak, and not lie: though it tarry, wait for it; because it will surely come, it will not tarry* (Habakkuk 2:3). Wait patiently because God promises that our dreams, breakthroughs and blessings are certain to be realized. "Delay does not mean denial; wait, I say, on the Lord." Jeremiah informs us: *The LORD is good unto them that wait for him, to the soul that seeketh him. It is good that a man should both hope and quietly wait for the salvation of the LORD* (Lamentations 3:25-26).

Gary Hawkins, Sr., author of, *Fighting for Your Destiny*, said it well when he wrote: "Rest is the assurance that God heard our prayers through our worship. Rest means we now have the authority to pursue our destiny with God." Our first example of what it means to wait is in Genesis where God waited patiently for one hundred and twenty years while he chose and instructed Noah to build an ark. Noah also waited a mighty long time for the people to whom he preached to turn to God.

Although they waited for very long periods, people still did not obey God's commands or Noah's warning. Today God is still waiting for people to repent of their sins and turn to Him. Another incredible example of waiting is seen in the way that Abraham and Sarah waited for the son God promised them when Abraham was already an old man (seventy-five years old). In their minds, too old to sire a child. They waited for twenty-five years for God's promise to be fulfilled. Abraham was one hundred years old when Sarah gave birth to their son, Isaac.

The children of Israel waited for forty years in the wilderness. Jesus was in the wilderness for forty days. Paul was in the wilderness for three years. All those waiting periods were periods of testing; yet they proved to be a necessary part of the preparation for the transformation that took place in the lives of those individuals. Today it is no different for us.

Waiting is a challenge, but if we wait courageously in faith and trust, our results will be satisfactory. Confront the challenges as the young men in Daniel 3- Shadrach, Meshach and Abednego-who gained victory because of their courage. Waiting produces growth and success when it is done purposefully, courageously and prayerfully. Just as there are different seasons in the year and we have to wait for them to come, we go through different seasons in our lives, for which we must wait. We have two choices; we can either resist these times or embrace them. In order for us to embrace them we must pray, seek God and not grow weary. If we let down our guard, we will allow roaring lion to snatch us from God's plan. Frustration will come, but do not give up. Giving up would mean that you are giving in to the serpent of old, and it could cause you to abolish your dreams or the plans that God has for you.

Stand firm, hold on to His promises and know that during those waiting times, you are simply in process and preparation of the step-by-step plan of God. When it seems as though you have lost control, ask God for wisdom, understanding, revelation, insight and clarification. Then take the attitude that there is a process for everything in life and you must surrender to it. Stay connected with your divine source so as not to prematurely abort the plan He has for you. I have learned to be persistent and stick with the plan even when I feel like giving up. The psalmist said: *Be still in the presence of the Lord and wait patiently for him to act* (Psalm 37:7) (NLT). God said: *Be **still**, and **know** that I am God* (Psalm 46:10). God's Word is final.

PRINCIPLES FOR DAILY APPLICATION

(**1**) Seek the guidance of the Holy Spirit. Do not make the final decision without first consulting with God and allowing the Holy Spirit to guide you through the process. The mistake I used to make often was to get too comfortable and independent, thinking that I could get through this life process on my own strength; but when I learned this verse and decided to apply its principle, my thought process changed: *But the Counselor, the **Holy Spirit**, whom the Father will send in my name, will teach you all things and will remind you of everything I have said to you* (John 14:26).

(**2**) Pray and trust for direction in everything: *Trust in the LORD with* *all thine heart; and lean not unto thine own understanding. In all thy ways acknowledge him, and he shall direct thy paths* (Proverbs 3:5-6). *The LORD redeemeth the soul of his servants: and none of them that trust in him shall be desolate* (Psalm 34:22). Paul assures: *Anyone who trusts in him will never be put to shame* (Romans 10:11).

(3) Know the Source. You have to constantly remember that God is your source. Colossians has made it clear in this verse: *In him lie hidden all the treasures of wisdom and knowledge* (Colossians 2:3) (NLT.). We must understand that God does things in His own time, when He chooses, when He knows it is good and ready, and when His appointed and perfect time has come. In Isaiah, we see that the Lord has set the example for waiting and having patience just as He does: *But the Lord still waits for you to come to Him, so he can show you His love and compassion. For the Lord is a faithful God. Blessed are those who wait for Him to help them* (Isaiah 30:18).

(4) Do not give up hope. In Isaiah 49:23, the Lord said: *those who hope in me will not be disappointed* and David said: *Wait on the LORD: be of good courage, and he shall strengthen thine heart: wait, I say, on the Lord* (Psalm 27:14). *I wait for the Lord, my soul waits and in His word I put my hope* (Psalm 130:5). The Lord is ready to show His compassion. He is a just God and He blesses all who wait for Him. Wait on God for direction, wisdom, knowledge and understanding.

(5) Be patient and have confidence in the process knowing that there are benefits to waiting on the Lord. Abraham and Sarah waited patiently on God and God called Abraham righteous. Ask the Lord to help you to wait with watchful eyes, listening ears and a ready heart. Micah 7:7 states: *As for me, I look to the Lord for His help. I wait confidently for God to save me, and my God will certainly hear me.* David's patience exemplifies how patience is a virtue. I like David's attitude toward waiting; he said, *I waited patiently for the LORD; and he inclined unto me, and heard my cry. He brought me up also out of an horrible pit, out of the miry clay, and set my feet upon a rock, and established my goings* (Psalm 40:1). James advised us to be patient as we wait for the Lord's return (James 5:7-11). He gave an analogy of the farmers who eagerly looked for the rains in the fall and in the spring and how they patiently waited for the precious harvest to ripen. James further stated: *Job is an example* *of a man who endured patiently. Like Job, You will succeed in whatever you choose to do, and light will shine on the road ahead of you* (Job 22:28).

From Job's experience we see how the Lord's plan finally ended in all good. He is full of tenderness and mercy. James 5:11 also sheds more light on the purpose of waiting. It says that God will reward us for waiting on Him. Then Peter puts the icing on the cake, when He gives the ultimate purpose for waiting on the Lord. Peter announced: *And when the head shepherd comes, your reward will be a never-ending share in His glory and honor* (1 Peter: 4). What a wonderful end for those who use their faith, wait patiently, trust and obey the Lord!

(6) Wait in faith, be content and remain focus. The Lord wants us to have faith and be content, no matter what our circumstances may be. Paul exemplifies this when he declares: *Not that I speak in respect of want: for I have learned, in whatsoever state I am, therewith to be content* (Philippians 4:11).

(7) Pray, pray, pray, worship, and praise while you wait. Worship and praise God, through every trial. Have gratitude in every moment. Never lose sight of the fact that Jesus is always working on your behalf, will never leave you nor forsake you, and that He waits for you to be gracious even through the tough times. In the end you will get your breakthrough. David did it and so can we. As I mentioned before, Habakkuk gives us a thrilling reminder when he wrote: *For the vision is yet for an appointed time, but at the end it shall speak, and not lie: though it tarry, wait for it; because it will surely come, it will not tarry* (Habakkuk 2:3).

PRAYER:

Dear heavenly Father, I thank You that the greatest and best lesson that I have learned about waiting is that in all our waiting, our ultimate waiting is on the promises of Your return. As it is written in 1 Corinthians 1:7, we now know that we have every spiritual gift that we need as we eagerly wait for the return of our Lord Jesus Christ. Holy Spirit, please help us to have patience and endurance as we wait each day for Your loving directions. Help us not to grow weary in waiting as Your Word says in Galatians 6:9: *And let us not be **weary** in well doing: for in due season we shall reap, if we faint not.* We realize that during these times of waiting we will experience trials and tribulations, but we should remain strong, courageous and focused on the prize. We believe that waiting is an essential part of Your divine process and we count it all joy. Thank You for Romans 8:28 that let us know that all things work together for good, so that we know that even the trials and hardships we face have a purpose. Thank You that we will learn from them and be anointed with fresh oil to see new mercies each day as we wait in hope and confident assurance. I give You gratitude and honor in Jesus' name, Amen.

CHAPTER 11
WORSHIP IN HIS PRESENCE

*O **worship** the **LORD** in the **beauty** of **holiness**: fear before him, all the earth*
Psalm 96:9.

God is a Spirit: and they that worship him must
worship him in spirit and in truth
John 4:24.

And when he had consulted with the people, he appointed singers unto the
LORD, and that should praise the beauty of holiness, as they went out before
the army, and to say, Praise the LORD; for his mercy endureth for ever
2 Chronicles 20:21.

Giving thanks always for all things unto God and the
Father in the name of our Lord Jesus Christ
Ephesians 5:20.

We were created for God's purpose, and He desires our praise and our worship. The deceiver is vying for our worship and we must be aware of this. Our purpose is to please God, always and never give in to the deceiver. People worship in different ways, and we can worship God in everything that we do. As a matter of fact, many scriptures command us to worship God. Some popular ways of worshipping God are by praying, singing, dancing, praise and thanksgiving, giving cheerfully, partaking in the Lord's Supper and giving of our bodies as a "living sacrifice" in all things, such as in our daily activities.

When we worship God in prayer, we are praising and giving him thanks. Hebrews 13:15 states: *Therefore by Him let us continually offer the sacrifice of praise to God, that is, the fruit of our lips, giving thanks to His name* (NKJV). Likewise, when we sing, we worship God. As David proclaimed in Psalm 100:1-2: *Make a joyful noise unto the LORD, all ye lands. Serve the LORD with gladness: come before his presence with singing.* I recommend that you read this entire chapter of Psalm 100.

Dancing before the Lord is one of my favorite forms of worship. I love praying and all the other forms of worship, but when I dance with the Lord there is something special about it. It adds more intimacy to my relationship with Him. I feel a special spiritual closeness, which I believe has to do with faith and imagination. Think about it: Have you ever slow danced with your husband or significant other? How did it feel?

I always think about how David danced with the Lord. Listen to Samuel's report of this spectacular moment said: *And David danced before the LORD with all his might; and David was girded with a linen ephod .So David and all the house of Israel brought up the ark of the LORD with shouting, and with the sound of the trumpet. And as the ark of the LORD came into the city of David, Michal, Saul's daughter, looked through a window, and saw King David leaping and dancing before the LORD; and she despised him in her heart* (2 Samuel 6:14-16). People may despise you, think or say you are crazy when you worship God, but do not let that intimidate you; worship Him anyway, just as David did when he put the cares of life aside and whole-heartedly worshipped God.

David was amazing. It is no wonder that he won a place in the heart of God. David gave thanks, danced, praised and worshipped the Lord with all his heart. We should be doing the same thing. David said: *I give you thanks, O Lord, with all my heart* (Psalm 138:1). *Give thanks to the Lord for He is good* (Psalm136:1). *I will praise the* Lord *as long as I live. I will sing praises to my God with my dying breath* (Psalm146:2). David's passion for Christ is quite evident in the ways in which he worshipped Him. He expressed to God how, why and when he would praise and worship Him. David did not say I will Praise the Lord when I am happy, when my circumstances have disappeared, when my situation changes, when my fears disappear or when my finances are in order. David praised God regardless of his circumstances, because he knew this one thing: *Blessed is the man that endureth temptation: for when he is tried, he shall receive the crown of life, which the Lord hath promised to them that love him* (James 1:12).

Worshipping with our bodies shows the Lord that we understand that the body is His temple. Paul asked this question of the people in Corinth: *Do you not know that your body is the temple (the very sanctuary) of the Holy Spirit Who lives within you, Whom you have received [as a Gift] from God? You are not your own* (1 Corinthians 6:19) (AMP), and then He pleaded: *I beseech you therefore, brethren, by the mercies of God, that ye present your bodies a living sacrifice, holy, acceptable unto God, which is your reasonable service. And be not conformed to this world: but be ye transformed by the renewing of your mind, that ye may prove what is that good, and acceptable, and perfect, will of God* (Romans 12:1-2).

Observing the Last Supper is another way of worshipping. There is a message from Paul that declares: *For as often as ye eat this bread, and drink this cup, ye do shew the Lord's death till he comes* (1 Corinthians 11:26). My family and I have taken communion as the Holy Spirit led us. It brings to memory the death of Christ on the cross. Sometimes we get so busy in our everyday life that we forget to stop and think about what Christ did and what he says we should do. When we to do take the communion we examined ourselves, we believe we are worthy (1 Corinthians 11:28-29), and that God has removed our transgressions as far as the east is from the west (Psalm 103:12). In many churches Communion is given once per month, every quarter or once per year. The Bible says, *For as often as ye eat this bread, and drink this cup, ye do shew the Lord's death till he comes.* We need to show the Lord's death every day, but if we take communion every day, that would be considered ritualistic in our society. How often communion is taken/given could be up for debate, but whenever we take it, we are to make sure that we first examine ourselves, believe we are worthy and know that we are doing it to *shew the Lord's death till he comes.*

Praising God is a key factor of our worship. We should always give the highest response to God. Thessalonians 5: 16-18 reads: *Always be joyful, keep on praying. No matter what happens, always be thankful, for this is God's will for you who belong to Christ Jesus.* When we praise God He showers us with His blessings. Sometimes we might face discouraging situations and do not feel like praising God, but those are the times when we should praise Him with all we have. Remember, always praise God no matter what you are going through. Whatever you (the believer) are going through at this moment or at any moment, just trust in the Lord and know that He is going to carry you through it. As the popular saying goes, "This too shall pass." He has promised not to give us any more than we can bear and to take our burdens. Do not be afraid to open your mouth and praise Him and open your heart to let Him in.

When we praise God with all our might, the father of lies has no choice but to step back, and tremble as he did when Joseph praised God. The more we praise Him, the more the ruler of the world will try to attack us, but the less effect the adversary's can have on us. God has promised to deliver us from our enemies when we are believers in Jesus. Jesus loves us so much that He waits patiently for us to worship Him in spirit and in truth. David has written numerous inspiring Psalms that give us examples of how we too can praise God. His last chapter truly sums it up:

Praise ye the LORD. Praise God in his sanctuary:
praise him in the firmament of his power.
Praise him for his mighty acts: praise him
according to his excellent greatness.
Praise him with the sound of the trumpet: praise
him with the psaltery and harp.
Praise him with the timbrel and dance: praise him
with stringed instruments and organs.
Praise him upon the loud cymbals: praise him
upon the high sounding cymbals.
Let everything that hath breath praise the LORD. Praise ye the LORD
(Psalm 150).

When we praise and worship God, we are giving Him thanks, and this is when miracles happen. During our times of praise and worship, miracles and supernatural things take place because God hears us. I often hear this phrase used: "When the praises go up, the blessings will come down." Praise Him in the morning, at noon and in the evening when the sun goes down. In other words, do not stop praising God. Imagine this: When Paul and Silas were put in prison, incredible salvation and transformation happened. They were beaten, thrown into captivity, humiliated and stripped of their dignity. This is what happened next: *And at midnight Paul and Silas prayed, and sang praises unto God: and the prisoners heard them. And suddenly there was a great earthquake, so that the foundations of the prison were shaken: and immediately all the doors were opened, and everyone's bands were loosed* (Acts 16:25-26). This is an amazing report; read the continuation of it in Acts 16. One song writer says; "Praise is what I do." According to Psalm 50:23, whoever offers praise, glorifies God, and those who keep His path to them will He reveal His salvation.

Psalm 50:23 in the New Living Translation, reads: *But giving thanks is a sacrifice that truly honors me.* We have heard the story of the one Samaritan woman many times, but hardly of the Samaritan man. Here is a man who knew what it meant to be thankful. As the narrative expresses, Jesus healed ten lepers who asked Him to have mercy upon them. Sadly, of the ten men whose requests were granted, only one man returned to give thanks. The report says in Luke 17:16: And he fell on his face at Jesus' feet, and thanked Him (emphasized). Jesus told him to get up and go, because his faith had made him whole. Our healing could depend on our praise and worship to God. We do not have to wait for the healing to occur before we give God praise. By faith, we must believe that God has already done what we ask according to His promises. Basically, he promised us everything we need, including healing. We just need to praise and give Him thanks, for He has already done His part.

Thanksgiving is another way in which we can worship. Sometimes when we go to pray, we have so much to request that we forget to give thanks. Before you pray for anything you should give God thanks for the blessings that you have already received and for the ones you will receive. There was a time in my life when I did not recognize all my blessings. Then I realized that I am alive, and that is my number one blessing. I have clothes to wear, and I considered that blessing number two, I have food to eat; blessing number three, and I really did not have to look too far to see number four and all my subsequent blessings. Look around, reminisce/recall and you will recognize your blessings as well.

Now that you have seen them, start praising the Lord for every blessing, great and small, and more blessings will be realized. I recall one songwriter, writing: "Count your blessings; name them one by one, and it will surprise you what the Lord has done." He has done so much for us and we fail to do the one thing that He desires of us, which is to commit our ways to Him. Commit to Him, and you will never let his blessings go unnoticed. Jesus said in Luke 14:33, that no one can become His disciple without giving up everything for Him. As I bring this chapter to a close, I am reminded of an article that Dave Faagau, a fitness specialist wrote about gratitude one Thanksgiving. It made me take a second look at how I express gratitude. Taking into consideration that gratitude is also a form of worship. Quoting with permission, here is what he had to say:

"Most people do not realize the many health benefits of gratitude. Studies indicate that thankfulness is directly linked to physical, mental, emotional, and spiritual well-being. Compared to people who do not live a lifestyle of thankfulness, research shows that grateful people:

1. Experience higher levels of alertness, enthusiasm, determination optimism and energy
2. Experience less depression
3. Better manage stress
4. Are more likely to help others
5. Exercise more regularly
6. Make more progress towards their personal goals
7. Have stronger immune systems
8. Have fewer symptoms of physical illness

Those are some impressive benefits that can be yours without even increasing your physical activity or changing your nutrition plan. All that is required is a grateful heart. Are you a thankful person? If you are unsure, it may be in your best interest to consider the following questions:

Are you the type of person who dwells on the good or on the bad things that happen to you?

Do you tell others about the blessings in your life as much as you tell them when things go wrong?

Are you considerate of the people closest to you, or do you often take them for granted?

Are you thankful only when things are going well, or do you look for blessings even when bad things happen?

Is there someone you admire who is a thankful person? What other attributes do you admire about them?

Are you leaving a legacy of thankfulness by which others will remember you?

There is nothing complicated about showing gratitude. Being thankful is simply a choice. To say we feel grateful is not to say that everything in our lives is great. It just means that in spite of all we see that is worthy of complaint, there is far more we can choose to focus on that is worthy of thankfulness. Why not choose to extend the tradition of giving thanks through the entire year, instead of limiting it to the Holiday Season? Your physical, emotional, and spiritual health will all reap the benefits of a thankful heart. The choice is yours." Dave Faagau, Fitness Specialist and owner of Total Body Training.

PRINCIPLES FOR DAILY APPLICATION

(1) Sing and read the Psalms when you are up on the mountain top and when you are down in the valley. Incorporate them and other scriptures into your daily prayers. Consider this verse: *Is any among you afflicted? Let him pray. Is any merry? Let him sing Psalms* (James 5:13). Read Psalm 2:11.

(2) Worship always. Whatever you do, do it as unto the Lord. He deserves your best: *But the LORD, who brought you up out of the land of Egypt with great power and a stretched out arm, him shall ye fear, and him shall ye worship* (2 Kings 17:36). Read Psalm 29:2; 66:4, 1 Chronicles 16:29 and 2 Chronicles 7:3; 20:18-19; 29:28-30.

(3) Do not quench the Spirit. Express yourself in worship, whatever brings God glory. If He tells you clap, run, walk, shout, cry or be quiet, do it without worrying about what the person sitting beside, behind or in front of you has to say. The scripture warns: *Do not quench (suppress or subdue) the [Holy] Spirit* (1 Thessalonians 5:19) (AMP).

(4) Know that your style of worship may be different from others. For example, while you may lift up holy hands in worship, someone else may clap their hands; still others may dance or kneel. Do whatever works for you as long as it is biblical. Read, Exodus 15:20, Psalm 149:3; 150:4, 2 Samuel 16:14, Matthew 11:17, Luke 15:25 and 1 Timothy 2:8.

(5) Praise God in all situations, even when it means that you or a loved one has to suffer. It is difficult to give praise while suffering, but it is better to praise Him than to curse or get mad with Him, as some people do. *Praise him for his mighty acts: praise him according to his excellent greatness* (Psalm 150:2). Read Hebrews 13:15.

(6) Give thanks and show gratitude to God and to others, not only for the big things but for the small ones as well. *O give thanks unto the LORD, for he is good: for his mercy endureth for ever* (Psalm 107:1). Read Psalm 79:13 and 100:4.

(7) Pray, pray, pray. *Be cheerful no matter what; pray all the time; thank God no matter what happens. This is the way God wants you who belong to Christ Jesus to live* (1 Thessalonians 5:16-18) (MSG).

PRAYER:

Dear heavenly Father, I bow before You in the name of Jesus and I ask You please, to forgive me of my sins, whether by thought, word or deed. As it is written in Psalm 35:2, and 102:2, hide not Your face from me and stand up for my help. Thank You that I have learned to be grateful. I give You glory, I praise You, I love You, I honor You, I magnify Your name, and I worship and adore You. Father, I give You thanks for Your faithful love that endures forever. Thank You that through Your grace I can find peace in all the circumstances of my life. Thank You for the confidence in You to control those things that I do not have control over. Thank You for helping me to understand when to take action and when to rest. Father God, I thank You for taking my burdens when I face difficult situations as I travel through this world, where sin is compromised and You are often ignored by many. Please forgive those who ignore and do not believe in You, Lord. Open their eyes that they may see You. I thank You for giving me all that I need to overcome the challenges that I face. Thank You that I know how to take life one day at a time. Lord I fully surrender to Your will. I am Your instrument; mold me and use me for Your glory now and forever, Amen.

CHAPTER 12
FAITH IS THE SUBSTANCE

*While we look not at the things which are seen, but at the
things which are not seen: for the things which are seen are
temporal; but the things which are not seen are eternal*
2 Corinthians 4:18.

Now faith is the substance of things hoped for, the evidence of things not seen
Hebrews 11:1.

*For therein is the righteousness of God revealed from faith
to faith: as it is written, The just shall live by faith*
Romans 1:17.

*And Jesus answering saith unto them, Have faith in God. For verily
I say unto you, That whosoever shall say unto this mountain,
Be thou removed, and be thou cast into the sea; and shall not
doubt in his heart, but shall believe that those things which he
saith shall come to pass; he shall have whatsoever he saith*
Mark 11:22-23.

*For in Jesus Christ neither circumcision availeth any thing,
nor uncircumcision; but faith which worketh by love*
Galatians 5:6.

*For by grace are ye saved through faith; and that
not of yourselves: it is the gift of God*
Ephesians 2:8.

*Abraham never wavered in believing God's promise. In fact, his
faith grew stronger, and in this he brought glory to God*
Romans 4:19-20.

*Now **faith is** the **substance** of things hoped for, the evidence of things not seen* (Hebrews 11:1) This is the Hebrews writer's definition of faith, and it is the first thing that comes to my mind when I hear or think of faith. Secondly, I think that faith means, believing in God, in His Son Jesus and in the Holy Spirit. Then I think about my faith and wonder to what extent I truly use it. Faith is the criteria by which God works through us. It is easier to talk about faith than to actually live by it. Faith is the substance of everything. It is the main thing that keeps us divinely connected to Jesus Christ, yet it is one of the most difficult principles for us to exercise, because we like to be independent. Faith requires dependence on God. Faith is what makes God move mountains out of our way. Faith is indescribable.

When God revealed to me that faith was another area of my life that needed to be transformed, I literally cried out to the Lord for help in this area, because I was truly struggling with it (and I am still working on it day by day). He began to show me numerous scriptures regarding faith. I have grown a great deal since the day I discovered the need to deepen my faith. I still have a long way to go, but because I know how important faith is for those who walk with God, I am determined to get my faith to a level where doubt is only a shadow in my past. I heard Joyce Myers once said: "Faith is what cranks God's tractor." Since our faith is what makes God moves to action on our behalf, we definitely need to maximize it.

I have looked at the closeness of Jesus and His disciples and the fact that, although they were right there with Jesus, where they could physically touch, see and hear Him, they had challenges in the area of their faith. They had to ask God to increase their faith, so that they could perform the daily tasks that He assigned to them. Likewise, we cannot physically see or touch Jesus, but we are expected to exercise our faith to the fullest extent.

The good thing is, we can touch Him with our faith, as did the woman with the issue of blood, blind Bartemaeus, Jairus, or any of the characters we read about in the Bible who had personal contact with Jesus Christ as a result of their faith. We do not have to be discouraged by the fact that we cannot physically see or touch Him, because we have the advantage of the Word of God. We can take the Bible in our hands, open it, read it daily, and have great experiences, as we hear from God.

God's Word teaches us how to use faith and allows Him to move on our behalf in all our circumstances. The definition of faith in Hebrews 11 has helped me to understand that, although I cannot touch or see God physically, if I believe and act upon my belief through such things as prayer, service to others, gratitude and spreading His Word, I am exercising faith.

According to the *Strong's Exhaustive Concordance*, the Hebrew word for faith is *pistis,* which means *belief, trust, and assurance* and often refers to the Christian system of belief and lifestyles. The Webster's Online Dictionary gives the following meanings for faith: "A strong belief in a supernatural power or powers that control human destiny; complete confidence in a person or plan; institution to express belief in a divine power and loyalty or allegiance to a cause or a person." Without faith we cannot have a relationship with God. Therefore, we need to ask God to develop and deepen our faith. With faith we can see manifestations and receive the promises of God.

Remain in an attitude of faith daily. Even though it is not always easy to exercise faith, we are required walk by faith, and it is possible. When we do we can overcome the world. *Who is he that overcometh the world, but he that believeth that Jesus is the son of God?* (1 John 5:5). Many of us believe that Jesus is the son of God, but we are not taking the authority that comes with being a son or daughter of the King of kings and Lord of lords. Nor are we using the power that we have been given to remove limitations and to manifest the promised greatness for our lives. We must release faith in all areas of our lives and believe without a shadow of doubt that the Lord is working on our behalf. We cannot accomplish the things that Jesus left for us to do if we do not stretch our faith, put it to action and trust in Jesus.

Often when my faith is challenged I think of the faith of Abraham, Sarah, Noah and Moses' parents; there is no doubt in my mind that faith is the most important ingredient in the recipe of life. Faith is strengthened by reading the Word and meditating on it every day. *So then faith cometh by hearing, and hearing by the word of God* (Romans 10:17). Faith is magnificently magnetic. It draws us closer to God and allows us to have a deeper relationship with Him.

We can have an abundant life by erasing fear and releasing faith. We often doubt the voice of God. We are afraid to do what God tells us to do. We need to take a page out of the books of those people of faith of whom the Bible speaks. Those great men and women heard God's voice, lived by faith and laid the foundation for us. In Genesis, we read of Abel's sacrificial offering to God because of his faith. Also in Genesis is the remarkable story of Sarah, Abraham's wife; she is the epitome of a woman of faith. Then we hear of how much God desired Enoch because of his faith, that He took him up to heaven while he was still alive. I encourage you to read Hebrews, Chapter 11 for greater insight into this very important topic of faith and in the lives of people who demonstrated faith. This chapter is remarkable and informative.

The story of Noah is an incredible faith story. As the story goes, Noah built an ark under unusual circumstances because God told Him to build it. I believe he must have encountered a great deal of negative comments, but he built the ark regardless. He lived a life of faith for one hundred and twenty years and his faith allowed him to build the ark on dry land. Because of his faith, he believed in the vision that God had revealed to him and he completed the task by putting action to faith. Noah was also a grateful man. To show God his gratitude for saving him and his family from the destruction of the flood, he built an altar of sacrifice to God. His life exemplifies the life of a true believer today. A true believer will not give up, even when going through tough times with many trials and tribulations. No matter what situation we may be facing, we need to have faith while carrying out an assignment from God.

Next we read of Abraham, the believers' spiritual forefather. Abraham had steadfast faith to which he held tightly, with determination, even through heaps of trials, tribulations, questions, and relentless waiting. Through it all, he never quit. He believed in God. He had a mission to please God; he endured to the end. Abraham held his vision in the forefront of his mind and kept his and faith based on the promises of God. Though at times he wavered, he kept believing.

Abraham pressed toward the mark and had coveted results: *And he received the sign of circumcision, a seal of the righteousness of the faith which he had yet being uncircumcised: that he might be the father of all them that believe, though they be not circumcised; that righteousness might be imputed unto them also* (Romans 4:11). God will declare us righteous also if we believe in Him, because we are beneficiaries of that same promise that God gave to Abraham.

Sometimes when I feel as though my faith is being challenged, I reflect on the scripture about the mustard seed faith. The Holy Spirit helped me to get a better understanding of the mustard seed faith. As I was praying with the intercessors in church one day, I visualized a tree with roots in the ground stretching deep and spreading endlessly. I asked, "What is that Lord?" and the Holy Spirit said: "This is how a mustard seed can grow and deepen." That experience boosted my faith, and that picture remains in my head to remind me that faith is the substance and always a priority. I must act upon my faith, nurture it and allow it to deepen and strengthen. As I take mustard seed steps, I expect my faith to mature to the point where I am confident enough to take giant steps. I had that vision at a time in my life when I was seeking God and praying for deeper faith. Since then, the Holy Spirit has been taking me through a process where my faith is being strengthened and developed daily.

The apostle Paul explains in Romans 3, that our acquittal from sin is not based on our good deeds, but it is rather based on our faith. *God makes people right only through faith* (Romans 3:30). He further goes on to say: *Only when we have faith we truly fulfill the law* (Romans 3:30). Why do we need to fulfill the law? Because these are the Words of Almighty God and His Words remain forever. He said, *Heaven and earth shall pass away, but my words shall not pass away* (Matthew 24:35).

Whatever God does for one true believer, He will do for another. God has been doing a new thing in me, because I have asked Him to help me with this very important piece of spiritual matter called faith, and He is helping me in this area every day. This gradual process has been taking me to a deeper place in Him. I now realize that faith is the key as Paul puts it in Romans 4:16. *Therefore it is of faith, that it might be by grace; to the end the promise might be sure to all the seed; not to that only which is of the law, but to that also which is of the faith of Abraham; who is the father of us all.* In Ephesians 6:16, Paul wrote: *In every battle you will need faith as your shield to stop the fiery arrows aimed at you.* The shield of faith will defeat the tempter's tactics. It will protect you from everything that people say about or do to you. As I conclude this chapter, I would like to encourage you to utilize your shield of faith in every situation; for example, when you learn that your employer has planned layoffs or to close the business, trust that God will move you to a better job or opportunity. Draw on your shield of faith when your coworkers conspire and plot against you and God will show you a more excellent way. What God has done for others, He will do for you.

Apply your shield of faith when your children are rebelling against the principles you have taught them, when your husband or wife is acting insane, when your family members put unnecessary pressures on you, and when it seems like the world has turned against you. In other words, keep your shield of faith up at all times and remember to keep working with the measure of faith you have been given. The more you use it, the more it matures, deepens and serves its purpose. As believers lives are being transformed, they need their faith to accomplish their destinies as they need air to remain alive.

PRINCIPLES FOR DAILY APPLICATION

(1) When things and time get tough and you feel as though all hope is gone, have faith, do not doubt, believe that God will provide whatever you need. Develop and deepen the measure of faith that He has given you, because without faith, it is impossible to please God. The Word says: *God hath dealt to every man the measure of faith* (Romans 12:3). Believe and see possibilities: *all things are possible to him that believeth* (Mark 9:23) Depend on God. Self-reliance suggests inability or refusal to exercise faith: *And Jesus answering saith unto them, Have faith in God* (Mark 11:22).

(2) Demonstrate faith in all aspects of your life. Believe in the promises of God without doubting; you will see His manifestations in your life. Acknowledge that faith is essential and you will not be afraid to take action. *Because of faith also Sarah herself received physical power to conceive a child, even when she was long past the age for it, because she considered God Who had given her the promise to be reliable and trustworthy and true to His word* (Hebrews 11:11) (AMP). Sarah and many others in the Bible applied their faith based on the promises of God, and those are the same promises we have today.

(3) Allow faith to make you appreciate, and have gratitude for your life just the way it is today. Exercise faith when you are going through your wilderness or valley experiences. Your wilderness and valley experiences are those times when you are at your lowest and everything seems to be going wrong in your life. It is when you feel as though you cannot get a grip on things, and you feel it is taking too long to get your breakthrough and to see manifestations. When you get those feelings that Jehovah Nissi has distanced Himself from you, replace those feelings with faith. Do not get discouraged when you are not seeing God at work, because He is our banner and is always present with us. The Word says: *For we walk by faith, not by sight* (2 Corinthians 5:7).

(4) When going through trials and tribulations apply faith. During times when everything seems to be going wrong-your finances are in bad shape, your health is failing and you have spent all you have to pay for healthcare, your family does not understand, and you are at your lowest point-the son of perdition will use those opportunities to confuse and distract you, but God in His infinite power will use the ploys of the wicked one to strengthen you-what the enemy means for bad, God means for good. He will eventually destroy every trick the ruler of this world uses against you. Faith will help to break barriers down and makes you: *mount up with wings as eagles* (Isaiah 40:31). So, *Fear none of those things which thou shalt suffer: behold, the devil shall cast some of you into prison, that ye may be tried; and ye shall have tribulation ten days: be thou faithful unto death, and I will give thee a crown of life* (Revelation 2:10).

(5) Be consistent in your faith. Sometimes we want to deviate, because we cannot see the full picture. Keep your eyes on Jesus. Peter began to sink when he took His eyes off Jesus. Have you been where Peter has been? I have. You must be grounded in your faith, so that you can resist the devil: *Submit yourselves therefore to God. Resist the devil, and he will flee from you* (James 4:7).

(6) Apply faith and give out of your need. Give of your service, using faith to take your focus off yourself and become a blessing to those around you. Apply faith when you are quiet and listening to hear from God about what service you should be rendering and to whom. When you give, you may not receive from the people to whom you give, but know that if you remain faithful, your heavenly Father will reward you at the right time. Never lose faith in God or in your giving: *Give, and* *it shall be given unto you; **good measure, pressed down**, and shaken together, and running over, shall men give into your bosom. For with the same **measure** that ye mete withal it shall be **measured** to you again* (Luke 6:38).

(7) Pray, pray, pray and remain in an attitude of faith at all costs. Pray for your faith to be developed, deepened, strengthened and cemented. Have faith in the promises of God. He will fulfill them, because He cannot lie. Hebrew 6:18 says: *So God has given both his promise and his oath. These two things are unchangeable because it is impossible for God to lie. Therefore, we who have fled to him for refuge can have great confidence as we hold to the hope that lies before us.*

PRAYER:

Dear heavenly Father, You have promised to give us a crown of life if we remain faithful to You, and for this, I thank You. Please help me to be like father Abraham, whom the scripture says never wavered in His faith and was declared righteous. Father, help me to realize that the same promises that You made to Abraham belong to me and the same miracles you worked for the woman with the issue of blood, the blind man, Peter and many others, you will work for me. Forgive me of my doubtfulness and independence. Help me to make a significant turn from doubt, fear, sin, unbelief and disobedience to trust, belief and obedience to You. Help me as I make this vow to live a new life in You and through Your grace and mercy. Please help me to strive to be in Your perfect will. Thank You for the measure of faith that You gave me. I am determined to make it stronger and stronger every day, so that like father Abraham, I too will bring glory to You through my faith, and You will declare me righteous. In Jesus' name, Amen!

CHAPTER 13
HEALINGS, MIRACLES AND PROPHECIES

Dear friend, I hope all is well with you and that you are
*as **healthy** in body as you are strong in spirit.*
3 John 2 (NLT).

He sent out his word and healed them, snatching them from the door of death.
Psalms 107:20.

Lord replied, "Listen, I am making a covenant with you in the presence of
*all your people. I will perform **miracle**s that have never been performed*
anywhere in all the earth or in any nation. And all the people around you
will see the power of the Lord—the awesome power I will display for you."
Exodus 34:10.

A person who speaks in tongues is strengthened personally, but one
*who speaks a word of **prophecy** strengthens the entire church*
1 Corinthians 14:4.

Do not neglect your gift, which was given you through a prophetic
message when the body of elders laid their hands on you
1 Timothy 4:14 (NIV).

And he said, Unto you it is given to know the mysteries of the
kingdom of God: but to others in parables; that seeing they
might not see, and hearing they might not understand
Luke 8:10.

In my years of attending different churches, I have not seen enough emphasis placed on the topics of healing, miracles and prophecies; yet these things were the very essence of Jesus' ministry when He was on earth. I have not had the privilege to be a part of any church that offers a comprehensive teaching and application of the Word. Emphasis is usually placed on selective areas of the Bible and other areas get brushed over or ignored. Before Jesus left to be with the Father, He said, we shall do the things He did and even greater things shall we do. Are the sick getting healed in the churches? Are the people being prophesied to? Too few churches are actually doing this. Who are working miracles? Since many churches are not doing these things, does that mean that the members have to go to different churches to get the basic necessity they need to live life fully? I believe the reasons why so many people in the church suffer from all kinds of sicknesses and diseases, are unsure of their purposes and unable to recognize their miracles, are due, in part, to the inability of church leaders to perform the requirements of their jobs as pastors, and in assisting the church members in activating and administering their gifts.

There are many people who have not realized or recognized their gifts and are therefore missing out on working in the areas of their calling. I believe the leaders in the church are responsible for assisting their members to discover, acknowledge and execute their spiritual gifts. Often, this is not the case, because the pastors are too self-absorbed, caring too much about the tithes and offerings, or are too far from the reality and truths of the scriptures. They have immature, mediocre relationships with God, and as a result they minimize their God-given potential and responsibilities. Jesus said in John 14:12: *Verily, verily, I say unto you, He that believeth on me, the works that I do shall he do also; and greater works than these shall he do; because I go unto my Father.*

I congratulate the pastors who have incorporated a comprehensive teaching and application model in their church program and are manifesting Kingdom principles. In speaking of healing miracles and prophecies, I am certain that I have experienced them all and believe most people have, even though they may not notice or acknowledge them.

Healing:

Healing was one of the cornerstones of Jesus' ministry-hence the reason it should be embraced and practiced by the church today. It is written in James 5:14-15: *Is any sick among you? let him call for the elders of the church; and let them pray over him, anointing him with oil in the name of the Lord: And the prayer of faith shall save the sick, and the Lord shall raise him up; and if he have committed sins, they shall be forgiven him.* Matthew tells us:

And Jesus went about all Galilee, teaching in their synagogues, and preaching the gospel of the kingdom, and healing all manner of sickness and all manner of disease among the people (Matthew 4:23).

Jesus healed all kinds of sicknesses, physical, mental/emotional and spiritual. In the previous chapters, I wrote about a number of things that I have incorporated in my daily life to help improve the quality of my life; however, ultimately; true and permanent healing comes from God. Everything else offers temporary relief. It is only God who has promised and has delivered divine healing. Regardless of how many times we visit our doctors or how many things we use to enhance our health and well being, we must rely on God for divine healing.

In my book, *Living in Clarity,* co-authored with many other authors in the best-selling series: *Wake Up, Live the Life You Love,* I wrote about my physical healing. I discussed my physical and emotional healing as well as my spiritual growth. I received physical healing from Fibromyalgia and emotional healing after many years of trying to "fix" my husband, myself and other people, without having the common sense to know that by myself, I was fighting a losing battle. For example, I was always worrying about my husband not communicating with me as often as I thought he should. I wasted a lot of time trying to get him to communicate better, so to speak. Then one night I had an awakening. The Holy Spirit asked me; "Why are you worrying about those things? Don't you know who is in control? Change your tune; you can't change your husband. You need to change the way you think and do things." I trembled when I heard this voice.

That night I surrendered in obedience to the Holy Spirit, by making a decision that I would no longer do things on my own, but instead, I would seek God's guidance and allow Him to handle the things I am not able to. Based on this decision, my life has never been the same. Prior to that experience, I used to do things that made me feel good, such as, "regurgitating" all over my husband and spilling my guts about what I did not like about his actions. I was often whining about things that were not going my way. I used to think everything was about Royston and me, but suddenly, I realized it was never about us. It was always about God and what He wanted to accomplish in our lives. Emotionally I felt better.

Unfortunately, I was ignorant of that very important fact for too long. I wished I had that awakening earlier in our marriage. I simply changed my approach. I decided I was not going to talk to my husband about what I considered to be issues anymore, so I stopped. Surprisingly, this new approach did not work for very long either! I discovered that not voicing my opinions became a problem for me. It was killing me slowly as everything was boiling up inside; I had no outlet and that was affecting my health. That was when the Holy Spirit came to my rescue again and showed me exactly what I needed to do. He said that this is not how I should do it; as it is senseless to stop communicating with my husband-lack of communication between the two of us would be an even worse disaster. I asked Him: "What do I do then?" The Holy Spirit said that I had not fully surrendered and was still trying to do things my way; so I should let it all go-change the way I view things and leave the rest up to the Lord.

I confessed and told God that I was sorry for carrying unnecessary burdens-which I could not do this anymore by myself and was ready to give it all to Him. At that moment, peace overcame me. It was a feeling I will never, ever forget. This was the absolute best approach I had tried in our then seventeen years of marriage. God acted on our behalf. He did not only heal me physically and emotionally; he also healed our marriage. God has a pathway to your healing, and He will help you find your way. With all the things I use on a daily basis to optimize my health, I know without a doubt that my ultimate healing comes from God. That is why we must seek first the Kingdom of God. In Chapter I have discussed marriage.

In 1 Peter 2:24, God promised me that I am healed by His stripe. The Lord says: *I am the one that heals you. You will live and not die.* I have searched the Word and found several scriptures about healing;

such as, In 3 John where it is written that it is God's wish that I should prosper and be in good health. In Isaiah 53:3-5 I read: *He is despised and rejected of men; a man of sorrows, and acquainted with grief: and we hid as it were our faces from him; he was despised, and we esteemed him not. Surely he hath borne our griefs, and carried our sorrows: yet we did esteem him stricken, smitten of God, and afflicted. But he was wounded for our transgressions; he was bruised for our iniquities: the chastisement of our peace was upon him; and with his stripes we are healed.* And again in Matthew 8:1 it is written that: *This fulfilled the word of the Lord through the prophet Isaiah, who said, He took our sicknesses and removed our diseases.* Now I must trust God and continue to do everything in my power to maintain my healing.

I am grateful to God for healing me. I cement myself in His Word that when the devil comes back to me with his lies that my body is aching; I speak God's Word, such as; I have been healed by the stripes of Jesus, sickness and disease are far from me, and no evil disease can cleave to my body. These affirmations break the power of the enemy. Do you have a disease, an infirmity or an affliction and do not know where to turn or what to do? Look to God, call upon Him. He can heal you. You can place your hand on any part of your body and heal yourself with steadfast faith in God's power and under the anointing of the Holy Spirit. It has been declared in His Word that He is the God who heals. We have read in the Bible that He has healed many, and we constantly hear of and see many people who have been healed in our day.

Miracles:

What are miracles? "Miracle" comes from the Hebrew word *neeseem* which means *wonder*. Do you think that the fact that you are alive is a miracle? The process from conception to birth is a miracle; the continuation of life to death is also a miracle and so is the promised life after death. Having faith in God is a miracle. In our day we do not have to look very far for miracles. Miracles are happening around us every day. The problem is that some of us do not recognize them, perhaps because we are too immersed in the issues of life, tradition, stubbornness or simply because of spiritual blindness. Maybe some of us are just like the Pharisees and the Sadducees who kept looking for more signs after witnessing Jesus performed so many miracles in their faces; from turning water into wine at the wedding at Canaan, to feeding more than five thousand people with only five loaves of breads and two small fish, or raising the widow's son, Jairus' daughter and Lazarus from the dead.

We see miracles when the doctors give someone six months to live, and that person lives for seven more years or longer. Miracles happen when lives are transformed when people make changes in relationships, when they make discoveries. Miracles are seen when people discover their purposes and embrace them; their lives are often changed positively, and forever. Miracles happen when people discover the awesome power within themselves and move from mediocrity to places of empowerment. Miracles are the prayers we see answered, and they are the prayers we pray for those who the doctors have given up on and through faith and effective prayers they live for many more years.

I have seen a recent miracle in my church. A mother and father were told by their doctor that their baby would not live beyond the birth canal, due to a rare condition. That baby is a year old today. We hear and read every day stories of miraculous survival. Many people have recovered from illnesses deemed terminal by their doctors, such as cancer, strokes, brain tumors, aneurysms, heart attacks, and even serious vehicular accidents. We also see and hear of people surviving through tragic natural and unnatural disasters, while others perish under those same conditions. Many have told their stories of "near-death" experiences or of having died and returned to life. All these things are miracles.

I believe we have had enough miracles in our day to know the nature of God and believe that He exists in the Trinity. He is a never, changing God. In the Bible we are told of numerous miracles from Genesis to Revelation. There are stories of; Noah's ark, the tower of Babel, Lot's wife turning into a pillar of salt, Abraham's son, Isaac, being born when Abraham was one hundred years old and Joseph's survival and victory after being thrown into a pit and left to die by his own siblings.

Then there are the miracles of Moses, where God spoke to him from a burning bush; the dividing of the Red Sea to allow the Israelites to cross, and the rod turning into a snake. There are miracles of Esther and Ruth and many more. These are just a few of the many miracles in the Bible, but the Bible is our greatest miracle itself and I do not understand how any person could deny it. The Bible tells stories and backs up every word with confirmations. Its narratives are inspired and written by different authors who confirm what God said and what each author wrote.

Prophecies:

Prophecy is another area that is highly neglected in many churches. I am simply amazed that God has given us such power and authority and yet we refuse to activate and use them. Prophecy is described in Revelation as: *the testimony of Jesus is the spirit of prophecy* (Revelation 19:10). There are hundreds of prophecies mentioned in the Bible and many of them have already been fulfilled, while there are many yet to be fulfilled. I believe our lives would be far better if we were implementing the principles that are in the Holy Book. Prophecy, in essence, is one of the spiritual gifts mentioned in the Bible and it is something about which God inspires an individual to speak to others for edification (Amos 3:1-8), exhortation (Habakkuk 2:6-8) and comfort (Micah 4:1). If the church cannot assume this responsibility, who can? The inability of the church to provide these services has made people turn to psychics.

All believers need to be edified, exhorted and comforted. I have had experiences in my own life where prophets spoke to me and confirmed things that God had already shown me in the Spirit, or they spoke truths that comforted and assured me in areas where I had uncertainties. God has also used me to speak into the lives of many people; and I believe that prophecy is here today as it was in olden days. Why not use it? Prophecy is God's Word and I will say it again: His Word remains forever. *Heaven and earth shall pass away, but my words shall not pass away* (Matthew 24:35). This is what the Lord said, and he also said: *So shall my word be that goeth forth out of my mouth: it shall not return unto me void, but it shall accomplish that which I please, and it shall prosper in the thing whereto I sent it* (Isaiah 55:11).

Prophecy must be activated in the church as a way of fulfilling God's will for the church. *He that speaketh in an unknown tongue edifieth himself; but he that prophesieth edifieth the church* (1 Corinthians 14:4). Prophecies were spoken in the Old Testament by many men who were inspired by God, from Moses, Joshua, Elijah, Elisha, Zechariah to Malachi and Jesus, Matthew, Peter to John the Baptist, in the New Testament. These are a few of the men who were inspired by the Holy Spirit to prophecy. We read in 2 Peter 1:21: *For the prophecy came not in old time by the will of man: but holy men of God spake as they were moved by the Holy Ghost.* The prophets did not take credit for the prophecies that they brought. John the Baptist made it very clear that he was just a spokesman and that he took no credit at all for the words that came out of his mouth. He declared: *I am the voice of one crying in the wilderness, Make straight the way of the Lord, as said the prophet Isaiah"* (John 1:23). John the Baptist made the way for the greatest prophet, Jesus.

If the gift of prophecy was taken more seriously in our day, we would have fewer people doubting themselves and God, being fearful, lacking faith and trust, feeling hopeless, giving up on life, going to psychics or living below the standards by which God requires His creation to live. Unless we make some drastic changes now, I am afraid that our world is going to fall apart and away from God, even further because of the lack in application of biblical principles.

Some may argue that **prophecy** is not important-only love is because 1Corinthians 13:2 reads: *If I had the gift of **prophecy**, and if I understood all of God's secret plans and possessed all knowledge, and if I had such faith that I could move mountains, but didn't love others, I would be nothing.* Take a look at what was said in verse 1 of Chapter 14: *Let love be your highest goal! But you should also desire the special abilities the Spirit gives—especially the ability to prophesy (1 Corinthians 14:1).* Some may even argue that there are false prophets, which there are, but the Word of God said His sheep knows His voice, so those who know the Lord should be able to discern His true prophets, who speak with the voice of God. What are your views on miracles, healing and prophecies and what does God's Word say about them?

PRINCIPLES FOR DAILY APPLICATION

Healing:

Apply Biblical principles from Genesis, Exodus, Leviticus, Numbers, Deuteronomy and all the books of the Bible; both Old and New Testaments.

(1) Know that it is God's will that you live a healthy life, free from sickness and diseases. In 1 Peter 2:24, He promises that you are healed by His stripe. The Lord says: *I am the one that heals you. You will live and not die.* You have been healed from all infirmities because Jesus carried your sickness and disease. He will ensure that your body functions the way He designed it to function. In Isaiah 53:3-5, it is written: *He is despised and rejected of men; a man of sorrows, and acquainted with grief: and we hid as it were our faces from him; he was despised, and we esteemed him not. Surely he hath borne our griefs, and carried our sorrows: yet we did esteem him stricken, smitten of God, and afflicted. But he was wounded for our transgressions, he was bruised for our iniquities: the chastisement of our peace was upon him; and with his stripes we are healed.* Matthew 8:1: *This fulfilled the word of the Lord through the prophet Isaiah, who said, He took our sicknesses and removed our diseases.*

(2) Pray the scriptures that address healing and confess your sins to God, so that His healing will take effect in your life.

(3) Surrender to Him and let Him know you need Him, because you cannot heal yourself without His help.

(4) Believe the promises of God and believe that He has healed you. Do not give in to satan's bait to have doubts: *That it might be fulfilled which was spoken by Esaias the prophet, saying, Himself took our infirmities, and bare our sicknesses* (Matthew 8:17).

(5) Be aware that the father of all lies will try to tell you are still sick, but you have to renounce him and believe what God says.

(6) Memorize this verse and have faith in it: *Beloved, I wish above all things that thou mayest **prosper** and be in **health**, even as thy soul **prospereth*** (3 John 1:2). God wants you to be in the best of health.

(7) Pray, pray, pray that no disease will cleave to your body and always give God thanks in everything.

Miracles:

(1) Read the Bible, there are examples of many miracles from Genesis to Revelation-some of which I have mentioned above.

(2) Look for the miracles that are happening in your daily life, around you and in the lives of others. Train your eyes and your ears to notice them. They come through acts of obedience. Read 1 Kings 17.

(3) Give God thanks for your miracles.

(4) Trust in God to continue performing miracles in your life.

(5) Ask Him to help you see and understand His miracles.

(6) Live in the Spirit so He can work with you. The flesh will prevent you from seeing, accepting or appreciating the supernatural elements of God.

(7) Pray, pray, pray that you will be able to recognize the miracles of God and differentiate them from demonic performances. The magicians in Egypt were able to do the same miracles that God worked through Moses. Physics are able to tell people about their future, but do you believe they really see the future?

Prophecies

(1) Believe in prophecy, but be careful to whom and what you listen, because there are some false prophets: *Beloved, do not **believe** every spirit, but test the spirits, whether they are of God; because many false **prophets** have gone out into the world* (1 John 4:1. Seek God for revelation and direction

(2) Use the prophecies you read in the Bible as well as those you receive from living prophets to help keep your focus on God's promises. He promised to prosper us through the prophets: *and they prospered through the prophesying of Haggai the prophet and Zechariah the son of Iddo* (Ezra 6:14).

(3) Search the scriptures and learn what they say about prophecies and prophets).

(4) Study the lives and works of the prophets.

(5) Know that the purpose of prophecy is to edify, encourage and Exhort.

(6) You will prosper if you believe that what God said to the prophets also applies to you: *Believe in the LORD your God, so shall ye be established; believe his prophets, so shall ye prosper* (2 Chronicles 20:20).

(7) Pray, pray, pray that you will be able to receive and appreciate the prophecies from God's true servants and that you will be able to discern false prophets and false prophecies.

PRAYER:

Dear heavenly Father, I know that Jesus performed many miracles, through His healings and prophecies, while He walked the earth. Thank You for sending Jesus and for being El-Shaddai, the Almighty and all sufficient God. Thank You for creating us in your image and for teaching us to be like Jesus and for giving us the authority to do great and mighty things. Thank you Jesus that when You were leaving the earth, You said: *Verily, verily, I say unto you, He that believeth on me, the works that I do shall he do also; and greater works than these shall he do; because I go unto my Father* (John 14:12).

I pray that all leaders in the churches will pay attention to and obey Your Word. Help us to recognize our daily miracles and be grateful for them. I am grateful that through Your grace and Your mercy and through my faith and trust in You, I can recognize the miracles that You perform in my life and the lives of others every day. Please open the spiritual eyes of those who are still looking for more signs and miracles, after all the personal and natural disasters that we have already experienced, and also after all the blessings that You have already bestowed upon us. Help us to believe Your prophets, so that we may prosper in the place of our assignments and help us to desire the spiritual gifts-especially the gift of prophecy. Lord, thank You for removing the blinders from our eyes and for assisting us in applying Your Word to our lives daily; Amen.

PART III

TRANSFORMATION CHANGES EVERYTHING

At its heart, spiritual transformation refers to a The process of character formation is defined by the Greek word paideia which is translated as "training" or "formation" in the Bible. (2 Timothy 3:15, 16). Formation involves transformation (morphe) which is a change in the inner man or essence. (Romans 12:2; Galatians 4:19). It is the continual change in the life of a teacher, mentor, coach, or even parent, student that calls forth a continual change in the life of a student, mentoree, client, or even a teenager.
Dr. Joseph Umidi, Author of Transformational Coaching

fundamental change in the place of the sacred or the character of the sacred in the life of the individual. Spiritual transformation can be understood in terms of new configurations of strivings
Kenneth Pargament

Spiritual transformation is defined here as :dramatic changes in world and self views, purposes, religious beliefs, attitudes, and behavior. These changes are often linked to discrete experiences that can occur gradually or over relatively short periods of time.
Spiritual Transformation Scientific Research Program

Transformation is to change in composition or structure; to change the outward form or appearance; to change in character or condition.
Mirriam-Webster's Online Dictionary

I beseech you therefore, brethren, by the mercies of God, that ye present your bodies a living sacrifice, holy, acceptable unto God, which is your reasonable service. And be not conformed to this world: but be ye transformed by the renewing of your mind, that ye may prove what is that good, and acceptable, and perfect, will of God
Romans 12:1-2.

CHAPTER 14
FORGIVENESS IS A MUST

*So shall ye say unto Joseph, **Forgive**, I pray thee now, the trespass of thy
brethren, and their sin; for they did unto thee evil: and now, we pray
thee, **forgive** the trespass of the servants of the God of thy father*
Genesis 50:17.

*If my people, which are called by my name, shall humble themselves, and
pray, and seek my face, and turn from their wicked ways; then will I
hear from heaven, and will **forgive** their sin, and will heal their land*
2 Chronicles 7:14.

*Blessed is he whose transgression is **forgiven**, whose sin is covered*
Psalm 32:1.

*And **forgive** us our debts, as we **forgive** our debtors*
Matthew 6:12.

*For if ye **forgive** men their trespasses, your
heavenly Father will also **forgive** you*
Matthew 6:14.

*But if ye **forgive** not men their trespasses, neither
will your Father **forgive** your trespasses*
Matthew 6:15.

*Then came Peter to him, and said, Lord, how oft shall my
brother sin against me, and I **forgive** him? Till seven times?*
Matthew 18:21.

Forgiveness is to excuse someone for a fault or an offense; to pardon! according to the dictionary. It is certainly not easy to forgive those who have hurt you, but it is a command from God that we forgive others. Practice the act of forgiveness by first forgiving yourself. We are naturally hard on ourselves, remembering and carrying the sins for which God has already forgiven. He asks us to forgive one another as He has forgiven us, yet we heap bags of hatred, envy, jealousy, pride, bitterness, feelings of rejection and other things that hold us hostage to forgiveness. Everyone has to learn the act of forgiveness in order to have joy, peace, harmony, good health and to be in obedience to God.

For if ye forgive men their trespasses, your
heavenly Father will also forgive you:
But if ye forgive not men their trespasses,
neither will your Father forgive your trespasses.
(Matthew 6:14-15).

God has forgiven us of our sins once and for all. He does not even remember our sins, yet we keep remembering them. Colin Tipping, the Author of *Radical Forgiveness* wrote: "Radical forgiveness is the key to empowerment and being able to forgive easily and quickly." Is there anyone you need to forgive today? To get close to God and please him we must choose to forgive. *Follow peace with all men, and holiness, without which no man shall see the Lord* (Hebrews 12:14).

The word forgiveness and related words are used almost 100 times in the Bible; therefore, the act of forgiveness must be of significance to God. The enemy would have us believe that our sins are not forgiven. He constantly reminds us of past sins and tries to keep us stuck in thoughts about our past, but we can be like Jesus. He showed us examples of forgiveness when He forgave those who hurt and caused Him pain and anguish. Jesus cried out to His Father:

Father, forgive them; *for they know not what they do* (Luke 23:34). God declares in Isaiah 43:25: *I, even I, am He who blots out your transgressions for My own sake; And I will not remember your sins.*

That, my friend, is absolute forgiveness!

It is painful to think that many of our hurts come from our family-our own blood relatives (mother, father, sister, brother, uncle, close family friends and so forth). On the other hand, there are others, such as bosses, co-workers, friends and associates with whom we spend many hours on any given day, and by whom we are a hurt also. It does not matter who they are or what they have done; we must choose to forgive them. That is the reason the Bible warns: *Love your enemy.* The truth is that we live in a broken world that is painted with human frailties and none of us is free from faults, hurt or un-forgiveness.

We can choose to forgive, or, we can continue to live in bitterness and hold on to hurt. I have heard it said many times, "I can forgive, but I can't forget." When God forgives us He does not remember our sins (Hebrews 8:12) . Why would someone want to remember the hurt he has done to someone or the hurt that someone has done to him? It is good to remember what happened in the past, in order to make wiser decisions in the future, but certainly one should not dwell on those things. Carrying a grudge can be dangerous to one's health. It causes stress, heart problems and anxiety, among other diseases. The burden of un-forgiveness is an unhealthy habit that not only robs people of their physical wellness, but of spiritual, social and emotional wellness. Forgive and enjoy emotional, social, spiritual and physical freedom.

What happens when we forgive? It frees us from the conditions listed above, and God in turn forgives us. It is in the Lord's prayer we learn the following:

And forgive us our debts, as we forgive our debtors. For if ye forgive men their trespasses, your heavenly Father will also forgive you. But if ye forgive not men their trespasses, neither will your Father forgive your trespasses (Matthew 6:12, 14-15).

We have the privilege of asking God to forgive us of our debts on condition that we are willing to forgive others. Therefore, if we refuse to forgive others, we should not expect God to forgive us either.

Un-forgiveness interferes with and damages relationships. People often get into squabbles and end up being angry at one another. When the damage is done, the only thing that can mend it, is forgiveness. Again holding on to past hurts does not solve the problems. Instead, it builds resentment, and anger which sometimes lead to hatred and even causes violence. In focusing on, and practicing love, we learn to forgive. If there is someone you need to forgive, do it today-do not wait until it is too late. Tomorrow is not promised, and life is short.

However, if it is a tough issue for you, in order to prevent a situation from escalating, a cool off period is sometimes necessary to give the people involved time to heal. Forcing a premature conflict resolution may lead to further conflicts. There truly is a time for everything...be sensitive to that. When you are guided by the Holy Spirit, go ahead and do what needs to be done. If someone refuses to accept your forgiveness, do not worry about it; you have done your part and it is no longer your problem or burden. George Herbert said it best: "He who cannot forgive breaks the bridge over which he himself must pass." Choose to forgive and free yourself from the tensions imposed by un-forgiveness. Then live life to the fullest with the knowledge that God has forgiven you and you are indeed free.

Jesus saith unto him, I say not unto thee, Until seven times: but, Until seventy times seven" (Matthew 18:22).

This was the instruction Jesus gave to Peter when Peter asked the question about how many times should a person forgive another person. The day-to-day offences that we encounter are nothing to compare to what Jesus encountered. In conclusion, I would like to reiterate that when we fail to forgive others, we harbor the stronghold of bitterness. In order for us to inherit God's kingdom we have to cleanse ourselves of all bitterness by letting go of the hurts that others have caused us. It is only when we release them that our spirits are set free. We also benefit from the act of forgiveness even more than the recipient.

When we learn to forgive, our prayer life gets stronger and more meaningful:. *Therefore if you bring your gift to the altar, and there remember that your brother has something against you, leave your gift there before the altar, and go your way. First be reconciled to your brother, and then come and offer your gift* (Matthew 5:23-24). It is inevitable that we will be offended by others throughout our lives, but what really matters is how we handle the offenses. Regardless of how we handle them, we simply must choose to forgive. It is the will of God that we forgive others, as He has forgiven us. The choice to forgive helps others release their guilt and sets the mind, body, spirit and soul of the forgiver free.

PRINCIPLES FOR DAILY APPLICATION

(1) To claim your divine destiny, you must embrace the act of forgiveness. If you struggle with this or feel it is too hard, ask God to help you. There is nothing too hard for God to (Jeremiah 32:27; Genesis 18:14). With God all things are possible (Matthew 19:26; Mark 10:27).

(2) Do not harbor bitterness, hatred, jealousy, pride, envy, malice or un-forgiveness.

If you have an issue that needs to be worked out with someone, do it now, tomorrow is not promised. *Make allowance for each other's faults, and forgive anyone who offends you. Remember, the Lord forgave you, so you must forgive others* (Colossians 3:13). Paul wrote in Romans 12:18: *If it be possible, as much as lieth in you, live peaceably with all men.*

(3) Forgive others, before going to God to offer your gifts of prayer, offering, worship or service. *Therefore if you bring your gift to the altar, and there remember that your brother has something against you, leave your gift there before the altar, and go your way. First be reconciled to your brother, and then come and offer your gift* (Matthew 5:23-24).

(4) Be eager to forgive. Forgive often and for as long as the need exists. As recorded by Matthew and Luke, when Peter asked Jesus how often he should forgive, *Jesus saith unto him, I say not unto thee, Until seven times: but, Until seventy times seven* (Matthew 18:22, Luke 17:3-4).

(5) Do not have preconceived thoughts of what their reactions might be. Simply go with a selfless attitude and with no expectation. What really matters is that you do your part: forgive yourself, accept God's forgiveness and forgive others: *In whom we have redemption through his blood, the **forgiveness** of sins, according to the riches of his grace* (Ephesians 1:7).

(6) Be responsible, and forgive those you need to forgive. Accept forgiveness if offered by someone. Help those who have a difficult time forgiving others to understand the importance of forgiveness. Forgiveness does not mean that you have to agree or accept the behavior of those who have wronged or hurt you. It just means that you are freeing yourself some something that could be potentially dangerous to your health and other things that you value.

(7) Pray, pray, pray and ask God to give you the courage, love and spirit of forgiveness. Then give Him thanks as if you have already received your request. Helpful verses for additional reading are: (Heb. 8:12; Phil. 3:13-14; Eph. 4:32; Mark 3:28-29, 11:25-26).

PRAYER:

Dear heavenly Father, Your Word says in 1 John 1:9, that, *if we confess our sins, he is faithful and just to **forgive** us our sins, and to cleanse us from all unrighteousness.* I come today in the name of Jesus to tell You that I know I am a sinner saved by Your grace. I ask You to forgive me this day of all my sins especially the sin of un-forgiveness ,if there is any in me, whether by thought, word or deed. Thank You for being Jehovah-Tsidkenu, the Lord of our righteousness. I pray that forgiveness will become a part of humanity's lifestyle, so that our world will be a more peaceful place to live in. I pray for the healing of those of us who have been wounded due to lack of forgiveness, and I pray that people will begin to call on You for assistance in this very difficult area called forgiveness as well as in the areas of their lives in which they are weak.

You said in Your Word, in 2 Chronicles 7:14: *If my people, which are called by my name, shall humble themselves, and pray, and seek my face, and turn from their wicked ways; then will I hear from heaven, and will forgive their sin, and will heal their land.* I come to You as an intercessor on behalf of the people, and I ask you to transform their minds and heal their hearts so that they will conform to your standards and can be better citizens of Your kingdom. Thank You, Lord, that we follow what the scriptures say: *Forbearing one another, and forgiving one another, if any man have a quarrel against any: even as Christ forgave you, so also do ye* (Colossians 3:13). *So likewise shall my heavenly Father do also unto you, if ye from your hearts **forgive** not everyone his brother their trespasses* (Matthew.18:35). Thank You, Lord, for forgiving us and for teaching us to forgive wholeheartedly, in Jesus' name, Amen.

CHAPTER 15
UNDERSTANDING RELATIONSHIPS

Honour all men. Love the brotherhood. Fear God. Honour the king
1 Peter 2:17.

*We who believe are carefully joined together, becoming a holy
temple for the Lord. Through Him you Gentiles are also joined
together as part of this dwelling where God lives by His Spirit*
Ephesians 2:21-22.

*And it came to pass, when he had made an end of speaking unto
Saul, that the soul of Jonathan was knit with the soul of David,
and Jonathan loved him as his own soul. Then Jonathan and
David made a covenant, because he loved him as his own soul*
1 Samuel 18:1and 3.

*A man that hath friends must shew himself friendly: and
there is a friend that sticketh closer than a brother*
Proverbs 18:24.

The subject of relationship can be a very sensitive one, because of the dynamics involved. One of the most prominent dysfunctions I have seen in my lifetime is relationship issues between families and among friends. I must admit that this is a tough area for me; I struggle to understand why people behave the way they do. After several failed relationships and questions about the reasons why, I found that I needed to seek God's guidance in this area of my life, just as in all the other areas.

Not very long after I poured out my concerns to God, I began to clearly recognize the relationships that were genuine and deserved to be nurtured and those that needed to remain where they were as well as those that needed to be ended. I used to think that I should have a good relationship with everyone of my family members, friends and associates. When I entered a relationship I thought the other person felt the same way I felt about it. I expected honesty and unconditional love. I was confusing "relationship" with the commandment to love everyone. As a result, I entered every relationship with a high expectation and that there would be mutual love and understanding. As time went on, I came to the sad reality that I was wrong. I have come to the conclusion that some relationships are genuine and a blessing, while others are a big mistake.

The problem is that in relationships we sometimes have a tendency to judge others, formulate opinions and expect too much from them, with no intention of reciprocating, whether in love, time, service, or with material things. Some people are like parasites; they will drain you of every bit of your energy. Some are freeloaders, who have no regard for the rights of the individuals being used or abused. However, I do believe every relationship serves a purpose, however, whether good or bad.

According to the Webster Online Dictionary, *relationship* is described as:

1. A relation between people; "relationship" is often used where "relation" would serve (as in "the relationship between inflation and unemployment") preferred usage of "relationship" is for human relations or states of relatedness; "the relationship between mothers and children"; A state of connectedness between people (especially an emotional connection); "he didn't want his wife to know of the relationship";

2. A state involving mutual dealings between people or parties or countries.;

3. State of relatedness or connection by blood or marriage or adoption.

Since relationship means that we have mutual connectedness, then we should learn the art of connecting and how to handle relationships better than we normally do. The problem is that in our human flesh, we are inefficient in many arenas. Therefore, in order to have a good, true and meaningful relationship, we must first have a true relationship with Jesus so He can teach us the art of relationship. Jesus' relationship with His Father is the blueprint of a true and lasting relationship. It is not possible to have a good relationship with God, unless we open up all areas of our lives and allow Him to enter in freely.

We should not take His relationship for granted, or any of our earthly relationships, for that matter. We should have a great relationship with God, not because of what He has done and can do for us, but because we love Him, and we respect and obey His commandments. In the same way, we should not enter into earthly relationships because of what people can do for us. Hold on to what is truly important in a relationship and respect your position as well as the other person's. Form a solid relationship with God, trust Him, put your focus on Him, and He will guide all of your subsequent relationships. When you do this, you will be surprise to see which of your relationships get dissolved.

What value do you place on the relationships with the people who are most important in your life? Do you value your husband, your children, your friends and your relatives? Do you tell them that you love them daily? I believe if there is any static in saying *I love you* to your family and friends, the relationships need to be evaluated. It might need some work. Cherish the relationships with which God has blessed you, and treat your family and friends right. Treat them the way in which you would want to be treated by them. I received an e-mail that has some excellent ideas about relationship; allow me to share it with you. I do not know the author to whom credit is due, but here it is:

"People come into your life for a reason, a season or a lifetime. When you know which one it is, you will know what to do for that person. When someone is in your life for a REASON, it is usually to meet a need you have expressed. They have come to assist you through a difficulty, to provide you with guidance and support, or to aid you physically, emotionally or spiritually. They may seem like a God-sent, and they are. They are there for the reason you need them to be. Then, without any wrong doing on your part or at an inconvenient time, this person will say, or do something to bring the relationship to an end. Sometimes they die. Sometimes they walk away. Sometimes they act up and force you to take a stand. What we must realize is that our need has been met, our desire fulfilled; their work is done.

The prayer you sent up has been answered and now it is time to move on. Some people come into your life for a SEASON, because your turn has come to share, grow or learn. They bring you an experience of peace or make you laugh. They may teach you something you have never done. They usually give you an unbelievable amount of joy. Believe it; it is real, but only for a season. LIFETIME relationships teach you lifetime lessons-things you must build upon in order to have a solid emotional foundation. Your job is to accept the lesson, love the person and put what you have learned to use in all other relationships and areas of your life. It is said that love is blind, but friendship is clairvoyant. Thank you for being a part of my life, whether you were a reason, a season or a lifetime."

I hope those powerful insights into relationships have inspired you, as they inspired me. The next time you begin to think about the hurt or wrong that someone has done to you or something unkind that has been said about you, instead of getting upset, think of the source and remember that this person is a human being, just as you are-made of flesh and blood, born in sin and are therefore capable of erring. Also remember Ephesians 6:12 which tells us: *For we wrestle not against flesh and blood, but against principalities, against powers, against the rulers of the darkness of this world, against spiritual wickedness in high places.* Although, we do not always follow it, the Golden Rule states that we should treat others the way that we would like them to treat us: *Do for others what you would like them to do for you. This is a summary of all that is taught in the law and the prophets.* (Matthew 7:12) (NLT). The golden rule should be a practiced habit throughout our lives. I see no wiggle room for compromise. 1 Peter 2:17 is a fitting scripture to insert here.

Another important consideration about relationships is that you could lose valuable time seeking approval or expecting too much from others. Many of the people from whom you seek approval may be in worse situations than you, even though it does not appear to be that way. Sometimes their outward lives reflect quite the opposite. The tricky thing about this is that they just manage to use the cover-up technique skillfully. Most relationships have problems, ranging lack of communication to stress. This is why we should put our trust in God only and *look to the hills from where our help comes* (as it is written in Psalm 121). You can find everything you need, and get every question answered through the Word of God, which will teach you how to employ the Holy Spirit as your source for direction, counseling and guidance. Nurture your meaningful relationships, let go of the ones that drag you down and let your focus on God be your priority and the one relationship in which you can fully trust. The Bible warns that we should use our energy to please God, because only what we do for God will last.

PRINCIPLES FOR DAILY APPLICATION

Study this simple prayer by Saint Francis of Assisi and use it in every relationship situation that you may find yourself.

Lord make me an instrument of your peace.
Where there is hatred, let me sow Love;
Where there is injury-Pardon;
Where there is doubt-Faith;
Where there is despair-Hope;
Where there is darkness-Light;
And where there is sadness-Joy.
Lord, grant that I may seek rather
to Comfort than to be comforted,
to Understand rather than to be understood,
to Love than to be loved.
For it is by Giving that one receives,
by Forgiving that one is forgiven,
and by Dying that one awakens to Eternal Life.

PRAYER:

Dear heavenly Father, please help me to see that it really is not that people want to be nasty to me and treat me badly, but it is the evil one that tries everything to prevent me from having the kinds of relationships that matter and that you would have me to have. Lord, Your Word in John 10:10 is a reminder that the enemy comes to kill, steal and destroy, while You come to give life and to give it more abundantly. I trust in Your promise of abundance in all areas of my life, which include the area of relationships. I renounce all of abbadon's tricks that he uses to keep us from having good relationships. Thank You, Lord that You have the final say in my life. I will not be deceived by the accuser. Thank You for Ephesians 6, which I can declare over my life to defeat the liar. I take up the shield of faith, and I fight the fiery darts of the enemy. *For we wrestle not against flesh and blood, but against principalities, against powers, against the rulers of the darkness of this world, against spiritual wickedness in high places (Ephesians 6:12).* Lord, I thank you for Your Word, the Sword, which I can use as a shield against the adversary, to fight him when he comes to destroy my relationships. Thank You Lord that I am blessed in my relationships. In Jesus' name, Amen.

CHAPTER 16
HOW TO SURVIVE AND THRIVE IN MARRIAGE

And the Lord God caused a deep sleep to fall upon Adam, and
he slept: and He took one of his ribs, and closed up the flesh
instead thereof; And the rib, which the Lord God had taken form
man, made he a woman, and brought her unto the man
Genesis 2:21-22.

*The man said, "This is now **bone** of my **bone**s and flesh of my*
flesh; she shall be called woman, for she was taken out of man
Genesis 2:23.

*Therefore **shall** a **man leave** his father and his mother, and*
***shall** cleave unto his wife: and they **shall** be one flesh*
Genesis 2:24.

He who finds a wife finds a good thing. And obtains favor from the LORD
Proverbs 18:22.

Let the husband render unto the wife due benevolence:
and likewise also the wife unto the husband
1 Corinthians 7:3.

And if one prevail against him, two shall withstand him;
*and a **threefold** cord is not quickly broken*
Ecclesiastes 4:12.

Wherefore they are no more twain, but one flesh. What therefore
***God** hath **joined together**, let not man put asunder*
Matthew 19:6.

Amarriage, in my opinion, is a consented, committed, mutual relationship between a man and a woman. It is a model of God's original couple, Adam and Eve-the first man and woman relationship documented in the scriptures. Before the fall in the Garden of Eden to sin, they had a beautiful life, the way a marriage relationship should be. The union of marriage is potentially good and beneficial when a couple can work out their differences and maintain a loving, caring and responsible attitude toward each other.

The world has several versions of what constitutes a marriage, but the marriage I am referring to is the one between one man and one woman. There is biblical support in Ephesians 5 which states that when a MAN is grown and no longer lives with his parents, because he is able to make his own decisions, and find a wife, (hopefully the one God ordained), the two become one. She is *bone of his bones and flesh of his flesh* (Genesis 2:23). Adam and Eve seemed quite happy and content with that arrangement.

The Webster Dictionary describes marriage as a legal union of a man and a woman for life, as husband and wife; wedlock, matrimony, vow or contract. These are very strong nouns that should be taken seriously. Marriage should not be entered into unless the partners are absolutely clear about their decisions. They should ask questions that need to be asked of the person with whom they intend to spend the rest of their lives, and the questions should be answered with sincerity.

Deceit should not be allowed to find its way into the marriage. In light of so many failed marriages and divorces, it is critical to take the right steps and make the right decisions initially. Couples can seek marriage counseling before entering the union of marriage. This would give them time to learn more about each other and to hear the perspective of couples who have been married, at least, for a while and who have offered counseling to many.

Two persons living together with completely different values, personality traits, characteristics and interests are bound to have some forms of disagreements. It is the attitude and reaction toward the disagreements that determine the response and results. Marriage is not a bed of roses, even though sometimes it appears to be that way. In the married relationship each partner must submit to the other, not for each other's sake, but for Christ's sake. Together they submit to the church which is the body of Christ. Our Lord, Jesus Christ loves us so much-so very much- that He died for our sake. He did this so that we may live a holy and pure life through obedience to His Word. Read 1 Corinthians Chapter 7 for more on the principles of the married life.

There has to be unconditional love, and mutual respect in the marriage relationship. Spouses should share in all aspects of the marriage. Share in the joys, sorrows, decision making and anything that impacts the marriage. In this relationship there should be no form of abuses-unfortunately too often times, there are. It is easy to recognize physical abuse, but emotional abuse and verbal abuse are easily pushed to the side by either or both spouses. Subtle abuses exist in arrogance, ego trips, anger, competition, and refusal to admit faults and apologize when in error. They are also seen in inappropriate language which destroys the partner's self-esteem, character insults and mean or controlling behaviors. These actions or inactions are bound to cause emotional scars. Learn to recognize these things and nip them in the bud before they get out of hand and someone lives to regret them. Do not be afraid to confront these issues because the scripture assures: *For God hath not given us the spirit of fear; but of power, and of love, and of a sound mind* (2 Timothy 1:7).

When certain things are ignored or neglected in a marriage, the relationship suffers and quite often ends in a divorce. Divorces often end in feuds, with the partners, hating each other, saying bad things about each other and causing innocent children to become victims. This has got to be the worst thing about a divorce. Children usually find security in the harmony and love that their parents exhibit. When such security is violated, the children are most often deeply affected. There are couples who stay in bad marriages "for the sake of their children." They do not want their children to be affected by the stress that comes with a divorce, but the children end up being affected anyways, by the tension between the parents in the home. This is where we would say, six of one and half a dozen of the other. I do wish that more marriages would withstand the trials and keep the vows.

Mutual respect and understanding are important for a peaceful marriage. When the foundation is built on Christ, it is easier to achieve this. As with everything else, Christ has to be in the marriage. In Ecclesiastes 4:12, we are taught this lesson: *And if one prevail against* *him, two shall withstand him; and a **threefold** cord is not quickly broken.* With Christ in the marriage, there is a mediator who does not show favoritism. Therefore, when an issue arises that both partners find difficult to resolve and they take it to God, He fixes it. There is nothing too hard for God to do.

The statistic of Christian marriages that end in divorce is incredible, but the fact remains that God is in control of all marriages. Christians whose marriages end in divorce have allowed the tempter to enter the relationship, without realizing it was not solely the partner's fault. It is however, the partners' responsibility to recognize the temptations of the roaring lion and to resist them. I can hear you saying, "It is easier said than done". Trust me, I do understand. I have been there and think I know what I am talking about. If there are other reasons for divorces, I simply do not know them. I read in the Bible that God hates divorce and I know that the evil one loves anything that God hates. I heard an elderly woman say that the Lord told her that her husband is her burden to bear. If each partner can think in these terms, it would help to tolerate the bearable burdens by applying love all the time, and casting the ones that are too big for you on to God. I believe if couples do this, it would help couples learn how to stay married.

Always be careful about what you verbalize; this is one of the enemy's weapons of destruction for marriages. He knows that words hurt and cause damage; they are irreparable for those who refuse to forgive others. You say something negative to or about your spouse, and the devil takes it, runs with it and you cannot take those words back. The Bible warns: *Death and life are in the **power** of the **tongue:** and they that love it shall eat the fruit thereof* (Proverb 18:21). Do you want a dead marriage or one that has life, love, joy, peace, harmony and understanding?

Sometimes it is better not to respond right away when you and your spouse find yourselves in a situation leading to an argument. It helps to take a breath, regain your composure or simply walk away. Wait until later when the atmosphere changes to then revisit and discuss the issue. Refrain from saying anything bad about your spouse to others, as it could come back to haunt you. I can recount a few instances in which I have seen this happen. In one particular case I recall an acquaintance who was separated from her husband, she told me that he was impotent, in addition to other not so good things. To my surprise, they were back living together in a few months and gave birth to a child. The marriage eventually ended in divorce. The point I am trying to make is: "Be careful what you say about your spouse." Minimize the negatives and focus on the positives in your marriage, realizing that the wicked serpent uses tactics to keep you focusing on the negatives. The solution I find, is to ask for God's help and to seek His guidance through His Word.

Remember, once the hurtful words are spoken and wrongful acts committed, they cannot be reversed. The damage is already done and there are regrets. Apology, confession and forgiveness are all in order, in circumstances where we have hurt our partners. It is as simple as saying, *I am sorry* and it is simple doing this; *forgive.* The memory will remain, and the power of darkness will try to use it against us, but we must remember that what the enemy means for evil, God means for good. Once you have made your confession to Christ, you must forgive yourself, accept His forgiveness, accept the other person's forgiveness and move on to the greater things that await you for the rest of your life.

The things we call mistakes are actually learning experiences. Our heavenly Father knows that we are weak in our flesh and do make bad choices at times. He allows us to make mistakes which we later must use for the accomplishment of His purposes for our lives and His Kingdom. We should use the experiences as testimonies to help minister to others. Mistakes are inevitable, but we must find the lessons in them, vow not to make the same mistakes again and move beyond.

When our daughters were in Catholic school, we used to carpool with a woman to drive our children thirty minutes across town to attend a school. One day she recommended that I read the book, *Men are from Mars and Women are from Venus.* In the same breath she commented, "It is such a good book. I want my *ex* back, I wish I had read it before I divorced him." I was curious about what made her say that, so I bought the book. As I read through the book, I understood why she felt that way. Learning about the differences in men and women through this book has helped me in my marriage. Today, Wednesday, June 23, 2009 my husband, Royston and I celebrate our Silver Anniversary-25 years! We feel this is truly an accomplishment in today's society. However, it has not been a perfect journey.

The information in John Gray's book that helped me the most was the part about what a woman should do when a man goes into his "cave." Prior to this insight I was wondering what on earth was wrong with my husband. Being nurturing and caring as most women are, I was doing all the things that drove him further into the cave, or kept him staying there longer. Nowadays when he goes into his cave, I do not try to get him out; I let him stay there while I find something of interest in which I engage. That way I am not spending my time trying to do the impossible, by trying to figure out what is wrong with him-why he is so quiet when I want to talk. Best of all, my husband gets his time for himself, undisturbed.

I believe the essence of a good relationship is to love unconditionally, understanding and knowing each other very well, communicating, accepting and learning to live with each other's differences. It is never, ever, taking each other for granted. John Gray said that the primary love needs of men and women are different in that, "men need to receive trust, acceptance, appreciation, admiration, approval and encouragement," while women need to receive caring, understanding, respect, devotion, validation and reassurance. The first thing I did after reading this, was to analyze these criteria to see how this applied to Royston and me. I then gave him the book to read and we had a discussion. We thought we fared pretty well, but we both agreed to pay more attention to Mr. Gray's comprehensive list.

Paying more attention to, and putting these principles into practice made an amazing difference in our marriage. For a marriage to thrive it requires extra work and creativity. I can remember us being creative throughout our marriage, creativity seems to add some excitement. One of the things that stands out very vividly was a period of time when we wrote each other notes every day. Sometimes it is the little things, such as calling your spouse everyday to let her know you got to work safely and to say, "I love you," one more time before beginning your day's work, that makes a difference and leave a lasting impression on your spouse.

Marriage is good, but as should be expected, there are challenges. There will be times when you may need some outside help. It is recommended that when you do, you should seek help from reliable sources. There are numerous resources available in the forms of books audio tapes, online articles, pastors and marriage counselors. Utilize them, but most importantly, read the Bible yourself and seek God's guidance on how to have a healthy marriage relationship.

In some marriages, one partner sees the necessity for growth and development and the other does not; one partner sees that the marriage is in trouble, and the other is in oblivion; one partner wants to talk about it and the other could not care less, does not know how to, or just refuses to do so. The problem is, changes cannot occur if only one partner is making the effort. Each person has an equal responsibility to work on the relationship.

As I conclude this very important Chapter, I would like to encourage sit together at times, and reflect on your earlier years together. Talk about some of the fun things you did and enjoyed doing together before you got married, or in the earlier years of your marriage. What are your unforgettable moments? I always reflect on the things that caused our earliest attraction-what made us become best friends before we got married. What memories keep you smiling? Reverting to the memory bank, and extracting beautiful memories help with refocusing when tension begins to build up.

You to know that the person to whom you are married is not your enemy, even though at times it may appear to be that way. This is your partner to love, to have, and to hold-"in sickness and in health, for better or for worse and for as long as you both shall live." Invest in your marriage by consistently putting effort into knowing the person better, forsaking all others, depositing in his/her emotional bank account, reading self help-books, listening to tapes on related topics, reinforce the vows. you made to each other and grow in intimacy. Those whom God has joined together, should not allow anyone or anything to put them asunder. May God bless your marriage.

PRINCIPLES FOR DAILY APPLICATION

(1) Give serious thoughts to the mandates and demands of marriage before deciding to marry anyone. Make sure that is what you want, what God intended, and that you are ready to commit. Seek the Holy Spirit's guidance: *Therefore **shall** a **man leave** his father and his mother, and **shall** cleave unto his wife: and they **shall** be one flesh* (Genesis 2:24).

(2) Secure you relationships by putting God in the center of them. Put selfish ambition aside and think of your partner as one who deserves the best. Encourage and affirm your spouse. Do not embarrass him or her in front of others; do not humiliate the person you love. *Let the husband render unto the wife due benevolence: and likewise also the wife unto the husband* (1 Corinthians 7:3).

(3) Communicate and cultivate the kind of relationship that will blossom into a beautiful relationship as you grow together. You will find that over time your love for each other will grow stronger. Speak with your partner so that there can be no guess work or misunderstanding about anything. Please be honest and speak the truth.

(4) Plan romantic get a-ways. You need time together-alone without the children. Use your imagination, write love notes/love letters. Use positive words of praise, affirmations and acknowledgement. From time to time, take a trip down memory lane and reminisce about the fun and exciting times you have had together.

(5) Have mutual agreements on how to raise your children, how to share the house work and how to run the household budget.

(6) Support each other's interests. For example, sacrifice you personal time to spend time with your spouse while he or she is doing something in which you may not be interested. I am not a football fan, but I watch the game with my husband sometimes.

(7) Pray, pray, pray. Fight for your marriage. Take your marriage seriously and not as a joke. Some marriages end up in divorce even before they get to know each other: *Wherefore they are no more twain, but one flesh. What therefore* **God** *hath* **joined together***, let not man put asunder* (Matthew 19:6).

PRAYER:

Dear heavenly, I thank You for the privilege of marriage. I pray that my spouse and I will grow together as You intended wives and husbands to do, according to Your Word in Genesis 2:18, 23-24, Ephesians 5, 1 Corinthians 7 and also in Ecclesiastes 4:11. Heavenly Father, please help me to understand what it means to have companionship, mutual understanding, good communication, oneness and intimacy with my spouse. Forgive me for my sexual sins and guard my heart, eyes and thoughts so that I may not lust after others. You said in Your Word that if I even have the thought and have not committed the sexual act, I have still sinned, so I ask You to please give me the strength to overcome my sexual weaknesses. Lord, let my marriage be like Your relationship with Israel, where nothing can come between my spouse and me. Please help my spouse and me to live in oneness, remain pure and allow no man to put us asunder. Thank You, Lord, that we respect and honor our vows, *until death do us part*, for Your name's sake. Amen.

CHAPTER 17
THE HUSBAND THE HEAD

*Therefore shall a man leave his father and his mother, and
shall cleave unto his wife: and they shall be one flesh*
Genesis 2:24.

The man who finds a wife finds a treasure, and he receives favor from the Lord
Proverbs 18:22.

*So ought men to love their wives as their own bodies.
He that loveth his wife loveth himself*
Ephesians 5:28.

Husbands, love your wives and do not be harsh with them
Colossians 3:19

*In the same way, you husbands must give honor to your wives. Treat
your wife with understanding as you live together. She may be weaker
than you are, but she is your equal partner in God's gift of new life.
Treat her as you should so your prayers will not be hindered.*
1 Peter 3:7

Husbands should love their wives as the Lord loves the church, and they are to submit to God as their wives submit to them. They must love their wives and forsake all other women and men. I have heard of husbands who have said that they do not love their wives. How can this be? If a husband says he does not love his wife, does that mean that he does not love himself? According to Ephesians 5:28, he does not!

This means that a man should know who he is and learn to love himself, before marrying another man's daughter. Marriage requires that a man loves his wife; as he loves his own body. When he does this, it will be easier to love his wife with the love that God has commanded. It is important that you tell your wife that she is special to you and you appreciate her, before she decides to leave you. I have seen and heard men making embarrassing insults about their wives to others or in front of others. This is a no-brainer; such behavior is of the flesh; it is egoistic and it destroys marriages.

When you see a woman, whether at church, the mall or at work, what you really are looking at is only flesh, until you really get to know the spirit of that individual. Do not be deceived by the outward appearance of the women you see each day as you go about your business. Sometimes a husband ends up falling in love with another woman and forms a relationship that wrecks his marriage. The result is often suffering, mental anguish and many times dysfunctional behaviors in children. Why ruin a marriage or a relationship to satisfy the flesh for a while? Only the things that we do for Christ will last. If you can remember this each time that you are tempted to make a move or stare lustfully at another woman, you might be able to keep things in perspective.

Husbands are the head of their household. Assume that responsibility-do not domineer her with power and control. Treat your wife with Godly respect; be the provider, support and protector that you were created to be. Apply the principles as they are divinely laid out to guide you, and you will prosper in all areas of your life: *Likewise, ye husbands, dwell with them according to knowledge, giving honour unto the wife, as unto the weaker vessel, and as being heirs together of the grace of life; that your prayers be not hindered* (1 Peter 3:7). Do you want your prayers hindered? I was stunned when I first read this verse. I am sure if men are aware of this verse they will treat their wives better.

Adhere to the principles in the scriptures and use common sense to do little things, such as taking or sending flowers to her or giving compliments on the meals she prepares, her new outfit or hair style. Remember special days such as, birthdays, anniversaries, and so forth. Open the car door, pull the chair out for her to sit and call from work to let her know you are thinking of her. Tell her she is beautiful and tell her often that you love her. Take a walk down memory lane sometimes and rekindle the admiration you had when you first met her. Those earlier memories hold the key-they are your *why*-the reasons you fell I love with her.

Do the things she asks you to do to get things in order in the house; do not wait and let her do them herself. The reason she asked you could be because it was a difficult task for her. Would you want her to ask another man to come into your home to do the task that you have ignored for days, weeks or months? Honor her in front of her children and friends at all times. Make an effort to align with your wife, have harmony and create synergy and balance in your marriage. Remember, you are the *head*. According to the Miriam-Webster Dictionary online, the head is the "seat of the intellect; one in charge." If you are in charge, you must lead, and leaders are expected to demonstrate exemplary characteristics.

Sometimes people who are newly-wed find it difficult to create a balance in their relationship because they are still looking out, perhaps to friends and family or they are self-absorbed. It is important to note that it is no longer about "me, mine, or me, myself and I (the unholy trinity)." It is now "we, us and, ours." Marriage is a mutual affair-it is between two people, yet there must be oneness. It is binding and it is fun when divine principles are applied. It would help if you set some standards, and expectations together prior to marriage-that is a good place to start. Make a list of the things you think an ideal marriage should reflect or that you would like to see happen in your marriage. Discuss it with your partner. Before getting married, Royston and I verbally agreed upon certain things that we still practice after twenty-five years of marriage. We honor the verbal contract out of pure love, respect, and for the sake of keeping our promise to each other.

As a newly-wed, a man may sometimes find it hard to separate from his friends and the life he was accustomed to living, but it should not take him too long to adjust to the new lifestyle he has chosen. If the man does not wake up to his new role as a partner in marriage, this can put a strain on the relationship. It is essential for newly-weds to spend as much time as possible with each other. I believe it is harder for the man to come to terms with the fact that he is no longer single and needs to spend quality time with his wife.

Communication is another sore topic for many men, yet it is the icing on the relationship cake. It is extremely important for the man to listen to his wife and respond, so that she knows that she has been heard, understood and taken seriously. Keep the line of communication wide open. Turn off the tube and turn on the passion. She should be your best friend, after Christ. You are the head of the household, so take the lead as Joshua did. Joshua contended: *But as for **me** and my **house**, we **will serve** the **LORD*** (Joshua 24:15**).**

According to a story in Acts 16, a jailer asked Paul and Silas what he should do to be saved. They told him that he needed to believe in the Lord Jesus and he, along with his entire household, would be saved. When the man takes the lead, as God intended, it makes a profound impact on the household. I pray that as the man takes the responsibility to lead in his household, he will know, that it is just as important to be willing to have open communication with his wife.

I would like to leave with you this email that I received some time ago; it very beautifully depicts the expectation and value of a woman:"Be very careful if you make a woman cry, because God counts her tears. The woman came out of a man's rib. Not from his feet to be walked on. Not from his head to be superior, but from his side to be EQUAL. Under the arm to be PROTECTED and next to the heart to be LOVED." I do not know to whom credit is due for this, but it is brilliant!

PRINCIPLES FOR DAILY APPLICATION

(1) Put God first in your life, marriage, work and in everything else you do. Maintain your individuality, but do things in oneness and with mutual understanding. *But **seek** ye **first** the kingdom of God, and*

his righteousness; and all these things shall be added unto you (Matthew 6:33).

(2) Love God first then your wife as yourself. ***Husbands, love your wives****, just as Christ* **love***d the church and gave himself up for her* (Ephesians 5:25).

(3) Respect your wife. No other person should come before your spouse or between you and your spouse. Princess Diana said her marriage was "a bit crowded" because of Camilla's presence which contributed to her broken heart; there were three people in that marriage. Make sure the third person in your marriage is God. He fixes problems, He does not cause them: *And if one prevail against him, two shall withstand him; and a* ***threefold cord*** *is not quickly broken* (Ecclesiastes 4:12). When you are overwhelmed with circumstance in your marriage, be aware that your wife is never the enemy. Abaddon is constantly trying to destroy anything that God created. The Word instructs*:* ***Husbands, love your wives****, and be not bitter against them* (Colossians 3:19).

(4) Spend quality time together. Make a date each week. It can be as simple as going for a walk together, going out to dinner or to the movie. Plan to get away, just you and your wife, as often as possible, especially on your wedding anniversaries. Look for a couple's retreat and attend. These are just a few things that can enrich your marriage. This is difficult to do when you have children, but you can hire a babysitter or utilize family and friends who you trust.

(5) Have a sense of oneness, mutual understanding, planning, and agreement-especially when children are involved. Be consistent in the rules you agree upon for the family.

(6) Support her interests and desires. Feel her pain and show some emotion. Rejoice in each other's victories. Be your wife's best friend and confidant.

(7) Set goals with her. Review, revise, revamp, agree, and commit. Make decisions, pray and seek God's guidance when things get tough and you feel like giving up on her, your children or even life.

PRAYER:

Father God, the Father of all fathers, I honor and submit to You. Thank You for blessing me with my beautiful wife, whom I cherish.

I confess any wrongs that I have done to her, and I ask You to forgive me. I promise to be the best husband that I can be. I will have no other woman, besides her. I will love my wife unconditionally. I will not cause her to feel any less than You created her to be. I will respect her, protect her, love, support and care for her in all her Godly endeavors. Please help me to be a better communicator. I responsibly accept my role as the head of our household, and I will lead according to Your precepts. In Jesus' name, Amen.

CHAPTER 18
THE WIFE THE VIRTUOUS WOMAN

Wives, submit to your **husbands***, as is fitting in the Lord*
Colossians 3:18.

House and riches are the inheritance of fathers:
and a prudent wife is from the LORD
Proverbs 19:14.

For the husband is the head of the wife, even as Christ is the
head of the church: and he is the saviour of the body
Ephesians 5:23.

In the same way, you wives must accept the authority of your
husbands, even those who refuse to accept the Good News. Your
Godly lives will speak to them better than any words. They will
be won over by watching your pure Godly behavior
1 Peter 3:1-2.

She considereth a field, and buyeth it: with the
fruit of her hands she planteth a vineyard.
She girdeth her loins with strength, and strengtheneth her arms.
She perceiveth that her merchandise is good:
her candle goeth not out by night.
She layeth her hands to the spindle, and her hands hold the distaff.
She stretcheth out her hand to the poor; yea, she
reacheth forth her hands to the needy.
She is not afraid of the snow for her household: for
all her household are clothed with scarlet.
She maketh herself coverings of tapestry; her clothing is silk and purple.
Her husband is known in the gates, when he

sitteth among the elders of the land.
She maketh fine linen, and selleth it; and
delivereth girdles unto the merchant.
Strength and honour are her clothing; and
she shall rejoice in time to come.
She openeth her mouth with wisdom; and in
her tongue is the law of kindness.
She looketh well to the ways of her household,
and eateth not the bread of idleness.
Her children arise up, and call her blessed; her
husband also, and he praiseth her.
Many daughters have done virtuously, but thou excellest them all.
Favour is deceitful, and beauty is vain: but a woman
that feareth the LORD, she shall be praised.
Give her of the fruit of her hands; and let her
own works praise her in the gates.
Proverbs 31.

Proverbs 31 is a fascinating chapter, filled with wisdom for every woman. The union of marriage is a continuous work in progress, and everyone who has ever been married can attest to that. There are happy moments, and sad moments, but no matter what moment it is in a marriage, it should be embraced, as each moment serves a purpose. God has a plan for every marriage and sometimes His plan hurts, but His plan is still the best. God's grace helps us to prevail through every storm. I have learned to put God in the center of my marriage, and I have seen that there are great benefits to doing so. It is harder for the enemy to penetrate and cause chaos. The deceiver will work overtime to prevent a wife from submitting to her husband. He entices her with the, I want my own independence attitude.

As a young wife, I struggled with the idea of submitting to my husband, because I did not fully understand what it meant to submit to him. As I matured and began to spend more time reading God's Word and seeking His guidance, I found out how important it is to submit to my husband. I must admit, I am still working on it, in certain areas. The Word of God says, wives are to be submitted to their husbands, just as the husbands should submit to Christ. If I am dedicated to live for Christ, I am obligated to study, understand, and apply His Word to my marriage and life with wisdom.

What does it mean to submit? To ascertain that I was following this principle, I researched the word submit and I found this: The Greek verb *hypotasso* means, "to put in subjection, subject, and subordinate, put under, obedient." As I read through this list of words, I asked myself: Do women want to be all these things to their husbands? And I thought, maybe not, but as children of God that is the mandate we have been given. A wife must be willing to follow the dictates of the Word. The Word declares that the husband is the head of the wife, as Christ is the head of the husband and of the church. The Greek word for wife, *issa*, literally means, "*woman*, in contrast to man."

Men are different from women because God created them that way. They think differently, are built differently, and do things differently from the ways in which women do them. This is a fact of nature by design, which is irreversible and should be understood by wives. We women sometimes forget our position in the marriage, but the scripture quoted above-1 Peter 3:1-2, clearly states that wives are to accept the authority of their husbands. There is no doubt that this could be a difficult task for some wives, because of the irresponsibility of some husbands, but that does not change or alter the mandate.

God knew the circumstances that couples would face in marriages; hence the reason He gave us 1 Peter 3:1-7. There are many instances when a woman gives her life to Christ, but her husband is not ready to do so. This can create problems and tension in a marriage. When this happens, the best thing to do is to pray and ask God to change his heart, and be patient with him. The worst thing you could do is try to change or push him to accept Christ. Remember, just as God made the change in you, He will make changes in your husband at the right times. Be the best role model for him, and he will desire what you have. The gift of salvation is most desirable when it is exercised in the right way. He will not be able to resist the ways of the Lord for too long.

Women are naturally nurturing, with a caring mother-nurture attitude and instinct. We like to assume responsibility and get things done when we want them done. Quite often this can be a disadvantage, because we end up end up taking on our husbands' roles. Wives-the truth is that we should excuse ourselves from the man's role. The sooner we realize the importance of this biblical principle, the better our marriage relationships will be! As wives, there are components that we need to bring to our marriage to support our husbands. Wives are their husbands' "help meets," and every husband needs a wife who is going to stand with, and help him meet the necessities of the marriage. This popular saying is a reminder: "Behind every successful man is a strong, supportive and good woman."

When you have done all you can, just stand, and let God do the rest. An acquaintance of mine (newly-wed) recently took me back to my earlier years of marriage, when she told me that she consults her husband about everything. (I mean everything), especially financial decisions, before she makes a purchase-even as small as two dollars. I remember being that way myself. That might be a good thing, after all-she is still happily married!

As my husband and I became more seasoned in our marriage, we allowed each other to make small financial decisions, but we found that it was always important to consult each other before making financial decisions that required larger sums. We have an example in Sarah, Abraham's wife. The scripture says: *For after this manner in the old time the holy women also, who trusted in God, adorned themselves, being in subjection unto their own husbands: Even as Sara obeyed Abraham, calling him lord: whose daughters ye are, as long as ye do well, and are not afraid with any amazement* (1 Peter 3:5-6).

To submit does not mean to bow down and be our husband's footstool. The only One to whom a woman should bow is her heavenly Father. Submission simply means to respect him and allow him to assume his role as the head of the household, as God designed him to be. If this law is violated, it infringes on the man's ego and could cause self-esteem issues, which will then backfire in the sense that the wife has to live with a husband who is miserable, due to low self-esteem. The key is to understand the principles and apply them consistently.

Do not be anxious to *fix* your husband, because you simply cannot do it. We wish we had found this out earlier in our marriage. Royston and I celebrated our twenty-fifth Wedding Anniversary this year, June 23, 2009. After twenty-five years of marriage, I know for a fact that you cannot fix your husband, but one thing I do know is that there is a Man who can. I could give you quite a few nuggets, but most importantly is this one: Do not argue with your husband about the things you consider to be constant or consistent issues, if together you have not been able to resolve them. This would be like beating your head against a rock and being a nagging wife. That might cause contention and the Bible warns against that: *A continual dripping on a very rainy day And a contentious woman are alike*; (Proverbs 27:15) (NKJ).

Instead, take all of your concerns to Almighty God, give them to Him, and ask Him to deal with them. He will deliver and set you free. He will give you peace as you ride out the storms in your marriage. Just trust Him! He may not do it all at one time or in the way you expect, but He will be right on time. Getting to a place in your marriage where you can relax in peace and harmony is a gradual process. It takes time for God to chisel away at habits in both the husband and the wife in order to bring a couple to a more common ground.

You will discover that one of the key pieces to surviving and thriving in a marriage is not to waste your time and energy fighting with your husband over small stuff. The husband's responsibilities are different from yours and you are responsible for fulfilling yours. Have faith in God, and trust Him with any battle you face in your marriage relationship. He does a far better job than you, any counselor or pastor can. The solution is not to look for an escape route, such as a separation or a divorce. It is rather to see the lessons in every trial, and learn from them. Muster up with all the strength you have and let satan know that you are in charge, not him; therefore you will not listen to His lies. If tempter tells you to talk at, yell, throw things, scream or belittle your husband ignore him. Be aware of these traps that the evil one will tempt you to use against your husband: "you are worthless," "you never," "you always (in a negative tone)," recalling and dwelling on old unpleasant memories, trying to correct him, not talking to him, or leaving your husband. These things really do not help God's plans to be accomplished. The solution I find that works all the times is asking the Holy Spirit to help me to take everything to Jesus, and let Him work out those things that I find are difficult for me to work out by myself or with my husband.

PRINCIPLES FOR DAILY APPLICATION

(1) Love your husband unconditionally, and allow him to be the head of the household. Do not ever try to change him; only God can do that. Sometimes, it may seem to you that he changed from the person you married. Understand that people do change some of their habits over time, but the person you married is still the same person, no matter what circumstances may arise. As the saying goes, "men will be men." Allow him to be the man. *For the husband is the head of the wife, even as Christ is the head of the church: and he is the saviour of the body* (Ephesians 5:23).

(2) Know and understand his likes and dislikes and try to do nice things for him to keep the love light burning. Cook his favorite meals, especially on special occasions. See him off when he leaves for work, and be there to greet him when he returns home. Sometimes you have to deny yourself to meet his needs. He may not communicate his love to you the way in which you hope, but you can know if he really loves you by his actions.

(3) Do not take revenge, because two wrongs do not fix the situation, but could potentially make matters worse. You will need to agree to disagree and find a middle ground. Have mutual understanding. Throw the darts at the enemy, not at your husband. Cut him some slacks!

(4) Offer to pick up the tabs for the movie, dinner out or vacation get away. You leave the tips sometimes. Give him the support he needs and avoid intimate relationships with other all other men.

(5) Acknowledge his efforts and show gratitude and appreciation for the special help he
offers and the extra things he does. Stroke his head, especially if it is bald. He will like it and it will be a soothing feeling to you as well.

(6) Keep yourself well groomed. Be aware of your physical appearance. Get in a fitness program. Keep yourself up, just as you give your car check-ups to make sure it is in good running condition.

(7) Pray, pray, pray for God's divine hedge of protection around your marriage. Be thankful for your husband. Do not give up on your marriage too easily. Your husband needs you, even when his actions do not convey that. The deceiver will try to make you give up, but always remember your reasons for falling in love and for getting married in the first place.

PRAYER:

Dear heavenly Father, I honor You, and I submit to my husband, as he submits to You. I thank You for blessing me with my handsome husband, whom I appreciate and love. I am sorry for the times I treated him in an ungodly way, for lack of knowledge. Father God, Your Word said in Hosea 4:6 that Your people perish for lack of knowledge. I pray, Lord, that we will no longer remain ignorant to Your Word and Your Principles. Give me the courage to educate myself through reading, meditating on, and praying Your Word. I release my husband to take authority as the head of our household, and I thank You that I am a faithful help meet. I submit to Your will now, totally and completely so that Your Spirit can have His way in my life and teach me how to be the best wife to my husband. Please teach me how to be an un-biased and committed wife. I will no longer walk in darkness or ignorance of the truth, because there is no darkness in You, the omniscient One. Help me to practice being the light and salt of this earth, as well as being a virtuous wife, as the woman in Proverbs 31. I realize that I am Your daughter, and Your Holy Spirit leads me according to Romans 8 verse 14. I resist the evil one and all his temptations. I abide in You and Your truth sets me free. I humbly bow before You in reverence now, and forevermore, Amen.

CHAPTER 19

TO THE PARENTS-YOUR CHILDREN
THE BLESSINGS FROM THE LORD

Children are a gift from the Lord; they are a reward from Him
Psalm 127:3-5.

Train up a child in the way he should go: and when
he is old, he will not depart from it
Proverbs 22:6.

Children's children are the crown of old men; and
the glory of children are their fathers
Proverb 17:6.

And now a word to you father. Don't make your children angry
by the way you treat them. Rather bring them up with
the discipline and instruction approved by the Lord
Ephesians 6:4.

Except the LORD build the house, they labour in vain that build it:
Psalm 127:1.

Parents have the responsibility to teach their children how to live spiritually and effectively in the fullness of who God created them to be. Parents should set Godly examples and affirm their children often and appropriately. It is the responsibility of the parents to let children know that they have an incredible destiny. Children need to hear from their parents that they can do all things-anything that they put their minds to. They should be well equipped to make the right choices in all of their endeavors.

Being a parent for the past 28 years, I am aware that I am my children's first role model. So I try my best to model behaviors that are congruent with that expectation. In looking at the lives of men such as David and Joshua I see true family men. Joshua knew it was his responsibility to be the head of the household and he proclaimed: *As for me and my house we will serve the Lord* (Joshua 24:15).

Teach your children to apply biblical principles. Help to understand the different experiences that they may face in life and equip them with ways of dealing with such issues. Give them examples of things you encountered along your life's journey. Let them know that they have a divine nature. Pray for, with, and teach them how to pray. Read the Bible to them, and show them how to connect to their power source from an early age. If they get in this habit early, they will never forget it when they grow up, even though they may stray along the way. The Word says to: *Train up a child in the way he should go: and when he is old, he will not depart from it* (Proverbs 22:6).

I vividly recall my earliest experiences. When I was growing up, my grandmother made me go to church every Sunday, even though I cannot recall her going, perhaps because she was too old to walk all that way. I went once in the morning for the service, and again in the afternoon for Sunday School. I also had to participate in seasonal church functions, often singing in the choir, memorizing and studying several Bible verses for recitations. I know my grand-mother did not know the career she was preparing me for and neither did I, but I am thankful for her training. I am forever grateful to all the people who helped to bring Jesus into my life at such an early age.

Children are an integral part of society; in fact they are tomorrow's teachers, leaders, caretakers, lawyers, doctors, civil servants, pastors and to make a long story short; they are the ones who will be assuming the roles and responsibilities that we now have. That is why we must teach them in the right way. I have seen many parents who have had difficult times with their teen aged children, simply because they did not bend the trees while they were young. If you wait until your children become teenagers before you start setting rules and giving guidelines to follow, you will be too late-it will not work. Children whose parents invest quality time in them exhibit attitudes and behaviors far different from those whose parents neglect to instill Godly values. I am not ignorant to the fact that some children who received biblical instructions, chose to do the opposite. Nevertheless, we cannot afford to neglect our parental responsibilities. We need to work on building our children's character in preparation for their roles in society. "Good people leave an inheritance to their children." Inheritance here, does not mean only money, but good behavior, discipline, character, attitude and other attributes. I read in Exodus 20 that whatever you do as a parent could affect your child to the third and fourth generation: *I punish the children for the sins of their parents to the third and fourth generations* (Exodus 20:5).

With this knowledge, every parent should be praying for generational curses and strongholds to be broken, and cast out of their family line so that these things do not follow their children and consequent generations. It behooves us to understand and assume our roles as parents to the best of our abilities. Children need to be brought up in the admonition of the Lord. Teach them the things you have learned along your life's journey and help to protect them from making the same mistakes you, and former generations have made. Solomon, the wisest man who ever lived, left the blueprint for us to emulate as we raise our children, and do other things in life. Solomon instructs: *In the fear of the LORD is strong confidence: and his children shall have a place of refuge. The fear of the LORD is a fountain of life, to depart from the snares of death* (Proverbs 14:26-27). Parents who fear the Lord do what He says, and their children often model.

Let me emphasize; parents, that it is your responsibility to teach your children biblical principles, because if you do not, there is no one to blame for their unacceptable behavior, but yourselves. It is not the teacher's or the pastor's responsibility. It is good that they help, but their responsibility is to their own children. Parents who train their children in biblical principles are not "rebellion proof." Many children who are taught principles rebel against their parents' teachings , which usually results in them learning some tough lessons.

Parents need not take their behaviors to heart, but pray, and trust God to take care of them. If you did your best and instilled the right values, stand still, because Jesus will take care of the rest. Children, like adults, have to learn lessons, and if they choose to learn the hard way, be at peace, even though it will hurt. Children may stray from the path that you have lead, but the lessons will be engraved in the innermost parts of their beings for life. That is what matters-you did your job.

Laying a solid foundation is key. Although a solid foundation does not guarantee that a child will turn out to be the super child every parent wishes to have-it does guarantee your confidence and satisfaction in knowing that you did your best as a parent. They may stray but most likely will return to the right way, and hopefully, not before it is too late.

In the Gospel of Luke a story is told of a prodigal (wasteful) son. In this narrative, the son grew up and decided to leave home. He asked his father for his inheritance. Let's say the son decided not to go to college or to work, so he took the money from his father, did not invest any of it and spent it unwisely until he had nothing left. Things got tough, and he decided to move back home. I believe the prodigal son's father laid the right foundation and that was the reason he was able to realize that he had to get out of the sad situation in which he found himself, and return to the life to which he was accustomed. Obviously, his father taught him well, so when he strayed, he knew how to turn back. A father should assume the responsibility as head of his household. This son's father was a good role model. Paul had some words for fathers when he proclaimed: *And you, fathers, do not provoke your children to wrath, but bring them up in the training and admonition of the Lord* (Ephesians 6:4) (NKJV).

When I heard on the news that children have stockpiled weapons or other dangerous items in their homes, I was amazed that parents could live in a house with their children and not know what they were doing. You have full access to your children's room when they are not at home and when they are at home, because you pay the mortgage or the rent. Until they leave for college or move out, you should be checking their rooms occasionally. I never announced to my children when I was getting ready to check their rooms. Trust me; you will learn a lot of things about your children that you might not have learned otherwise. You do not need to feel that you are imposing or snooping. You are responsible for whatever goes on in your home.

Children need to be protected, instead of being left unsupervised to raise themselves or to be left in the hands of irresponsible people. They should not be sent to a sleep over, unless you are familiar with what goes on in the house of the child who has invited your child to a sleepover. They need to be disciplined by their parents. Children should be taught how to have respect for themselves and others. They should be taught to respect boundaries. Get to know you children's friends; that will give you an indication of who your children really are. As the popular saying goes, "show me your friend and I'll tell you who you are."

Discipline is an aspect of childrearing that has slipped out the back door for many families. This principle seems to be forgotten, but "don't spare the rod and spoil the child." This does not necessarily mean that we should spank or physically abuse our children. The rod can be any form of discipline or even a teaching tool. Your children may get upset with you when you discipline them now, but be consistent; they will thank you for it later.

Discipline comes in many forms, such as withholding things from your child, but not food, shelter, appropriate clothing, education or love, which are a part of their basic needs and are essential for their survival. Children love the luxuries with which they are showered by family and friends. Luxuries such as video games, cell phones, visiting friends or having friends to visit with, watching television or any of the other extra privileges that your children often get. These are just a few of the things that can be withheld and will make them think before they misbehave again.

Do your best to train your children to aim high, and chose excellence over mediocrity an you will have nothing to regret.

PRINCIPLES FOR DAILY APPLICATION

(1) Love your children unconditionally. Children need to have the security of knowing that their parents love them. Hug them often so they may experience the power of a loving touch.

(2) Discipline your children. If you love your children, you will discipline them. When you discipline them in love, you are showing that you want the best for them. Help them to understand that tough love is for their good. The Bible says: *If you refuse to discipline your children, it proves you don't love them: if you love your children, you will be prompt to discipline them* (Proverb 13:24).

(3) Give them encouragement. Praise your children when they get good grades, behave themselves well, or do deeds of kindness. Do it as often as possible. Likewise, let them know when you are not pleased with their actions.

(4) Encourage open communication and trust. Get them to trust you, so that they will share important information with you, instead of with their friends. Let them enjoy life in their unique abilities. Sometimes we tend to forget that we were once children and used to do some of the same things that they are doing. Be transparent with your children, so that they do not make the same mistakes you made. Instill good values in them, teach them affirmations and how to affirm themselves.

(5) Listen to your Children. You can affect changes in your children's lives by listening to them, genuinely complimenting them when they do well. With our busy lifestyles, we do not spend enough time in active listening to our children. Active and reflective listening, show them that we care. The next time your child speaks to you, stop, listen and repeat what your child has said.

(6) Get the necessary skills you need to be the most effective parents you are capable of being. Receive the anointing of the Holy Spirit, so you can boldly speak God's Word into their lives. They may not see it at the time when you are telling them, but eventually they will, and they will thank you for it. Invest in your children's education and in their future. Stay connected with their teachers and functions at their schools. Volunteer at the school when you can. Monitor their education, make sure their education is not being compromised in any way and be their best advocate.

(7) Pray, pray, pray and teach your children how to pray and have gratitude. Help them to discover their talents and nurture their uniqueness. Help them to recognize their strengths and assist them to grow in those areas. For example, if your child is showing interest in music, explore the different aspects of music and musical instruments, starting with the child's visible point of interest. Support their interest and allow them to explore different options. This will help them to find their passion and make the best choices that will prepare them as future leaders. Your child can make use of what is offered at school, and you can pay to have your child take extra lessons in those areas.

PRAYER:

Dear heavenly, Father, thank You for giving me the responsibility of being a parent, by blessing me with children. Father I owe it to You to train my child/children in a Godly way. Thank You for equipping me with all the tools that I need to raise my child/children with unconditional love, support and discipline. Thank You for teaching me how to use biblical principles to perform my work as a parent. Bless me with wisdom and the anointing of Solomon, in every situation as I raise my child/children. Please help me to be an excellent role model for my child/children and help me to help other children who do not have parental support. In Jesus' holy and precious name I pray, Amen.

CHAPTER 20
TO THE CHILDREN GIFTS FROM GOD

*Honor your father and your mother, so that you may live
long in the land the LORD your God is giving you*
Exodus 20:12.

*Children, obey your parents in the Lord: for this is the right thing to
do. Honor your father and mother. This is the first commandment
with a promise: If you honor your father and mother, things will
go well for you, and you will have a long life on the earth*
Ephesians 6:1-3 (NKJV).

Children, obey your parents in all things: for this is well pleasing unto the Lord
Colossians 3:20.

*And this is the promise: If you honor your father and
mother, you will live a long life full of blessings*
Ephesians 6:3.

Even a child is known by his deeds, by whether what he does is pure and right
Proverb 20:11.

Children-listen to me! You are a gift from the Lord and you must obey your parents, because that is what the Lord says you are to do. Your parents are your gifts from God. Let Ephesians 6:1-3 be one of your favorite scripture readings. When I was a child I had to memorize these verses, and they would always surface when I was tempted to disobey. Most parents discipline their children when they disobey or misbehave. Good parents discipline children because they love them.

When you accept discipline from your parents, and from those to whose care you have been entrusted, you are wise. Read that for yourself in Proverbs 13:1. You can do it even if your parents are not supportive, or even present. The only time you should disobey your parents is if they tell you to do wrong things; sadly enough some parents do teach their children wrongs. For example, to get involved with drugs, beg, steal or to commit other kinds of crimes or sin. Read Exodus 20 and it will teach you the Ten Commandments. The Ten Commandments, sometimes, referred to as "the moral or royal law," is instruction that was given to Moses by God for all people to obey and follow. They are God's laws and the guide that help us to know what sin is and how we should live. When we obey them we learn how to avoid sin, and live our best lives. When you read these laws and adhere to the principles, you please God-the One who gave you life and instructions by which to live. As you follow these commandments, as well as the other laws in the Bible, you will find it easier to follow your parent's instructions.

Sometimes you do not follow through with your chores and other instructions that your parents give you. Maybe you do not feel like doing them, but when you follow the instructions of your parents, you are pleasing God and you are learning to be responsible. Being responsible is a quality that you will need to have as an adult in order to be a productive citizen in your community and world. When you become a man or a woman, you will have to work. Chores get you in the habit of working and they prepare you to face the challenges that you will encounter at work and in life. In the book of Proverbs, Chapter 10 verses 4 and 5, it is declared that, *lazy people are soon poor; hard workers get rich. A wise youth works hard all summer: a youth who sleeps away the hour of opportunity brings shame.* No need for me to explain this verse, it is self-explanatory.

Paul, an apostle of Jesus and the author of many of the books in the New Testament of the Holy Bible, wrote in the book of Philippians, Chapter 4:13 *I can do all things through Christ which strengtheneth me.* So can you, because you are God's own special creation. There is an inner person in you; some people may call it gut or conscience. I call Him the Holy Spirit. Listen to that inner person. He will guide, teach, and counsel you. You can be whatever God wants you to be. God created you with your own special, unique gifts. It is okay to want to be like a person who you admire, but always remember that you were created to be yourself, and to be like Jesus.

Affirm yourself every day by saying things such as," I am uniquely designed for God's purpose," "I am beautiful," (if you are a girl), or "I am handsome" (if you are a boy), "I am smart," "I am walking in my destiny," "I am a child of the living God," "I am wise," "I am excellent," "I am a genius," "I am exceptional," and so forth. When you affirm something, you are declaring that you believe that thing to be true. You will feel good about yourself when you understand and claim who you really are.

Allow your inner person to guide you to many good things. Psalm 139:13-14 tell us that God made all the delicate, inner parts of our bodies and knit us together in our mothers' wombs and that we are fearfully and wonderfully made. God knew you and assigned your special purpose before you were born. If you do not obey Him, the devil can ruin or take your life while you are still young. He can take away all the good things that you inherit from Jesus Christ. He can take away your courage, dignity, determination, strength, wisdom, knowledge, love, and all the good things that God gave you and wants you to keep.

Put your trust in God, no matter the situation in which you may find yourself. The Bible says: *Trust in the LORD with all thine heart; and lean not unto thine own understanding* (Proverbs 3:5). For example, if you are a child who was born out of wedlock, adopted, or living with a foster parent/parents or a single parent, you are to be grateful. You are no different from the child whose parents are married, who lives with his or her biological parents, has two parents, or who has wealthy parents who buy them everything for which they ask and more. God created you just as special as the other child who you may think is better than you are, for whatever reason. The real difference is in who you know you are and who you decide to become, how you will use your mind and all the gifts that God gave you. In a simpler term, it is the choices that you make that will determine how you fare in life.

Let me explain something to you. Since I have had firsthand experience with this situation. Many children were born to unmarried parents. If you were born out of wedlock, do not be concerned about it. Chances are that your parents have already repented of their sins, the

Lord has forgiven them, and they have moved on and found peace in that situation. Try to understand that God used your parents in that situation to be a testimony for someone. Your birth was not a mistake, because God has a purpose for your life. However, remember that this is not to say that it is okay for you to have children before you are married. It is not okay. I encourage you to abstain from having pre-marital sex, as it could ruin your life. Venereal diseases are contracted through sexual intercourse and you do not want these diseases.

For a long time it bothered me that I had a child before I got married, because I knew I disobeyed God. Fornication is having sex when you are not married. It is not a sin only when you get caught or when you become pregnant; it is a sin to have sex before marriage, period. That is why your parents teach you to abstain from having sex. Pregnancy can only occur through sexual intercourse. I regretted my disobedient action that produced my daughter out of wedlock, but I have never regretted having my child. Since having sex before you are married is wrong and abortion is wrong, the safest and best thing to do is to abstain from having sex until you are married. There is nothing wrong with doing that and according to Bible teachings, that is the correct way. Do not let your peers tell you otherwise.

My husband, Royston, who married me two years after our first daughter, Shauna was born, gave her love, and we raised her together as best we knew how. It was not too difficult for us because we had her in our early twenties-not in our teen years. We had completed the first part of our college education, and had jobs. The Lord has forgiven us for having a child before we were married, and we have moved on with our lives. Shauna turned out pretty well. She is a college graduate and a captain in the United States Army. She is married, and does not yet have a child. I am grateful that this generational curse of having children out of wedlock has been broken, and my prayer is that future generations will follow in her footsteps. Having had this experience myself, I am able to share it with you and I hope that it will help you to choose purity or abstinence over sex before marriage. If I have a chance to do things over again, I will choose abstinence.

If you are a teenager and you are not married, please think about the consequences of having sex. The best thing that you can do for yourself is to abstain and save yourself until you are ready to make a covenant with God and the man he will send to you (if you are a female) or the woman He will send you, (if you are a male), to be your spouse. If you have already made this mistake or any other, and have not asked for forgiveness, and moved on with your life, do it now. Your heavenly Father is waiting to hear the words, "I am sorry, Lord, please forgive me. I surrender my life to You and promise to abstain from sin." Do not let any past mistakes keep you from living in the fullness of what God has ordained for you.

For Christ's sake, once you have said that concise prayer, accept God's forgiveness and move on to the greater things that He has planned for you. God will supply all your needs, so you should depend on Him, and on no one else. He is the only one who will never fail you, and He will never ever leave you. If you find yourself in a lonely place, know that it may be lonely in the physical, but in the spiritual sense, your Savior is with you, and is always interceding with God on your behalf. Your seemingly tough situation will pass. Be patient with God. He is always patient with you.

God always speaks to His children who are willing to listen. There are times when you will hear another voice that tries to tell you to do bad things, but do not listen to that voice. That is the enemy trying to trick you into doing things with which Your Father in heaven would not be pleased. Always remember that your number one purpose is to please God. Do not discount Him in any way, even if you cannot figure out every little detail about what is going on in your life or in the lives of those around you. Proverbs 20:24 says that you can understand the road you travel, by knowing that it is the Lord who directs your steps.

Love is one of the main ingredients in the recipe of a successful life. You first need to know that God loves you very much. Read John 3:16. It is very important to love yourself. When you love yourself, you accept yourself just as you are. You will not want to be like others. You will also find it easier to love others as you love yourself. God has placed the love that you need within you. You are beautiful or handsome, depending on your sex. It does not matter how you may think you look or how others say you look, just know that in God's eyes you are beautiful or handsome. God created you in His image-as His very special design, and there is no one else like you. Someone may have said something to you that hurt your feelings, but all you have to do with that is shake it off, and keep on going. Martin Luther King, Jr., said: "No one can make you feel inferior, unless you allow them to."

If someone says something that is not nice to you, you do not have to receive it, unless that comment is in your best interest. No matter what people say about you, it cannot change who you are. Keep your character clean and no one will be able to steal your dignity. Use negative comments as sources of motivation, by turning them into positive actions. Use them in a beneficial way, knowing that you can choose not to let anyone blemish your character or steal your joy.

Jesus loves you, and wants the best for you. You will go through some challenges in life, but the Lord will remain with you through all of them. He promises: *I will never leave thee, nor forsake thee* (Hebrews 13:5). When you are facing challenging times and experiencing trials, be confident that you are sacrificing yourself for the Lord. The burdens you bear are tests that will make you stronger for each step on your journey with Christ. Jesus bore much more burdens for our sake when He died on the cross at Calvary. Ultimately, Christ takes our burdens when we trust Him. One psalmist said: Cast *thy burden upon the LORD, and he shall sustain thee: he shall never suffer the righteous to be moved* (Psalm 55:22).

Peer pressure might be one of the biggest issues that you face, but you can simplify things for yourself by making one of the only two choices you have in life: to do "good" (things to please the Lord) or "evil" (things to please satan). By choosing the former you are making God the first priority and ruler over your life, and also putting Jesus first. The Bible teaches that we should seek the Kingdom of God first and he will add everything else to our lives. I know this is the best and most important choice you could ever make in life.

Ask the Lord, Jesus Christ to direct your path and to show you right from wrong-every single day of your life, because you want to please Him. Paul encourages you to listen to the Word of God instead of giving in to peer pressure. He said: *Then we will no longer be immature like children. We won't be tossed and blown about by every wind of new teaching. We will not be influenced when people try to trick us with lies so clever they sound like the truth* (Ephesians 4:14) (NLT). Be aware that your peers do not know any more than you do, because they do not have life experiences-your parents do. They have been there and done that! They love you and want the very best for you, so be honest with them and they will advise and assist you. Trust in God; He has all the answers you need.

God is Jehovah Jireh, our provider. He has promised to give you everything you need. Expensive shoes and clothes should not matter. You should not become sad, or feel left out when your parents cannot afford to buy you the same types of clothing that some of your friends wear. Jesus said that we should not worry about these things, because they are just temporary things. Rather we must focus on the things of God-they are eternal. Be sure to read your Bible every day, and you will see for yourself the truth about what God really desires for you.

What will you decide to do? Will you walk with Jesus, or with your peers who are going the wrong way? Will you be yourself, and not try to be like anyone else? Remember what I said before-God created only one of you; there is no other person like you. People may tell you that you look like such, and such a person, or you act like so and so, but whether they are referring to your parents or someone else, that does not mean that you do not have your own identity and unique authentic self. No one can tell you who you are. Your physical appearance does not dictate who you are on the inside. God and you are the only ones who know this side of you.

As you go through life, you will find yourself struggling to find answers to some of your questions. When things puzzle you, and you ask your parents or others questions for which you cannot get the answers, ask God. If He does not give you the answer, save the questions for when you see Jesus, because there are some things we will never be able to figure out, or find the answers to while we are on this earth. The Bible tells us: *The secret things belong to the Lord our God, but those things which are revealed belong to us and to our children forever, that we may do all the words of the law* (Deuteronomy 29:29). I trust that it is your hope and desire to see Jesus one day. I love you, your parents love you more (even if at this moment you have valid reasons to believe differently), and Jesus loves you the most.

PRINCIPLES FOR DAILY APPLICATION

(1) Be obedient to your parents. You are promised a long life if you do. In the book of Ephesians are these instructions: *Children, obey your parents in the Lord: for this is right. Honour thy father and mother; which is the first commandment with promise. That it may be well with thee, and thou mayest live long on the earth* (Ephesians 6:1-3).

(2) Accept Jesus as your Lord and Savior and put your trust in Him. He will give you the directions for your life. Proverbs 3:5-6 encourages you: *Trust in the LORD with all thine heart; and lean not unto thine own understanding. In all thy ways acknowledge him, and he shall direct thy paths.* Read Matthew 6:33.

(3) Respect yourself and others. When you are dressed in clothing that reveals areas of your body that should be covered, that does not show that you respect yourself. If you do not respect yourself, others will not respect you. Girls, 1 Timothy 2:9 says that you should adorn yourselves in modesty. Modest means not showy or obscene.

(4) Love others. The Bible teaches that we should love everyone, even our enemies. Do not tease or bully other children, as that could affect their self-esteem for life. Do you like being teased or bullied? Be nice!

(5) Keep your priorities in order. Go to school and get a good education. Do not waste your years in idleness. Once you have an education, no one can take it away from you. If you do not have an education, that could be used against you when you want to progress in life. You could become miserable and feel hopeless.

(6) Figure out what your purpose in life is, and work toward that end. If you fail, try again until you win. You can figure out what your purpose is through prayer, by making observations of the things you like to do and have fun doing, by listening to your parents, teachers, mentors, coach, and by spending time speaking with your school counselors to find out the different types of careers that exist. Write and repeat your own affirmations and keep a journal.

(7) Pray, pray, pray. Prayer is a tool you can use to form a close relationship with God, while you are seeking His direction for your life. Be thankful always!

PRAYER:

Dear heavenly Father, I know that You have called me to great things. According to Your Word, I am the head and not the tail. I am the first and not the last; therefore, I will be a leader and not a follower. I thank You for blessing me with life, parents, brothers, sisters, teachers, counselors, coaches, mentors, pastors, friends and family. Lord, my peers and I do not know everything; my parents know more, and You alone, know everything. Please help me to accept my parents' discipline, so that I can be wise, as Your Word declares in Proverbs 13:1.

I confess all of my sins to You, now (name your sins). I ask You to forgive me and remove anything in me that displeases You. I thank You that my character is impeccable, my body is pure, my heart is clean, and I know You. I thank You for giving me understanding, clarity and revelation when I read your Word. Thank You for making me special and for ordering my steps. Thank You for my divine education, wisdom and knowledge. Thank You for rebuking the enemy from my life and for helping me to walk in pure light, that I am not misled by anyone in any way. I thank You that I do not rebel against You or disobey my parents. Thank You for sending the Holy Spirit and the angels to give me divine direction, favor, guidance, protection and help all the days of my life. In Jesus' name, Amen.

CHAPTER 21
MONEY IS A PART OF THE FORMULA

Now he that ministereth seed to the sower both minister bread for your food,
and multiply your seed sown, and increase the fruits of your righteousness
2 Corinthians 9:10.

*For the **love** of **money** is the root of all evil: which while some*
coveted after, they have erred from the faith, and
pierced themselves through with many sorrows
1 Timothy 6:10.

*For it is easier for a camel to go through a **needle's eye**, than*
for a rich man to enter into the kingdom of God
Luke 18:25.

The Lord is My shepherd; I shall not want
Psalm 23:1.

For unto whomsoever much is given, of him shall be much required: and
to whom men have committed much, of him they will ask the more
Luke 12:48.

Many people, especially those who were born and grew up in poverty have misconceptions about being rich or about becoming wealthy. Some of the misconceptions I have heard include: in order to be a Christian, one has to be poor; one cannot love God and want to have a lot of money; or only certain people have money.

My personal misconception was that there was no need for me to accumulate riches, as long as I had everything I needed because I am spiritually rich as a child of God. My reasoning was that it was not

193

worth storing riches here on this earth because I was going to leave it all when I go to heaven. This misconception changed when I became more aware of the vast majority of ways in which I could use a lot of money to impact people's lives at a greater level and help make the world a better place. There are many who suffer in poverty, some are malnourished, and others do not have what we consider to be the basic needs-water, food and clothing- much less healthcare. In addition, there are many organizations that are helping to feed hungry families, build wells for those who have no drinking water, build homes, spread the Gospel and support orphans among other charitable work.

Misconceptions are lies that keep people ignorant to the truth. There is nothing good about poverty. It is a sin that makes people do bad things such as gamble, starve, blame others, steal, justify wrong doings, fight, become addicted to substances and even commit murder and suicide. These things happen in generation after generation and need to be broken and put to an end-period.

The understanding and application of biblical principles can erase these misconceptions and bring people into their places of wealth, abundance and prosperity. In Genesis 1:28, God said, *Be fruitful, and multiply, and replenish the earth, and subdue it: and have dominion over the fish of the sea, and over the fowl of the air, and over every living thing that moveth upon the earth.* This verse is interpreted by many as referring to having children, but this verse encompasses all of God's creations, including money and every good thing with which you are involved. If you are wondering how you can multiply in the area of your finances, the principles are laid out in the Bible.

I made a decision to break out of the poverty mind-set and embrace the promises of my great provider (Jehovah Jireh). Releasing the stronghold of a poverty mind-set is a critical step. This has to be done by thinking positive thoughts and taking actions to eradicate negative ones. Begin to apply and accept the spiritual blessings of prosperity and abundance. Just as Christ came to deliver us from sin, He delivers us from the curse of poverty. *For ye know the grace of our Lord Jesus Christ, that, though he was rich, yet for your sakes he became poor, that ye through his poverty might be rich* (2 Corinthians 8:9). In John 10:10 we are reminded that Jesus came to give us an abundant life. This is the life we need to embrace. These are the thoughts we want to entertain.

Living in financial prosperity, requires will-power, an investment mind-set, making intelligent financial decisions, taking proper actions, having a steadfast determination and discipline to break the curse of poverty. Let me emphasize-we must believe that it is God's will for us to live an abundant life. The Lord says, *Beloved, I wish in ALL things that thou mayest prosper and be in health, even as thy soul prospereth* (3 John 1:2). Jehovah Jireh has promised prosperity to His children, and His Word never lies. In order to reap the benefits of God's promises we must stop believing the lies that enemy tells us about our finances. We must begin to take control over our spending habits, rid ourselves of the misconceptions that poison our minds from having a positive outlook on our financial lives. Can you envision the possibilities if we get it right?

Jesus told a parable in Matthew about a man who had three servants to whom he entrusted his money in order for them to invest it. Two of the men followed his instructions. They invested the money and doubled the amount as a result. The third man found all kinds of excuses and hid the money instead of investing it. Does this sound familiar?

In the end, all the money was taken away from the man who hoarded his money and was given to the men who invested the portions given to them. The investors were called faithful. I believe it is the same way the Lord treats us when it comes to money. This is a practical lesson to show us that if we are not good stewards of the money God has given us, He will not give us more or He may take what He gave us and give it to a better money manager. What will you choose to do with the money that God has entrusted to you? Invest, spend, squander, give or hoard? The decision you make will determine your financial status, future and the extent of your financial blessings. Only what is done for Christ will last; everything else is temporary. If your money is not being used for God's purposes, your money is not guaranteed to last. You must sow into the Kingdom in order to reap Kingdom reward. Kingdom reward is everlasting.

It is not a coincidence that verses such as these are in the Bible: *And that which fell among thorns are they, which, when they have heard, go forth, and are choked with cares and riches and pleasures of this life, and bring no fruit to perfection* (Luke 8:14); *And he said unto them, Take heed, and beware of covetousness: for a man's life consisteth not in the abundance of the things which he possesseth* (Luke 12:15*); Though while he lived he counted himself blessed and men praise you when you prosper, he will join the generation of his fathers, who will never see the light of life. A man who has riches without understanding is like the beasts that perish* (Psalm 49:18-20); Jesus said: *So is he that layeth up treasure for himself, and is not rich toward God* (Luke 12:21).

The psalmist said: *Lo, this is the man that made not God his strength; but trusted in the abundance of his riches, and strengthened himself in his wickedness* (Psalm 52:7). Jesus said, *But God said unto him, Thou fool, this night thy soul shall be required of thee: then whose shall those things be, which thou hast provided?* (Luke 12:20). Some people go to the extreme to hoard money. They love money so much that they forget to whom the money really belongs. It is written: *For the love of money is the root of all evil* (1 Timothy 6:10). With due respect to the rich, there are some who hoard their monies; watch people around the world starve; children die from malnutrition, and diseases. In spite of these grave conditions, many continue to hoard their monies and do nothing to help the poor and needy. Such individuals will have to give an account to God.

God will allow anyone to get rich, but if the wealth is not being used for the advancement God's Kingdom, it will be given to the righteous who will use the money for the sake of building God's Kingdom. The wise man Solomon explained it this way: *A good man leaveth an inheritance to his children's children: and the wealth of the sinner is laid up for the just* (Proverb 13:22). This verse clearly indicate that those who store up their wealth and do not use it for the Kingdom of God will lose it.

Read Psalm 73 for further insight into Proverbs 13:22. Psalm 73 supports the preceding statement and scripture. It will help the wealthy ungodly person to understand why it is written in the Bible that one should not be deceived, because God is not mocked. Psalm 73 will also help believers who are struggling to understand why they should not be disheartened by the fact that many unbelievers appear to be more prosperous than believers. The psalmist reminds: *Do not be overawed when a man grows rich, when the splendor of his house increases; for he will take nothing with him when he dies, his splendor will not descend with him* (Psalm 49:16-17) (NIV). The enemy is constantly working to keep the non-believing people blinded and the believers doubting. That is what happens when we view things with our natural eyes. We need to develop our spiritual insight.

Life is not about spending so we can live like the *Joneses-*, having a big house with ostentatious furniture or décor (one that we can hardly pay for). It is not about having a big car that loses value as soon as it is driven off the parking lot at the dealership. It is not about having fancy clothes, nails and hair. What does the Lord have to say about this? *And he said unto them, Take heed, and beware of covetousness: for a man's life consisteth not in the abundance of the things which he possesseth* (Luke 12:15).

Let us work on being good stewards of the money with which God has blessed us. This means we must look at the big picture, make a plan for our finances and seek God's guidance in the process. Up to this point I have not done my best, but with this new awareness, I look forward to a better financial future. Spending on impulse should not come into play. Sticking to a financial plan will help to control unnecessary spending. When we crave material things, things after the flesh or things that are temporal, we become distracted from the bigger picture and the main plan. We are often tempted to spend unwisely, but we have to keep the important things in mind. Life is about having balance in all areas and not neglecting the area of our finances, as many of us seem to do. It is impossible to discuss money without addressing the topic of giving. In the chapter that follows, we will take a look at giving and what the Bible says about it.

PRINCIPLES FOR DAILY APPLICATION

(1) Recognize and admit the reasons you are where you are financially. Take your eyes off of your circumstances. Focus on God so that you can see what He wants to do for you. Make a decision to change your current method, if what you are doing is not working for you. Come up with a plan. Think outside the box. Think prosperity and abundance, because this is a divine ordination of God for those who believe and trust Him. Jesus said: *I am come that they might have life, and that they might have it more abundantly* (John 10:10).

(2) Think about the poor and needy of the world; If you are already doing what you can to help, think of how much more you could do from your overflow: *He that **giveth** unto the **poor** shall not lack: but he that hideth his eyes shall have many a curse* (Proverbs 28:27).

(3) Break the cycles of poverty and help to prepare the next generations to have financial freedom and a better way of life. Erase those negative thoughts and misconceptions about people and money and take actions immediately.

(4) Hire a financial planner to get you started and help you stay on track.

(5) Resist the temptations to spend unnecessarily. Be sure you have a good reason for spending, and it should not be because the item is on sale. I used that line with my husband once when I was about to make one of those impulsive purchases, and he reminded me that there are always sales going on.

(6) Think long term. What do you want your financial future to look like? Contribute to the financial plan, most commonly known as 401K, that your employer offers, even if there is no employer match. At one job that I worked, I was stunned to see that employees did not contribute to their employer's plan that offered a match. While I could not wait for my probationary period to be over so that I could get the benefit of contributing, employees who had been working there for many years did not make use of this benefit. Although God provides for us and tells us not to worry about the future, He expects us to be the Captains of the ships that he has given us. We must use common sense, and make wise decisions.

(7) Pray, pray, pray about finding the right investment tools. Investing your money is the key. There are several books on the market that teach investment strategies. Many authors have written concise instructions on how to get your finances in order. Give thanks for all the resources that are available to you and use them.

PRAYER:

Dear heavenly Father, thank You that You have taught us Your plan for our lives regarding money. Thanks for the principles that You have provided in Your Word. I pray that the body of Christ will embrace those principles in order that Your Kingdom will be enhanced, advanced and expanded. Help us to see money as a necessary part of life and for the building up of Your Kingdom here on earth, and not as something that is for a few people, but for all of us. Help us to understand that we should respect money and be good stewards of it. Help us not to hoard the money You have given us here on earth where it can be stolen, eaten by moths or get "rusty", according to Your Word in Matthew 6: 19. Show me avenues where I may invest and give freely toward Your causes; such as helping the poor and needy and for building Your Kingdom. Thank You, Father that as I make the effort to create a great financial future, and You transform me into a productive kingdom builder, I will be able to impact the lives of the poor and needy at a greater level. I honor, and give You all the praise in Jesus' name, Amen.

CHAPTER 22
A CHEERFUL GIVER

Give, and it shall be given unto you; **good measure, pressed down,** *and shaken together, and running over, shall men give into your bosom. For with the same* **measure** *that ye mete withal it shall be* **measured** *to you again*
Luke 6:38.

But this I say, He which soweth sparingly shall reap also sparingly; and he which soweth bountifully shall reap also bountifully. Every man according as he purposeth in his heart, so let him give; not grudgingly, or of necessity: for God loveth a cheerful giver. And God is able to make all grace abound toward you; that ye, always having all sufficiency in all things, may abound to every good work: (As it is written, He hath dispersed abroad; he hath given to the poor: his righteousness remaineth for ever. Now he that ministereth seed to the sower both minister bread for your food, and multiply your seed sown, and increase the fruits of your righteousness;)
2 Corinthians 6-10.

Every man according as he purposeth in his heart, so let him give; not grudgingly, or of necessity: for God loveth a cheerful giver
2 Corinthians 9:7.

When we speak of giving in the church, we mainly refer to time and money. These are the two main things that are needed for the church to function at a certain level. Without the giving of tithes and offerings, and voluntary services of the attendees, it is almost impossible to effectively keep a church in operation. The word *give* is mentioned in fifty three of the sixty six books of the Holy Bible and therefore, must be very important to God, and for us to do. The Miriam-Webster Online Dictionary gives many meanings to the word *give*, and many ways in which it may be used. For the purpose of this writing, I have selected two meanings; (1) To make a present of; (2) To put into the possession of another for his or her use. When we give, we want to make sure that we are not forced to do so. We must give freely and willingly for it to be effective. Giving of our money, and time to our Father's work is priceless. When we do this, we should do it cheerfully, as Paul declared: *Every man according as he purposeth in his heart, so let him give; not grudgingly, or of necessity: for God loveth a cheerful giver* (2 Corinthians 9:7). We also give of our time to the body of Christ, by offering our spiritual gifts. In 1 Corinthians 12:1-14 and again in Ephesians 4:7-16, Paul has given some clarification into the importance of this act.

My husband's and my finances began to become blessed when we stopped robbing God and started to tithe. We realized that the money belonged to Him, because He is the reason we receive it in the first place. Tithing is giving a tenth of your earnings to the work of God's Kingdom. It is written in Leviticus 27:32: *And concerning the tithe of the herd, or of the flock, even of whatsoever passeth under the rod, the tenth shall be holy unto the LORD.* The giving of one tenth of our earnings is indeed a foundational principle that began in Genesis, the book of beginnings. When Abram had victory over many kings in Kedorloamer, he gave Melchizedek, the King of Salem, and a priest of God Most High, *a tenth of all the goods he had recovered.* I know that many people do not believe in tithing, but it is a principle that we have seen work in our lives, and has made a huge difference.

In Malachi we are told to: *Bring ye all the tithes into the storehouse, that there may be meat in mine house, and prove me now herewith, saith the LORD of hosts, if I will not open you the windows of heaven, and pour you out a blessing, that there shall not be room enough to receive it* (Malachi 3:10). This principle will work for you if you apply it. My former pastor, Kim Brown, taught a lesson on the subject of *giving* and alluded to this: "Money is a current and therefore, it was meant to be released-it must move." Nonetheless, one must be careful as to how one uses his money and from what source it is received.

There was a time when Royston and I did not tithe. We believed we just needed to give generously-(less than ten percent of our earnings, of course). When we discovered the principle of tithing and began to apply it, our financial experiences began to change. Learning this principle has been quite a blessing. There were times when we thought that we would not have been able to meet all our financial obligations, but we were always able to, and we have attributed to us paying our tithes.

We have always thanked the late brother England who was a senior member at the AME church we attended in Virginia. He taught us the biblical principle of tithing; it has been a priority for us since. We make it our duty to write our tithe check before we pay any of our bills (and we do pay all our bills on time). We have never had to beg for anything, but we have always been able to give. Jehovah Jireh, our provider, continues to provide and open doors, enabling us to meet every need and obligation. There is nothing impossible with God, and He will come through for you when you least expect.

Another interesting thing we learned about giving is that if we do not pay our tithe on time, we have to pay twenty 20 percent interest. Does this 20% rule sound familiar to you? The world applies this principle to our monies if we are late with our payments for things such as; charge cards and other bills. It is a biblical truth that we must pay our tithe on time or pay twenty percent more. One of my former pastors, made a confession from the pulpit during a sermon, he said: "I held my tithe and I am having financial problems as a result." Go figure! I believed him, because for the six years I attended the church, I had never once heard him preach on the topic of tithing, so I knew it was not a tactic to encourage.

Here is the biblical proof relating to what was discussed above about not paying your tithe. : *And all the tithe of the land, whether of the seed of the land, or of the fruit of the tree, is the LORD's: it is holy unto the LORD. And if a man will at all redeem ought of his tithes, he shall add thereto the fifth part thereof* (Leviticus 27:30-31). In Galatians, we are given this reminder: *Be not deceived; God is not mocked: for whatsoever a man soweth, that shall he also reap* (Galatians 6:7). We intend to tithe for the rest of our lives and we hope that you will too. We do not believe we have anything to lose but instead, much to gain. After all, God gives us 100% and he only asks us to give Him back 10%.

A friend once told me; "I give money to charity and I consider that tithing, even though it is less than ten percent. I am not giving anybody ten percent of what I make." There was a time when I also thought that ten percent of my earnings was too much to give back to God. Here is a reminder for anyone who thinks this way: *But thou shalt remember the LORD thy God: for it is he that giveth thee power to get wealth, that he may establish his covenant which he sware unto thy fathers, as it is this day* (Deuteronomy 8:18). On the other hand, some people like to give, but are shy to receive from others. I believe this is due to pride. Giving and receiving are reciprocal, so it is just as good to be a cheerful and grateful receiver as you are a cheerful and willing giver. That stimulates harmony. There is another biblical principle regarding money that I did not learn until a few years ago. I learned it from my former pastor and from Paula White. This of course, is different from the tithe and offering. This is a fairly new concept for me; therefore, I am exploring it for more clarity. I recently asked my biblical mentor about the principle of first fruit, he explained that Jesus became our first fruit. He read the Leviticus passage with me and clarified that this principle as it pertains to our earnings, does not apply to us today. So what would first fruit look like for us today.

The Hebrew word for first fruits is *bikkurim* which means, "promise to come." It is about exercising faith and being obedient, and a principle that God established from the beginning and honors. When practiced, it allows God's promises of blessings to be manifested in our lives. Read Leviticus 23:10 for more information about this principle. It reinforces the practice of Matthew 6:33, which is to put God first in every area of our lives. Here is what I do to offer my first to God daily.

The first thing I do upon waking up in the mornings is pray and read my Bible. I also worship God with other believers on the first day of every week. What are the benefits? Applying biblical principles help us to stretch our faith, obey and believe in God to bless as we do our part. It is written: *Now he that ministereth seed to the sower both minister bread for your food, and multiply your seed sown, and increase the fruits of your* righteousness (2 Corinthians 9:10).

Instead of looking at giving as "losing something," think of how rich our heavenly Father is, how much He has given you and how much better are spiritual riches than financial gains. Jesus asked His disciples: *For what is a man profited, if he shall gain the whole world, and lose his own soul? Or what shall a man give in exchange for his soul?* (Matthew 16:26). Jesus wants us to realize the importance of giving our souls to Him and not to the world. Whatever we give to God He multiplies. As the popular saying goes, "the more you give, the more you get." If you give sparingly, you will reap sparingly, but when we give, we are planting seeds. Seeds take time to grow, so we must be patient. In Genesis 8:22 we are informed that: *While the earth remaineth, seedtime and harvest, and cold and heat, and summer and winter, and day and night shall not cease.* Think about it; if you plant one kernel of corn, you could reap approximately eight hundred kernels from it. Can you imagine what would happen if you sow ten? .Give more, and see what happens.

The story of Elijah and the widow in 2 Kings 17 is an inspiration for us to trust and obey God; He will supply all our needs. In this story the Lord provided for Elijah by sending him to stay by a brook, from which he would be able to drink and get fed by a raven during the drought. The brook dried up, and again God looked out for Elijah. This time, telling him to go to Zarephath, where a widow would feed him. Elijah did as God told him to do, but when he got there and asked the woman for a bite of bread along with a cup of water, she replied: *As the LORD thy God liveth, I have not a cake, but a handful of meal in a barrel, and a little oil in a cruse: and, behold, I am gathering two sticks, that I may go in and dress it for me and my son, that we may eat it, and die* (1 King 17:12).

The widow did not want to use up the little supply she had left for only just one meal, but Elijah assured her that it was okay because the Lord promised that she would always have plenty of oil and flour left until the Lord sent rain and caused the crops to grow again. The widow used her faith and did as Elijah told her, and all three of them had plenty to eat for many days after. When we put our faith to work, trust in God and obey Him; He works miracles in our lives. This illustration has taught me that I do not have to have a surplus from which to give, but I must always give-even when I am in need. I shows how faith and obedience on both Elijah's and the widows' part worked together for their good. I give contributions to programs that spread the Word across nations, since I have not been personally able go around the world to spread the Good News, as God's Word commands. We have to do what we can, where we are and with what we have.

PRINCIPLES FOR DAILY APPLICATION

(1) Give cheerfully and think outside the box. Think prosperity and abundance, because this is a divine ordination of God for those who believe and trust Him. Think about the poor and needy of the world and how you can help them with your giving. John 10:10, 1 John 2

(2) Get out of the mind-set of giving sparingly, to giving abundantly, without looking for anything in return. Luke 6:38.

(3) Get an attitude of being more of a giver than a receiver. Jesus said, *It is more blessed to give than to receive* (Acts 20:35). To give does not only mean money. It could be giving of your time, love, praise and just about anything. People who give receive also receive; it is a natural law or the law of reciprocity, that cannot be reversed by anyone but the Maker, and He says that His words are everlasting. Therefore, I doubt that there will ever be a reversal of the law. This does not only mean money, but honor, glory, praise and anything that belongs to Him. Read in Ezekiel 28:14-15, Genesis 3:1, to learn how the enemy tried to take from God and the results. Luke affirmed: *Give, and it shall be given unto you;* ***good measure, pressed down,*** *and shaken together, and running over, shall men give into your bosom. For with the same **measure** that ye mete withal it shall be **measured** to you again* (Luke 6:38). Whatever you put out will come back to you. Everything we give to God, He multiples abundantly. It is written: *One man gives freely, yet gains even more; another withholds unduly, but comes to poverty* (Proverbs 11:24).

(4) Since we like instant gratification, we must be mindful that we should not become discouraged or give up when we do not immediately see returns on our investments. The Word says: *Cast thy bread upon the waters: for thou shalt find it after many days* (Ecclesiastes 11:1).

(5) Learn to be a receiver as much as you are a giver. Some people like to give but they have a hard time receiving. It can be awkward to receive freely when you are always giving, because if someone is always giving and it is not reciprocated, it throws the law of reciprocity out of balance. If you fall into this category, be conscious of it and learn to receive without static, but with gratitude, love and appreciation. 2 Corinthians 9:7

(6) Tithe at your church and give to charities that support worthy causes such as orphanages, world hunger, assisting the poor and so forth. A lot of times people are afraid to give because they do not trust the sources that they hear about. For a comprehensive list of reliable causes to which you can give, outside your local church and charities, read former President Bill Clinton's book, *Giving.*

(7) Pray, pray, pray that you will be open to giving as well as to receiving and let the Holy Spirit direct you in your giving as well as in all other areas of your life.

PRAYER:

Dear heavenly Father, I thank You for teaching me how to be a giver as well as a receiver. Thank You that I am a cheerful giver and I give according to Your Word in Proverbs 3:9, Malachi 3:10 and 2 Corinthians 9:7. Likewise, I thank You that I receive according to Your Word in 2 Corinthians 9:10 and 1 John 5:14-15. Thank You that I seek the Holy Spirit's guidance in how to give of my time, money and service. Thank You that I make love a priority and love teaches me when, why and how to give. Thank you for blessing me and my family as we give willingly and without counting the costs. Please help us to find opportunities to always give. Let sow seeds out of our needs and reap rewards as the woman to whom You sent Elijah. Thank You, Jehovah Jireh, for all Your provisions and blessings, in Jesus' precious name I pray, Amen.

CHAPTER 23
A UNITIED TEAM FOR THE KINGDOM

So we, being many, are one body in Christ, and
every one, members one of another
Romans 12:5.

Two *are* **better than one**; *because they have a good reward for their labour*
Ecclesiastes 4:9.

And let the peace of God rule in your hearts, to the which,
also ye are called in one body; and be ye thankful
Colossians 3:15.

Again I say unto you, that if two of you shall agree on earth as
touching anything that they shall ask, it shall be done for them of
my Father which is in heaven. For where two or three are gathered
together in my name, there am I in the midst of them
Matthew 18:19-20.

A team agrees on the same thing. A team has one common goal and works together to achieve that goal. The aim is always to win or succeed. The team concept started before man was created. Obviously, God had not been working alone. This evidence is apparent in Genesis where God said, *Let us make man in our image, and after our likeness* (Genesis 1:26).

God did not create man by Himself, not because He was incapable, but because He wanted to demonstrate the strength and power of togetherness and agreement. That was the reason He did not leave Adam by himself and also why He ordered Noah to bring a pair of every kind of animal into the ark. Even animals understand this concept. It is amazing how the tiny ants work together to create their own cities. When you see animals, they are always in a group, whether the smallest ants or the biggest buffalo. Animals know that by working in teams they are able to build strong affiliations that conquer their enemies or preys.

We are accustomed to seeing people in sports working in teams, but it is becoming equally popular in certain sectors of society, where the team concept is being adapted-from corporate businesses to classroom teachers. The result is that they experience success and have greater accomplishment. The body of Christ should work collectively to bring God glory. Jesus made a powerful statement regarding teamwork in Matthew, Chapter 18 and verses 19-20, as I have quoted above, the apostle Paul gave the reason why we need each other; the wise man Solomon said, *"two are better than one"* and the prophet Amos asked a very valid question; *Can two people walk together without agreeing on the direction?* (Amos 3:3).

Jesus had a core team of twelve men. The following two verses from Matthew are priceless guides for us, as Jesus depicts the power of teamwork: *Again, I say unto you, that if two of you shall agree on earth as touching anything that they shall ask, it shall be done for them of my Father which is in heaven. For where two or three are gathered together in my name, there am I in the midst of them* (Matthew 18:19-20). This is a promise that if indeed we work together God hears and acts on our behalf. In Jesus' prayer to God for us, He prayed that we would be unified (17:11).

Whether we want to believe or not, accept or not, we are all connected. Not because we want to be connected, but because we all have the same heavenly Father- the omniscient, omnipotent and omnipresent God. We can continue to fight and disagree with one another and defeat our destinies, or we can begin to work together and fulfill them. The choice is up to each and every one of us.

When we have the kingdom of God within us and we are sustained by joy, peace and righteousness, we can build God's kingdom externally by uniting with others for Christ's sake. I believe and I have heard it said over and again, "unity is strength." This concept seems to be quite difficult for some human minds to conceive, as we often see or hear of people fighting against each other instead of working peaceably together. The disunity I see is a big tug of war, where people constantly and forcefully pull against one another, rather than pull together to accomplish God's work.

Not only is Iraq fighting against America, Muslims fighting against Christians, and Jews and different ethnic groups fighting against each other, but fighting goes on right in our homes, churches, back yards, and places of employment every day. The horrid truth is that disunity is a common denominator amongst the human race, even among the people who say they are Christians or followers of Jesus Christ. It is a shame that a lot of fighting goes on in churches. This is one reason some people stay away from church. Groups within the church body fight against each other for non-paying positions, as if it is a contest or big competition of some kind. Can you imagine what would happen if they were actually getting paid to do the work they volunteer to do in church? The fighting amongst brethren would be even greater!

Look at what Paul said in Corinthians: *For as the body is one, and hath many members, and all the members of that one body, being many, are, one body: so also is Christ. Now ye are the body of Christ, and members in particular* (1 Corinthians 12:12, 27). In fact, I recommend that you read the entire chapter for an understanding of God's design for mankind's unity. Einstein said that you cannot solve a problem with the same mind that created it. We are all created for a specific purpose, and each of us is just a piece of one big puzzle. I can just imagine how displeased God must be to see how disconnected we are in the body. We need each other.

As I was waking up one morning, I saw my Life Cycle Plan or (Vision Board), as many people call it, appeared before me. My life cycle plan is nothing mystical, it is just a piece of cardboard that I have covered with pictures that I cut out of magazines. I do this as a visual reminder of what I desire my life to look like. On it, I have pictures of people whose work I admire, things I want to accomplish now and in the future, and things I want to possess. The cardboard is approximately twenty by forty inches in size; it is a reflection of my dreams and intentions. The entire surface is covered with pictures, but the only picture that I could recognize on the Life Cycle Plan at that particular moment of visualization was the one that read, UNITING PEOPLE IN

OUR COMMUNITY, and I heard a voice in the Spirit saying, "Tell my people I want UNITY." My heart began to pound as I lay on my back and I could not go back to sleep. I got up and called my prayer partner, Marilyn, at 3:32 AM, and we prayed. Luckily for Marilyn, it was 6:32 A.M. because she lives on the East Coast. One thing we have learned during our years of praying together, is that it is very important to get up and pray when God nudges us in the wee hours of the morning, even though we are not fully awake. We praise God for blessing us with the gift of intercession, because we have seen how God has come through for the people we have prayed for and for ourselves.

The focus of our prayer on that particular morning was for unity among people everywhere. Revelation tells us that Christ will unite us all in the end. Why not begin to experience Kingdom living now? Revelation gives us a glimpse of how we will be brought together in the end: *And the names of the twelve tribes of Israel were written on the gates* (Rev.21:12). *The wall of the city had twelve foundation stones, and on them were written the names of the twelve apostles of the Lamb* (Revelation 21:14). These groups are from different time periods in the Bible, but they are joined together in the end, because they have all served the same one God (the King of every nation).

The Father does not tell us to do anything that He has not done. Jesus had His team of disciples, Paul had his team which he called friends, and he warned against people who caused division. He said to stay away from them, because they are not serving Christ but their own personal interests. T. Harv Eker said it well: "The problem is, by ourselves, we can never see what's holding us back from reaching our full potential." I totally agree with this statement. When teams are in place, people bond, communicate, commit, inspire, empower, encourage, share knowledge and wisdom. They brainstorm, hold one another accountable, execute plans, and produce something that is valuable.

It is good news that no one has to try to reach full potential singly, as there are many people waiting to give their assistance. It only takes two simple steps: one is to find these people, and the other is to ask them. Our heavenly Father does not work alone. He works with at least three, including Himself - God the Father, God the Son, and God the Holy Spirit. He does not expect us to do it all alone either. That is why He gave us the privilege of having each other.

Do you think it would be a beautiful experience, if in our lifetime people begin to work in unity and be at peace? I heard the story of a group of people who have the "crab mentality." In this group there are people who desire to be productive and live a life of success; those who have no desire but to see that first group fail (they have no intention of doing anything to improve their lifestyles); those who want "to be" but fail to do the things that are necessary to support what they want "to be"; those who "talk about the others" in the group; and those who are "clueless".

None of these people really know how powerful, and productive they could be how much they could personally accomplish, if they would look inside themselves, see, and believe that they are created in the image of God to be like Him, and that working together would exemplify that. This is the reason we have teams, mentors, counselors, coaches and people who help others to implement strategies for maximum success. Allow me to share an experience that I had shortly before moving to Arizona, and one of the reasons this chapter was birthed:

One day a sister in Christ-Shirley, called me and told me that she reserved a room at a camp in Ashland, Virginia. I knew that the Lord had spoken to her, because I had been speaking to Him about making a way for me to get away to be with Him, undistracted for a few days. She told me that she was going to the camp for a few days, but I told her that I could not go because I was preparing to leave for a trip to Arizona in a few days. As much as I desperately wanted to take a trip such as that one, I did not want to miss the opportunity to visit the state, which for the past ten years, I had dreamed of making my home.

At first I told Shirley thanks for letting me know and that I would have really liked to go, but I had other plans. As I was about to say goodbye and hang up the telephone, the Holy Spirit uttered a reminder that this was what I had been seeking from God for the past couple of weeks. I realized this was indeed an opportunity to get away to spend some time with the Lord. I quickly told Shirley to make sure that there was a place in the car for me, because I had decided to go, regardless of prior plans. I felt it was important for me to go, even if I had to return a day early; which I did.

Filled with excitement, I could not sleep that night. When I got out of bed the following morning I began to pray, thanking God for

Shirley's obedience to Him. As I prayed, one of my spiritual sisters popped up in my spirit, so I asked the Lord why He had put her in my spirit at this time. He said that I should get her to go to Ashland with us. Later that morning, I called Shirley and asked her if she had room for another person in her car, and she said, "Yes." I called Francine and told her about the trip, and invited her to come along with us. She was absolutely elated. She sounded even more excited than I was and began to tell me how she had been thinking of how she could get away for a while. The Lord is just so awesome, I thought! God looks out for us. He orders our steps while fulfilling His purposes in us.

On August 9, 2006, four sisters in the Spirit set a on the trip to the camp in Ashland, Virginia. I was already friends with Shirley and Francine, but I was meeting Jonnie Mae for the first time. As we drove along the highway, we listened to a sermon on CDs of Bishop Neil Ellis' message, from the Issachar Conference that I had attended at my church the week before.

The message was truly astounding. The profundity of his teaching had us so engrossed that we missed the exit for Ashland. As a result, we drove around, trying to find our way, until it began to get dark. Finally, we arrived at our intended destination-just in time to join the praise and worship service. We were exhausted, but not too tired to worship God and hear what He had to say. At the end, I did not feel as though I got much from the service; perhaps that was due to exhaustion from driving what would be an unusually long distance for me. I was the one behind the wheel. I asked God for what reason He brought me all this way, and I told Him, I know it has to be something more . I pleaded, please Lord, do not let me miss the purpose for which I came here over the next couple of days.

Day two came and God showed up. The Spirit weighed heavily on me, and I knew it was going to be a great experience at this camp. Before we went to bed that night, I felt the unction for all four of us to pray together, but as you may know, women tend to like to talk. We talked ourselves into lassitude, and started to fall asleep, so we could not pray together. We said our individual prayers and drifted off into the stillness of the night.

The following day, the Holy Spirit touched me early in the morning, woke me up before the other ladies, and told me to read the books of

Peter. I did as I was told, and God revealed some things to me about unity and working together. He told me to share what I had just read with the other ladies. I could not wait for them to wake up! As soon they woke up, I shared what the spirit had revealed to me about building a team for Christ.

He said we have many ideas and talents that the Lord gave to us, but we needed to work as a team to accomplish these tasks for the glory of God. After sharing, we prayed together, and in that instant we had prophetic revelations of our different talents. It was an absolutely amazing experience. It was very clear to me that the Lord wants believers to work together as a team for kingdom establishment, building, accomplishing, and achieving our destinies.

We had a great time at the camp meetings, eating, praying, meeting new people and dialoging with one another. The night before we left to return home, as I reflected on the events of those few days, I heard the Holy Spirit saying, "You are all doing this together now; what are you going to do when you leave here?" The Holy Spirit sent me to the book of Peter again, showed me more scriptures and told me to show them to my friends.

It was Saturday morning, and our time at camp was about to end. We all agreed that we would be back some time in the near future. We attended the morning teaching session before we left, receiving confirmation about the experiences that we were having. The lesson was about unity, love and working together. I believe that the Holy Spirit was warning us against selfish attitudes among the people in the body of Christ. Jesus wants to work with us to build His kingdom, but His feet are bound due to our lack of obedience, and trust, and also because of our rebellion.

There are many Christians who feel that God is far away and is not answering their prayers, but God has never left. It is the other way around, people move away from Him because it is easier to do that than to obey His laws and commands. Other reasons for which people turn away from him are due in part to lack of love, faith and trust. It is time to get things right with God, so he can use you and release the blessings He has promised and planned for us. God gives us free will, therefore we can choose to obey Him or satan. When the latter is chosen, it limits what God can do for us.

It is possible to do some things by ourselves but impossible to do other things without the help of other people; working as a team would help us to accomplish so much more. It is unfortunate that we have not yet realized that, or if we have, out of rebellion, we are simply refusing to do what we should be doing. Until each individual realizes that God has created every single one of us uniquely and that each person is a member of one body (the body of Christ) with a specific purpose, we will continue to fail in our attempts to have our own way, and digress instead of progress in our spiritual lives.

We must realize that, although each of us is unique, there is only one message for everyone. There is no need to be jealous of each other. We must learn to celebrate one another's accomplishments, because all people can accomplish anything when they work at diligently. Paul said: *For as the body is one, and hath many members, and all the members of that one body, being many, are one body: so also is Christ.*(1 Corinthians 12:12) *and Now ye are the body of Christ, and members in particular* (Corinthians 12:27). When this concept is understood, and embraced, people will begin to work more amicably. They will learn to live with and serve one another. That is when transformation will begin to happen.

I checked out the book, *The ABC's of Building a Business Team That Wins*, by Blair Singer (Warner Book Groups, September 2004) from the Library. I chose this particular book because when I reviewed the contents, I saw it had excellent information on how to build a team that wins. The author spoke about a code of honor such as the one the military uses. Some of the most disciplined team players I have encountered are people who have had military training. Everyone knows that the military gives the best training in discipline. As I read the book, I reflected on the scriptures to see how what Mr. Singer wrote matched up with scripture.

There are several points made in his book that have scriptural support. For example, he wrote: "One reason why businesses fail is because the people have no business skills. In the absence of rules, people make their own rules. Successful people and groups have a very clear code of honor that is easy to understand and is not negotiable." The Bible says: *My people are destroyed for **lack** of **knowledge*** (Hosea 4:6). When people do not understand what is expected of them, they do what they feel is the right thing to do or they do whatever comes to mind. They do not stop to consider the implications that their actions may have on the team. I recommend that Mr. Singer's book to anyone interested in this topic of team building, but above all, I recommend that you read the Bible for all your needs as it is the book that has all the codes needed for everything in life.

PRINCIPLES FOR DAILY APPLICATION

(1) Get in an attitude of accepting others as they are, in order to make it easier to work with them. Get an understanding of what the team stands for. Know their philosophy, their vision and mission, their rules and respect your leaders: *Their responsibility is to equip God's people to do his work and build up the church, the body of Christ* (Ephesians 4:12).

(2) Find out what your role is on the team and become the best team player you can possibly be. Use your talents, skills and abilities to the fullest. Strive to do your best, while supporting the other members of your team. *But eagerly desire the greater gifts. And now I will show you the most **excellent** way* (1 Corinthians 12:3). ***Bear ye one another's burden**s, and so fulfill the law of Christ* (Galatians 6:2).

(3) Accept responsibility and do your part. Show up when you are scheduled. Read Galatians 6, Matthew, Chapter 5 (the Beatitudes): Matthew 7 and pay attention to verse 7 (The Golden Rule). Also read Galatians 5: 22, 23 & 26 (The fruit off the Spirit), and 1 Corinthians 12:12-29 (The body of Christ).

(4) Put self-interest aside and commit to working for the common interest of the team. Read Proverbs 3:21-23. Celebrate all wins, not just your own. Make each day as pleasant and peaceful as you possibly can, because the word says: *This is the day which the LORD hath made; we **will rejoice** and be **glad** in it* (Psalm 118:24). Sometimes we let jealousy gets the best of us and we do not know how to celebrate when others win. We need to be happy about all wins, and wait for our winning day to come

(5) Be dependable, accountable, loyal, punctual, decisive, and maintain a winning attitude, even in times of high pressure, stress, trials and adversity. Say no when you know you cannot do something. Do not over commit. You will stretch yourself thin, experience burn-out, and eventually fail. It benefits the team when each member takes the responsibility to assume his or her role. Do not swindle your way out of your responsibility. Certain members of a team sometimes sit back and do the bare minimum, because they know that the rest of the group will get the work done. God's Word says: *We are many parts of one **body**, and we all belong to each other.* (Romans 12:5). In other words we need each other.

(6) Choose someone you trust to be your accountability partner. Make sure the person you choose has good integrity and boldness to objectively tell you the truth. This is a proven concept that will help you to do what you need to do when you feel like doing nothing. Be responsible. Do not blame others for your mistakes and do not judge; Jesus is the only one given the authority to judge. He is the only one who qualifies for this position, because He is already a just and righteous judge. Jesus said in the book of John: *I can of mine own self do nothing: as I hear, I **judge**: and my judgment is **just**; because I seek not mine own will, but the will of the Father which hath sent me* (John 5:30). For more on the topic of judging, read Matthew 28. Do not justify either. Read Romans 3 for more information on justification.

(7) Pray, pray, pray and be grateful that you have an opportunity work with people. Pray that no matter what, you will love yourself, the team members, and leaders. Develop an attitude of trust and respect for yourself, as well as for the team members. Always remember the golden rule in Matthew, Chapter 7, which teaches us to "do unto others as we would want them to do unto us." There will be times when your team mate may tick you off , but that happens you may apply this scripture: *Casting all your cares upon him; for he careth for you* (1 Peter 5:7). Peter also gave this suggestion: *Above all, love each other deeply, because love covers over a multitude of sins* (1 Peter 4:8) (NIV).

PRAYER:

Dear heavenly Father, it is quite evident that working in teams is difficult for many of us, but Lord, we realize that if we must please You, working together is necessary and is a piece of life's puzzle. It is not an option but a requirement. Help us to realize that we are one body with different parts. We need each part in order to function as a whole and complete our assigned tasks on this planet. Please help us to realize that we must be in agreement if we are to go in the same direction. Lord, You said in Matthew 18:20 that where two or three are gathered in Your name, You are there also. Help us to follow the principles that Your Word provides, even when it is seemingly difficult to do at times. Please help us to develop and grow ourselves in our areas of assignments and apply Your Word as it is written: **Study** *to shew thyself approved unto God, a workman that needeth not to be ashamed, rightly dividing the word of truth* (2 Timothy 2:15) and that we will understand what Romans 8:28 which teaches: *And we know that all things work together for good to them that love God, to them who are the called according to his purpose.* In Your precious name we pray, Amen.

CHAPTER 24
OBEY AND SURRENDER

*But if thou shalt indeed obey his voice, and do all that I speak; then I will
be an enemy unto thine enemies, and an adversary unto thine adversaries*
Exodus 23:22.

*And the people said unto Joshua, The LORD our God
will we serve, and his voice will we obey*
Joshua 24:24.

If you love me, obey my commandments
John 14:15. (NLT).

*And being found in fashion as a man, he humbled himself, and
became obedient unto death, even the death of the cross*
Philippians 2:8.

*So then, any of you who does not forsake (renounce, surrender claim
to, give up, say good-bye to) all that he has cannot be My disciple*
Luke 14:33. (AMP).

God wants our obedience to the Word that He has given us.
Everyone should have a mindset that being obedient to God's
will is a duty, not a burden. Obedience and surrender go hand in hand.
If we are obedient to God's Word, we are most likely going to surrender
to His will. When you surrender in obedience, and you are consciously
working on making obedience a habit, God will begin to work in your
life, and show you awesome things-things you have never heard or seen
before. You will be compelled to share them with others. I desire to

live in obedience and please God for the rest of my life, so I act daily to that measure. As David said: *I delight to do thy will, O my God: yea, thy law is within my heart* (Psalm 40:8). David knew that doing God's will brings freedom.

One has to be obedient to become a recipient of the great and eternal promises of God. Revelation 21:4, reminds me of one of these promises: *He will wipe every tear from their eyes, and there will be no more death or sorrow or crying or pain. All these things are gone forever.* Can you imagine a life without pain, sorrow, death or crying? That is one of the reasons I want to live in obedience to the Word of God-I long for that experience. I know for a fact that if we do not walk in obedience to His Word, we cannot get what God intended for us to have, nor will we get to the place He has gone to prepare for us (John 14:1-3).

Have you ever heard the saying, "obedience is better than sacrifice?" Did you know that it came straight from the Holy Book? *And Samuel said, Hath the LORD as great delight in burnt offerings and sacrifices, as in obeying the voice of the LORD? Behold, to obey is better than sacrifice* (1 Samuel 15:22). Samuel was speaking to Saul, who disobeyed God to please the people; he feared them, instead of God, and that caused him to miss the blessing of becoming king. Many of us do pretty much the same thing today-we think we can get God on our sides by doing busy, so called "good works," while side-stepping His Word. Sacrifice without obedience is unbalanced. We must be will to surrender to God's leading and direction.

I have heard the saying, "obedience is better than sacrifice," on numerous occasions, but when I decided that I want to live in obedience for the rest of my life, I sought clarity on the meaning of that phrase. I read the passage in Samuel, and I looked up the meaning of the word obedience in the Dictionary. I found the following: "submissive to the will of another" and; "implies compliance with the demands or request of one in authority." I also looked up the meaning of sacrifice and there was a sleight of meanings. "Sacrifice" means an act of offering to a deity something precious; especially: the killing of a victim on an altar; a destruction or surrender of something for the sake of something else and; something given up or lost. As I read these meanings the first thing that came to my mind was that Jesus was always obedient to God, the

Father, even to the point of death, God gave Jesus, His only Son, as a sacrifice for your sins and mine.

God allowed His one Son to die in order for the prophecies to be fulfilled, for us to be forgiven our sins once and for all and for us to understand what it means to *present our **bodies** a **living sacrifice**, holy, acceptable unto God, which is our reasonable service* (Romans 12:1). Emphasis placed. There is nothing that any of us can give, or do for God that could take the place of our obedience to Him. Let us reflect on one special action of Abraham for a minute. In obedience to God, Abraham was willing to sacrifice his son, Isaac. All Abraham wanted to do was to please God, even if it meant that his son had to die. How many of us would be willing to do what Abraham did? That was a test of Abraham's faith, as well as of his obedience. God is still testing our faith and obedience today. Are we passing these tests?

God created a beautiful world and because He has so much love, He created a man and a woman, Adam and Eve. I can just imagine how beautiful the woman must have been and how handsome the man must have been. God created them for His glory and pleasure. He gave them some specific instructions to follow for His own pleasure, but they failed the test of obedience, because they became too self-absorbed-were only concerned about the desires of their flesh, as many of us are today. What happened when disobedience occurred in the Garden of Eden? Adam and Eve failed God, their Creator, Master and King, and subsequently all of us. They brought sin into the world, for which we are still paying the consequences. We struggle with sin daily, even though Jesus came to rectify this situation-we still cannot get it all right. We are caught up in the *sins that are in the world, the lust of the flesh, and the lust of the eyes, and the **pride** of **life*** (1 John 2:16). Emphasis placed.

Although we have the freedom to choose through God's grace and His mercy, we often choose to disobey. In simple terms, if we do not consciously choose to obey, we are then consciously choosing to disobey. The result of disobedience is a vicious cycle of curses instead of blessings, strongholds instead of freedom and deliverance, disbelief and doubt instead of faith and serving satan instead of serving God.

When we read Hebrews, Chapter 11, we see that there is no question that obedience is the key to winning in God's Kingdom. Can you imagine what would have happened if Noah did not obey God and built the ark? His family and all those species of animals would not have survived the flood, and there would be no "us". If Abel did not obey God, he would not have witnessed God's righteousness and neither would we. If Enoch was disobedient, God would not have spared his life in such a unique way.

If Abraham was not obedient, we would not have seen the promises of God fulfilled, nor would his descendants, and we would not have an inheritance of which to look forward. If Isaac was not obedient, he would not have blessed his twin sons, and we might not have experienced what it means to be blessed. Moses had to obey God for the people of Israel to reach the Promised Land. If He did not obey, God would have chosen someone, as he has done in many cases, and Moses would not have been given the privilege of being the only prophet who saw God face to face, and if Joshua and the people of Israel did not obey God, the wall would not have come down.

Obedience to Christ also guarantees our blessings, favor and royal priesthood-ship. When we do obey God, divine blessings are guaranteed. It is written in Deuteronomy 7:13: *And he **will** love thee, and **bless** thee, and multiply thee: he **will** also **bless** the fruit of thy womb, and the fruit of thy land, thy corn, and thy wine, and thine oil, the increase of thy kine, and the flocks of thy sheep, **in** the land which he sware unto thy fathers to give thee.* Deuteronomy, Chapter 28 gives us a clear description of the many blessings that God showers upon those who obey Him. The first and second verses read: *And it shall come to pass, if thou shalt hearken diligently unto the voice of the LORD thy God, to observe and to do all his commandments which I command thee this day, that the LORD thy God will set thee on high above all nations of the earth: And all these blessings shall come on thee, and overtake thee, if thou shalt hearken unto the voice of the LORD thy God* (Deuteronomy28:1-2). Read verses I through 14 to get the full picture.

Obedience through faith guarantees us favor with God. That is why in Genesis 6:8, we are told that Noah found favor with God. Throughout the scriptures we read of many others, such as Joseph, Jeremiah, Esther, Daniel, David and others who found favor with God through their obedience. I read in Romans 1 that we receive grace and apostleship when we obey Christ through faith: *By whom we have received grace and apostleship, for obedience to the faith among all nations, for his name* (Romans 1:5.): Televangelist, John Hagee said it best, and I quote, "Favor is born in the womb of obedience and every act of obedience shortens the distance of the miracles of God." You will receive favor, blessings, protection, deliverance, freedom and everything you need when you obey God.

Obedience guarantees our destinies. Job 36:11-12, says. When we walk in Obedience, we are walking in the steps of the Father who set the blueprints for obedience. Jesus did everything that God told Him to do. He always consulted His Father before He did anything and Jesus fulfilled His destiny. We will fulfill our destinies, if we obey God. Job said, *So he will do to me whatever he has planned. He controls my **destiny*** (Job 23:14).(NLT). Daniel said, *God gives us the breath of life and controls our destinies* (Daniel 5:23) (NLT). God is the One gives us the breath of life, and controls our destinies, so why do we not obey Him? Look at what happened when Peter obeyed Jesus and casted his net.

Obedience to calling on the name of Jesus guarantees you answers. When you call on the name of Jesus with confidence, using the authority that God has given you, the enemy who tempts you to disobedience will have to flee. With the enemy out of your way, there is more room for Christ. I know that the name of Jesus is a very powerful tool to use against the enemy. In Psalm, Chapter 20 verse 59, we are told to call on the Lord in the day of trouble and He will answer. I had an experience with calling the name of Jesus, which I would like to share with you.

One mid–summer evening just after dusk, my husband, our three children and I were traveling home to Chesapeake, Virginia from a weekend trip with our friends in Wake Forest, North Carolina. As we drove on the dark road, Route 1, I suddenly realized that Royston was struggling to keep the car on the road. He swerved to the left and then to the right several times, just barely, missing the ditches on each side of the road. We had taken many road trips before and I had never experienced anything like this. Fear gripped my heart and held me at freezing point for a moment; a feeling of helplessness overshadowed me. I whispered to myself, "What can I do to help?" I realized that I could do nothing, so I affirmed myself: "Royston is a good driver; he will get this car under control and the best I can do is to remain calm." Although I wanted to scream. I contained my emotions so that I would not raise anxieties in our children.

Finally I built up the courage to turn my head and look at Royston's face. In a quick glance at my husband, I saw a helpless man. It appeared to me that he was temporarily under distress, trying as hard as he could to control the car. I knew that we were in trouble, and I was paralyzed by fear. The look on my Royston's face made me screamed, JESUS! The car stopped immediately. I felt major relief, I thanked God and asked Royston, "What just happened?" Apparently he tried to avoid hitting an animal that crossed the road. There is **power** in the **name of Jesus**. No one can convince me otherwise. This was not, "just a coincidence." This was the mighty power of God at work once again! We should obey the scriptures call on Jesus; He will answer. *And call upon me in the **day** of **trouble**: I will deliver thee, and thou shalt glorify me* (Psalm 50:15; 20:1).

Obedience to the Word, and the application of its principles will benefit us enormously. Here are some things that Jesus does for people who trust, submit, yield, surrender and obey Him. He protects, gives courage, wisdom and understanding, provides for every need and gives us supernatural blessings. He blots out our sins and keeps our names in the book of life as it is written in the book of Acts: *Repent therefore and be convened, that your sins may be blotted out, so that times of refreshing may come from the presence of the Lord* (Acts 3:19). Words cannot suffice to describe all that He does for those who do the above as well as, repent, have faith and love Almighty God. He said in Revelation that He will intercede for us as we remain in purity: *All who are victorious will be clothed in white. I will never erase their names from the Book of Life, but I will announce before my Father and his angels that they are mine* (Revelation 3:5).

I am thrilled that I have the freedom to choose, and that I have chosen to exercise repentance, faith, trust, love, surrender and obedience daily, through God's grace and mercy. I do this for the sake of salvation, sanctification and holiness. It is pleasing to know that God qualified Jesus to become the source of salvation for us who believe in Christ Jesus and obey Him. Through the power of His blood, we have freedom. The Hebrew Epistle says:

God qualified him as a perfect High Priest, and he became the source of eternal salvation for all those who obey him (Hebrew 5:9). This verse is referring to the fact that Jesus being God's son, was obedient and

God made Him a priest because of His obedience. It is a delight to be a transformed and not a droopy Christian.

Every believer can make the decision to be transformed and live life abundantly through the grace and mercy of God. I am a believer who has taken a stand for the Lord, and I am truly amazed at the joy that salvation gives. The joy of the Lord is truly my strength. My prayer is that all of mankind will have the same joy that some of us have found in knowing and having a true relationship with our heavenly Father. I get very elated and excited whenever I read verses in the Bible such as a prophecy in the book of Daniel which tells of the Kingdom of God that will be established, stand forever and all of God's children will inherit that kingdom.

Daniel said: *During the reigns of those kings, the God of heaven will set up a kingdom that will never be destroyed or conquered. It will crush all these kingdoms into nothingness, and it will stand forever* (Daniel 2:44). Another biblical truth that keeps me in obedience is that although we all sin, God's grace saves the ones who believe in him. The proof is found in this verse: *For all have sinned and fall short of the glory of God* (Romans 3:23). I have confidence in Cod's Word and as a result, I do not let my past sins prevent me from living my life fully today.

Paul did not stop there either; He went on to say that if we continue in sin our destiny is death, but if we receive Christ in our lives, our destiny is eternal life. He wrote: *For the wages of sin is death, but the gift of God is eternal life in Christ Jesus our Lord* (Romans 6:23) (NKJV). These are a few of the truths that give us hope, keep our faith alive and give meaning to each day. If Jesus had not died on the cross for our sins there would be no hope. Ephesians 2:1 declares: *And you He made alive, who were dead in trespasses and sins.*

Can you visualize this? In the kingdom that is to come, there will be no sin, sickness, depression, schizophrenia, dementia, Alzheimer's, obesity, high blood pressure, muscular sclerosis, Parkinson's or other nervous system diseases, diabetes, lupus, Fibromyalgia or any other muscular and immune system diseases, as well as no desire to commit suicide? God is absolutely awesome and deserves our continuous and steadfast obedience!

When we get to the point of total obedience, we can surrender to God. This shows that we appreciate and embrace His preeminence.

When we Surrender to God we stop fighting, give up control, submit, yield listen to what He is saying and obey. Surrendering to God means that we lay our lives down for Him; we love, trust and live daily in His presence. Surrendering is giving up worldly pleasures-the flesh, and allowing the Holy Spirit to take control. Surrendering is having the joy of full salvation and giving God the Glory in all things. Surrendering is everything that Judson W. Van Deventer, wrote in his hymn, *I Surrender All*. One writer reports: In his heartfelt explanation for writing this song, Deventer said: "At last the pivotal hour of my life came, and I surrendered All, and when I did that, a new day ushered into my life." Are you ready to surrender all to Jesus and allow a new day to usher into your life?

PRINCIPLES FOR DAILY APPLICATION

(1) Eradicate self-will and allow the Holy Spirit to guide you: ***Trust** in the* ***LORD** with all thine heart; and lean not unto **thine** own understanding.* In all thy ways acknowledge him, and he shall direct thy paths (Proverbs 3:5).

(2) Obey His greatest commandment which will compel you to aim at doing everything else right. *Thou shalt love the Lord thy God with all thy heart, and with all thy soul, and with all thy mind. Thou shalt love thy neighbour as thyself* (Matthew 22:37 & 39).

(3) Strive to have an intimate relationship with God, such that you desire nothing as much as you desire to please Him. Ponder this verse: ***Abide** in **me**, and I in you. As the branch cannot bear fruit of itself, except it **abide** in the vine; no more can ye, except ye **abide** in **me*** (John 15:4).

(4) Obedience is like faith. Just as it is impossible to please God if you have no faith in Him, you cannot disobey your Father and expect to have a good and lasting relationship with Him. Jesus said He did everything His Father told Him to do. That is obedience and surrender-a very simple model that we need to follow. Jesus surrendered all to God, and we should surrender all to Jesus, Who intercedes with the Father for us. Read or sing the song: "I Surrender All."

(5) If God tells you to run, run-do not walk. On that note, I would like to share an experience with you. While at home recuperating from a surgery, God told me not to return to my job, but I returned. I found that the job was not the same as it was before I went on sick leave, and my health was deteriorating. I was a Vocational Rehabilitation Counselor at the time, and one day while I was trying to catch up with work on some case files, I heard the Lord said, "What are you doing? I said it is finished." This time I knew it was over. I had to obey, surrender and let it go of that job. I submitted my letter of resignation the very next day, after discussing it with Royston. In two weeks I left the job. I surrendered that job to my heavenly Father, and He has blessed me immensely as a result of my obedience and willingness to surrender. Out of that decision came two books and a business.

(6) If God tells you to let your light shine and to salt the earth, do it: *But be ye doers of the word, and not hearers only, deceiving your own selves* (James 1:22). If he tells you to cast your bread upon the water, do it, because you shall indeed find it after many days (Ecclesiastes 11:1).

(7) Pray, pray, pray that God will direct your path and that you will be able to discern the Holy Spirit, resist the devil and that he will flee from you:

Submit yourselves therefore to God. **Resist** *the* **devil***, and he will flee from you* (James 4:7).

PRAYER:

Dear heavenly Father, our omniscient Creator, I am sorry for my sins of disobedience. I give my life to You as a living sacrifice, so that I might totally transform into Your likeness. Have Your own divine sweet way, and bind all that I am to all that You are, in the name of Jesus. I commit to do Your will for the rest of my life. Thank You for giving me wisdom to obey You and resist the devil. Thank You for being a just God Who rewards obedience. Thank You for all Your promised blessings, divine favor, everlasting life, prosperity, fighting my battles for me, giving me victory over my enemies, making me the head and not the tail, the first and not the last and for all the blessings listed in Deuteronomy 28:1-14. According to Psalm 115:12, Lord, You, are mindful of us and You bless us-for this I thank You. Thank You that sin and death cannot hold me because I have surrendered all to You. I am grateful that Your grace and mercy, coupled with my faith, obedience and trust in You, are sufficient for me to live a redeemed, holy and sanctified life. In Jesus' name, Amen.

PART IV

THE FUTURE IS FORETOLD

CHAPTER 25
JESUS FORTELLS THE FUTURE

Now the Spirit speaketh expressly, that in the latter times some shall depart from the faith, giving heed to seducing spirits, and doctrines of devils
1 Timothy 4:1.

*This know also, that in the **last days** perilous times shall come*
2 Timothy 3:1.

*Knowing this first, that there shall come in the **last days** scoffers, walking after their own lusts*
2 Peter 3:3.

For the Lord himself shall descend from heaven with a shout, with the voice of the archangel, and with the trump of God: and the dead in Christ shall rise first: Then we which are alive and remain shall be caught up together with them in the clouds, to meet the Lord in the air: and so shall we ever be with the Lord
1 Thessalonians 4:6.

For we must all appear before the judgment seat of Christ; that every one may receive the things done in his body, according to that he hath done, whether it be good or bad
2 Corinthians 5:10.

But of that day and hour knoweth no man, no, not the angels of heaven, but my Father only
Matthew 24:36.

Reading the books of the Bible that tell us about Jesus' coming, can be scary for some, but for others the scriptures in those books are actually very promising and exciting, even though some of the prophecies are not easily understood. Those who are prepared and are looking forward to Christ's second coming cannot help but be joyful about those scriptures, yet be sorrowful for those who are not prepared because they refuse to turn from their evil ways and practices. Amos 4:12 warns that we should prepare to meet our God. In this special Chapter, I have included Matthew, Chapter 24, and Daniel Chapter 12, along with other related scripture reference to verses that I think are of most significance to understanding what to expect in the end-time. I believe that we are indeed living in the last days. What do you think?

MATTHEW 24

"And Jesus went out, and departed from the temple: and his disciples came to him for to shew him the buildings of the temple.

And Jesus said unto them, See ye not all these things? Verily I say unto you, There shall not be left here one stone upon another, that shall not be thrown down.

And as he sat upon the Mount of Olives, the disciples came unto him privately, saying, Tell us, when shall these things be? and what shall be the sign of thy coming, and of the end of the world?

And Jesus answered and said unto them, Take heed that no man deceive you.

For many shall come in my name, saying, I am Christ; and shall deceive many.

And ye shall hear of wars and rumours of wars: see that ye be not troubled: for all these things must come to pass, but the end is not yet.

For nation shall rise against nation, and kingdom against kingdom: and there shall be famines, and pestilences, and earthquakes, in divers places.

All these are the beginning of sorrows.

Then shall they deliver you up to be afflicted, and shall kill you: and ye shall be hated of all nations for my name's sake.

And then shall many be offended, and shall betray one another, and shall hate one another.

And many false prophets shall rise, and shall deceive many.

And because iniquity shall abound, the love of many shall wax cold.

But he that shall endure unto the end, the same shall be saved.

And this gospel of the kingdom shall be preached in all the world for a witness unto all nations; and then shall the end come.

When ye therefore shall see the abomination of desolation, spoken of by Daniel the prophet, stand in the holy place, (whoso readeth, let him understand:)

Then let them which be in Judaea flee into the mountains:

Let him which is on the housetop not come down to take anything out of his house:

Neither let him which is in the field return back to take his clothes.

And woe unto them that are with child, and to them that give suck in those days!

But pray ye that your flight be not in the winter, neither on the Sabbath day:

For then shall be great tribulation, such as was not since the beginning of the world to this time, no, nor ever shall be.

And except those days should be shortened, there should no flesh be saved: but for the elect's sake those days shall be shortened.

Then if any man shall say unto you, Lo, here is Christ, or there; believe it not.

For there shall arise false christs, and false prophets, and shall shew great signs and wonders; insomuch that, if it were possible, they shall deceive the very elect.

Behold, I have told you before.

Wherefore if they shall say unto you, Behold, he is in the desert; go not forth: behold, he is in the secret chambers; believe it not.

For as the lightning cometh out of the east, and shineth even unto the west; so shall also the coming of the Son of man be.

For wheresoever the carcase is, there will the eagles be gathered together.

Immediately after the tribulation of those days shall the sun be darkened, and the moon shall not give her light, and the stars shall fall from heaven, and the powers of the heavens shall be shaken:

And then shall appear the sign of the Son of man in heaven: and then shall all the tribes of the earth mourn, and they shall see the Son of man coming in the clouds of heaven with power and great glory.

And he shall send his angels with a great sound of a trumpet, and they shall gather together his elect from the four winds, from one end of heaven to the other.

Now learn a parable of the fig tree; When his branch is yet tender, and putteth forth leaves, ye know that summer is nigh:

So likewise ye, when ye shall see all these things, know that it is near, even at the doors.

Verily I say unto you, This generation shall not pass, till all these things be fulfilled.

Heaven and earth shall pass away, but my words shall not pass away.

But of that day and hour knoweth no man, no, not the angels of heaven, but my Father only.

But as the days of Noah were, so shall also the coming of the Son of man be. For as in the days that were before the flood they were eating and drinking, marrying and giving in marriage, until the day that Noah entered into the ark, And knew not until the flood came, and took them all away; so shall also the coming of the Son of man be.

Then shall two be in the field; the one shall be taken, and the other left.

Two women shall be grinding at the mill; the one shall be taken, and the other left.

Watch therefore: for ye know not what hour your Lord doth come.

But know this, that if the good man of the house had known in what watch the thief would come, he would have watched, and would not have suffered his house to be broken up.

Therefore be ye also ready: for in such an hour as ye think not the Son of man cometh.

Who then is a faithful and wise servant, whom his lord hath made ruler over his household, to give them meat in due season?

Blessed is that servant, whom his lord when he cometh shall find so doing.

Verily I say unto you, That he shall make him ruler over all his goods.

But and if that evil servant shall say in his heart, My lord delayeth his coming;

And shall begin to smite his fellow servants, and to eat and drink with the drunken;

The lord of that servant shall come in a day when he looketh not for him, and in an hour that he is not aware of,

And shall cut him asunder, and appoint him his portion with the hypocrites: there shall be weeping and gnashing of teeth."

Take note: I will come unexpectedly as a thief! Blessed are all who are watching for me, who keep their robes ready so they will not need to walk naked and ashamed.
Revelation 16:15

DANIEL 12

"And at that time shall Michael stand up, the great prince who standeth for the children of thy people: and there shall be a time of trouble, such as never was since there was a nation even to that same time: and at that time thy people shall be delivered, every one that shall be found written in the book.

And many of them that sleep in the dust of the earth shall awake, some to everlasting life, and some to shame and everlasting contempt.

And they that be wise shall shine as the brightness of the firmament; and they that turn many to righteousness as the stars forever and ever.

But thou, O Daniel, shut up the words, and seal the book, even to the time of the end: many shall run to and fro, and knowledge shall be increased.

Then I Daniel looked, and, behold, there stood other two, the one on this side of the bank of the river, and the other on that side of the bank of the river.

And one said to the man clothed in linen, which was upon the waters of the river, how long shall it be to the end of these wonders?

And I heard the man clothed in linen, which was upon the waters of the river, when he held up his right hand and his left hand unto heaven, and sware by him that liveth for ever that it shall be for a time, times, and an half; and when he shall have accomplished to scatter the power of the holy people, all these things shall be finished.

And I heard, but I understood not: then said I, O my Lord, what shall be the end of these things?

And he said, go thy way, Daniel: for the words are closed up and sealed till the time of the end.

Many shall be purified, and made white, and tried; but the wicked shall do wickedly: and none of the wicked shall understand; but the wise shall understand.

And from the time that the daily sacrifice shall be taken away, and the abomination that maketh desolate set up, there shall be a thousand two hundred and ninety days.

Blessed is he that waiteth, and cometh to the thousand three hundred and five and thirty days.

But go thou thy way till the end be: for thou shalt rest, and stand in thy lot at the end of the days."

I recommend that you read all of the books in Daniel (pay attention to Chapter 9), Revelation, Zechariah, Isaiah 66:15, Mark 13:35-37, Acts 1:7, 11 ;2:17-18, 1 and 2 Thessalonians, 1 and 2 Timothy and 1 and 2 Peter. Many people are scared to read prophetic books, but the intentions of these books need to be understood- they are not to scare you, but to help you know what to expect and how to prepare yourself for the great day of Christ's return, and your inheritance of an eternal life. If you are unprepared you will inherit eternal damnation. By this I mean that if you do not accept Christ as your Lord and Savior, and live life according to God's Word-watching, serving, praying and waiting for His return you will go to hell, according to the Word of God.

On the other hand, a glorious end has been promised to the people who believe, trust and obey God. For example, it is written: *And it shall come to pass in the **last days**, saith God, I will pour out of my Spirit upon all flesh: and your sons and your daughters shall prophesy, and your young men shall see visions, and your old men shall dream dreams* (Acts 2:12; Joel 2:28), and in John 14:12, Jesus said that He is going to prepare a place for us, and that He will return to receive us, so that we may be with Him. I think these promises are absolutely lovely and only the people who are prepared will be able to receive these blessings. Another beautiful end time verse is this one: *But in the **last days** it shall come to pass, that the mountain of the house of the LORD shall be established in the top of the mountains, and it shall be exalted above the hills; and people shall flow unto it* (Micah 4:1).

Would you like to be one who flows into this mountain? You must be prepared. Jesus is preparing to return to meet you; are you preparing to meet Him. If you heed to the call of God and earnestly seek Him and do His will you will wear a crown. It has been declared in the book of Timothy: *And now the prize awaits me-the crown of righteousness that the Lord, the righteous judge, will give me on that great day of His return. And the prize is not for just me but for all who eagerly look forward to His glorious return* (2 Timothy. 4:8).

Here this: *Today you must listen to His voice. Don't harden your hearts against Him as Israel did when they rebelled* (Hebrews 3:15). People who continue to oppose and rebel against God will be judged accordingly. Psalm 76:10 reads: *Human opposition only enhances your glory, for you use it as a sword of judgment.* Who do you think that "You" in this verse is referring to? God, of course. If you oppose God, He will judge you based on those actions. Remember also that, those who disobeyed God, as we have read in the Bible; were punished. A good example can be seen in the narrative about Noah, where God warned His people and waited patiently for them while He instructed Noah to build the ark. Because of their rebellion and disobedience, only eight people in an entire nation were saved from drowning in the terrible flood. Those eight people were the obedient-Noah and his family.

PRINCIPLES FOR DAILY APPLICATION

(1) Know that as many as one hundred Bible prophecies that foretold the first coming of Jesus Christ were fulfilled (Isaiah 11:1,7:14, 9:1-2, 42:1-4, 53:9; Micah 5:2; Zechariah 11:12-13, 9:9, 13:7). There are other prophecies concerning His second coming, some already fulfilled, some are being fulfilled right now and others are yet to be fulfilled. I believe we ought to pay attention.(Mark 13, Luke 21, 2 Timothy 3:1-5).
(2) Jesus said he is coming back and He will destroy the earth with fire

(Matthew 24: 30; Psalm 37:10, 20; Matthew 13:40-42; Malachi 4:1,3; Revelation 20:9, 15, 22:12; 2 Peter 3:10). Those who trust and abide in Jesus need to be prepared to meet Him, because He is preparing to meet us (John 14:1-3; Revelation 21:1,4).

(3) Live each day as if it were your last; in expectation of God's return. Ask yourself, if Jesus comes or if He calls me to die today, would I be ready to live with Jesus in eternity? (Titus 2:12).

(4) Know the signs of His return. Read the books of Matthew 24, Daniel and Revelation.

(5) Do not give in to deception. Study the Word for yourself. Ask God for discernment. (2 Thessalonians 1:2:3, Matthew 24:5; Revelation 20:10, Matthew 25:41).

(6) The righteous (living and dead), will receive eternal life (1 Corinthians 15:51-54; 2 Timothy 4:8). The unrighteous (living and dead), will receive eternal destruction (Ezekiel 18:20; 2 Thessalonians 1;7-10; Revelation 14:14-20, 19:11-21).

(7) Pray, pray and be prepared! (Matthew 24:44; 1 Thessalonians 5:1-6; 2 Peter 3:11-14, Luke 21:36). There is a lot to learn, but it is possible. Just take it one day at a time.

CHAPTER 26
CONCLUSION

*And do not be conformed to this world, but be transformed
by the renewing of your mind, that you may prove what is
that good and acceptable and perfect will of God*
Romans 12:1 (NKJV).

*And be renewed in the spirit of your mind; And that ye put on the
new man, which after God is created in righteousness and true
holiness. Wherefore putting away lying, speak every man truth
with his neighbour: for we are members one of another*
Ephesians 4:23-25.

*But we all, with unveiled face, beholding as in a mirror the glory
of the Lord, are being transformed into the same image
from glory to glory, just as by the Spirit of the Lord.*
2 Corinthians 3:18 (NKJV).

*Let us **draw near** with a true heart in full assurance of faith, having our hearts
sprinkled from an evil conscience, and our bodies washed with pure water*
Hebrews 10:22.

In conclusion, I would like to emphasize that there is power in transformation. The Bible has given us the blueprint of how to access the Kingdom and live an abundant life through Christ Jesus; the choice is ours to follow it, let our light shine and live life to its fullest until Christ returns. I hope that I have conveyed a message about my own personal transformation that has touched your heart and soul; I pray that it has helped to transform one or more areas your life.

You can make the decision to actually live a renewed life by opening up all areas of your heart and life, allowing God to come in fully and use you daily. I can tell you that it works, because I am doing it, have been for a while, and would not change it for anything in this world. God will give you the desires of your heart when you surrender fully to His will. He has been and continues to do a marvelous work in me, and in others, as we allow Him to do so. He chisels at my flesh to the extent of uneasiness at times, but I want Him to do this until the acts of my flesh die, and I have total submission to the Holy Spirit.

The Holy Spirit shows me things about Pauline that I need to address, and He shows me things about others, that they need to address. He shows and speaks to everyone, but we do not always listen. Jesus desires our souls, our commitment to Him, and our trust in Him. One of the first things He told me when I told Him that I wanted to be like Him, was that my life should not reflect pride. I knew then that I would have to get rid of anything in me that would mirror pride. I struggled with this, because I did not want to believe that pride was one of my defects. After all, I came from a very humble beginning, so why should I be proud, I thought. This revelation opened my eyes to many things, and forced me to do a character check-more of a self-examination, if you know what I mean.

God took me to His Word, where I always go to find the answers to my questions, and He showed me scriptures such as Psalm 40:4, 101:5; Proverbs 15:25, 16:11; Luke 1:51 James 4:6 and 1 Peter 5:5. These passages, along with many others, have shown me that God does not like certain kinds of pride. I am handling this by swallowing my pride as Psalm 6:3 commands. He is working on me constantly, in as many areas to which I give Him the access. God will do the same for you. He will not work with people who do not allow Him. When He is permitted to work in our lives, He does a marvelous job, diligently and in a way that no one else can. As soon as I start thinking that I have it all together, surprise! He shows my other areas on which I need to work. I have resigned myself to the fact that I have not arrived, and I am a continuous piece of work in progress, but I know that when I give God my best, He gives me more than His best. Since it is impossible for me to reach perfection before Jesus comes, I have decided to work daily toward that end. This is not an easy journey; it has many challenges, but it is an exhilarating, possible and awesome path. I ask you to come and journey with me today.

I identify with the apostle Paul and consider my struggles to be similar to his in many ways. For this reason I started this book with excerpts from his writings and have also ended the book that way. My prayer is that all people will get to the point in their lives where they see the need for transformation and do whatever it takes to make it happen. Here is what I leave with you: If you consider your life as a work in progress, you can transform daily and God will help you, just as He did for Jacob, David, Jonah, Paul, and many others in days of old and just as He is doing today for numerous people. He will do the same for you if you give Him full access to your life. As mentioned before, Paul's teachings have had a great impact on my life, and that is the reason I have quoted him and used excerpts from his writings so often.

Like Paul, at the end of my days I want to be able to say: *I have fought a good fight, I have finished my course, I have kept the faith: Henceforth there is laid up for me a crown of righteousness, which the Lord, the righteous judge, shall give me at that day: and not to me only, but unto all them also that love his appearing* (2 Timothy 4:7-8), and like Jesus, I would like to say, "it is finished".

The apostle Paul wrote this prayer of spiritual empowerment for the people at the church in Ephesus. As you prepare for the return of Jesus Christ, it is my prayer that this book will empower you to live an abundant, wholesome and transformed life here on earth, as it is in heaven.

PRAYER:

For this cause I bow my knees unto the Father of our Lord Jesus Christ, of whom the whole family in heaven and earth is named, that He would grant you, according to the riches of His glory, to be strengthened with might by His Spirit in the inner man; that Christ may dwell in your hearts by faith; that ye, being rooted and grounded in love, may be able to comprehend with all saints what is the breadth, and length, and depth, and height; and to know the love of Christ, which passeth knowledge, that ye might be filled with all the fullness of God. Now unto Him that is able to do exceeding abundantly above all that we ask or think, according to the power that worketh in us, unto Him be glory in the church by Christ Jesus throughout all ages, world without end, Amen.(Ephesians 3:14-21).

REFERENCES

Holy Bible:

King James Version, from Hengeveld, Nick, BibleGateway.com, 1995-2008, Gospel Communications International

New King James Version, from Hengeveld, Nick, BibleGateway.com, 1995-2008, Gospel Communications International

New Living Translation, from Hengeveld, Nick, BibleGateway.com, 1995-2008, Gospel Communications International

New International Version, from Hengeveld, Nick, BibleGateway.com, 1995-2008, Gospel Communications International

Amplified Bible, from Hengeveld, Nick, BibleGateway.com, 1995-2008, Gospel Communications International

Parker, Phillip M. Webster's Online Dictionary Http://www.websters-onlinedictionary. Org

Wikipedia, the Free Online Encyclopedia: The Four Kinds of Love, by C.S. Lewis

Strong, James. LL.D, S.T.D. The Strongest, Strong's Exhaustive Concordance of the Bible

The American Heritage Dictionary. Houghton Mifflin Company, (1982). Boston, MA

Blair, Singer. 2004 The ABC's of Building a Team That Wins

Gray, John Ph.D. (1951). Men Are From Mars, Women Are from Venus